Suzy Gershman's

BORN TO SHOP

PARIS

The Ultimate Guide for People Who Love to Shop

11th Edition

Wiley Publishing, Inc.

For Pascale-Agnes Renaud Sahler, who has taught me Paris for over 20 years.

Published by:

Wiley Publishing, Inc.
111 River St.
Hoboken, NJ 07030-5774

ISBN-13: 978-0-471-79035-8
ISBN-10: 0-471-79035-4

Editor: Shelley W. Bance
Production Editor: Suzanna R. Thompson
Cartographer: Anton Crane
Photo Editor: Richard Fox
Anniversary Logo Design: Richard Pacifico
Production by Wiley Indianapolis Composition Services

For information on our other products and services or to obtain technical support, please contact our Customer Care Department within the U.S. at 800/762-2974, outside the U.S. at 317/572-3993 or fax 317/572-4002.

Wiley also publishes its books in a variety of electronic formats. Some content that appears in print may not be available in electronic formats.

Manufactured in the United States of America

5   4   3   2   1

CONTENTS

MAP LIST

ABOUT THE AUTHORS

Suzy Gershman is a journalist, author, and global-shopping goddess who has worked in the fashion and fiber industries for more than 25 years. Her essays on retailing have been used by the Harvard School of Business; her reportage on travel and retail has appeared in *Travel + Leisure, Travel Holiday, Travel Weekly,* and most of the major women's magazines. She is translated into French for Condé Nast's *Air France Madame* magazine. The *Born to Shop* series, now over 23 years old, is translated into eight languages. Gershman is also the author of *C'est La Vie* (Viking and Penguin Paperback), the story of her first year as a widow living in Paris. She recently sold her flat in Paris and now divides her time between San Antonio, Texas (her childhood home); a small house in Provence; and the airport. Suzy is currently working on a guide to the world's best shopping and also gives shopping tours; contact her at suzy@suzygershman.com for details.

Sarah Lahey retired from her career in home style to raise a family and recently rejoined the workforce as news director for the *Born to Shop* series. Sarah shows and sells English smalls at Northern California antiques fairs. She lives with her husband and dog, Bentley, outside of San Francisco and wears the same size as Suzy (so they can share clothes).

TO START WITH

When my Grandma Jessie used to speak Yiddish, she would then cover her mouth with her hand and say, "Oh! Pardon my French!"

So when I quote her and say *"Oy vey,"* you know I'm referring to the exchange rate between the U.S. dollar and the euro, the fact that many Americans have been dissing the French, and the news that some shopping ops in France have become less attractive, at least price-wise.

But never mind all that.

Paris is always gonna be Paris, and it's very much worth a visit. I lived here while I wrote and updated this book and have worked very hard to give you an insider's look at deals and goings-on, at different kinds of hotels, and at all sorts of best buys.

I thank the guys who helped me with the legwork and threw in their own opinions—my son, Aaron James; my assistant, Jennifer McCormick; and the various hoteliers who have shown me that you can live like a king without a palace.

Chapter One

....

BEST OF PARIS

J'ADORE PARIS

....

I hope you are reading this as you plan a trip to Paris. While the dollar-euro ratio isn't great, it's not that bad either, and the newspapers are filled with articles about how many Americans are traveling to Europe. If crowds are swarming around you, you'll need this book more than ever, because I've added many insider's tips and noted out-of-the-way places that aren't too touristy.

In these pages are shopping lists that will help get your *jus* flowing. Paris is filled with great things to look at and buy. If you shop wisely, you may even save money.

Putting the best of Paris into one list is an impossible task; it seems that every store I visit is the best in Paris. Every magazine has pictures of merchandise I must own because, surely, it is the best in Paris. Now that I spend several months a year here, I run around with a notebook in my handbag so that I can write down my latest finds to share with my readers. The notebook is bigger than this edition.

With that in mind, the selections in this chapter have been chosen for people in an incredible hurry, who have no time for leisurely strolling and shopping. If you have more time, you owe yourself the luxury of checking out the finds described elsewhere in this book. However, if you must hit and run, I hope these choices will be rewarding.

Paris

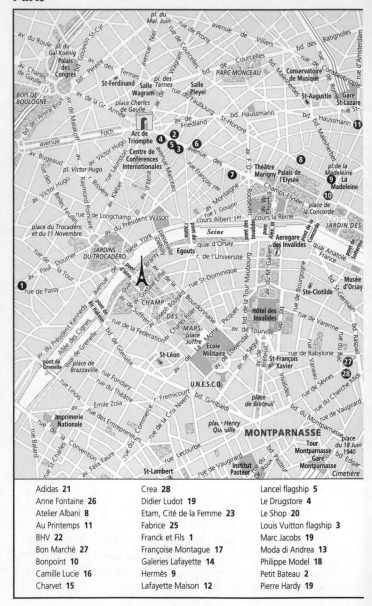

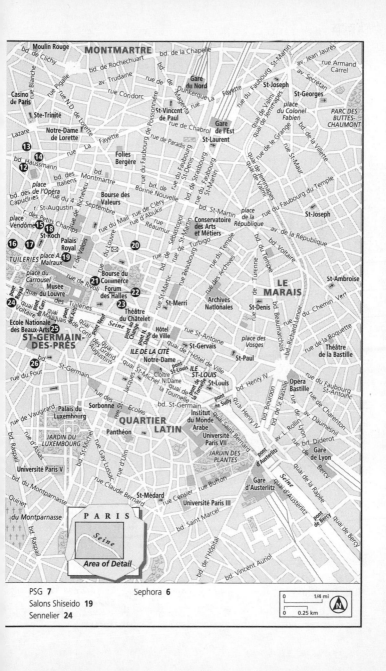

PSG **7**   Sephora **6**
Salons Shiseido **19**
Sennelier **24**

Best Specialty Perfume Shop

SALONS SHISEIDO
142 galerie de Valois, Jardin du Palais Royal, 1er
(Métro: Palais-Royal).

This tiny shop, with high ceilings and royal purple decor, is the showcase of makeup genius Serge Lutens. He used to create makeup for Christian Dior and has now been with Shiseido for decades. His perfumes are also divine; even if you buy nothing, just look around and breathe deeply. The Jardin du Palais Royal is another terrific shopping experience, so check it out while you're here. Plan to spend several hours in this little piece of hidden Paris, a shopping heaven.

RUNNER-UP

FREDERIC MALLE
140 av. Victor Hugo, 16e (Métro: Victor Hugo).

Come here for the specialty scents, a smelling booth, and do-it-yourself or custom-made fragrance.

Best Duty-Free Perfume Shop

CATHERINE
7 rue Castiglione, 1er (Métro: Tuileries or Concorde).

This small, intimate shop is family-run and can get crowded because it's very popular (good news travels fast). Catherine has an excellent selection of scents and specializes in hard-to-find perfumes. The salespeople will also help you to choose a new fragrance based on your skin type and lifestyle, or they'll help you pick a fragrance for a gift. There are also makeup and beauty goods by Chanel, Dior, Lancôme, and Sisley—which are the steal of the century at French prices. Also note the excellent handbags, watches, and souvenirs.

Confused about the whole duty-free issue? There's lots more information in these pages (see p. 53 for starters).

Best Mass-Market Perfume Shop

SEPHORA
70 av. des Champs-Elysées, 8e (Métro: Franklin D. Roosevelt).

I don't care if you have Sephora at your local mall. The French stores are different, partly because Sephora is a large French chain and the flagship is right smack on the Champs-Elysées. This branch is even open on Sunday.

Everything in the large shop is color-coordinated. Fragrances have their own section, with scads of testers and lots of scent strips. There's far more than perfume; in fact, you're better off not buying perfume here, since you'll get a better price from a discounter or duty-free shop. Sephora is good for bath and beauty products (an enormous selection, including its own line of shampoos and body lotions, makeup, and hair accessories).

This is a great place for girls, preteens, and women of all ages. The inexpensive sample-size products make fabulous gifts. You'll also find books, a *parapharmacie,* a mix-your-own perfume counter, and a computer to teach you everything you need (or want) to know. There's also a good détaxe rebate here (14%).

Aside from the flagship on Champs-Elysées and the many other Sephora locations, there is a relatively new shop on rue de Rivoli (no. 99) that's geared toward teens and tweens (it's located in one of the former Samaritaine buildings). Most branches have the same feel to them; it's just a matter of size, selection, and belles and whistles. (The belles wear uniforms and white gloves.)

Best French Gift Statements

- Glass and/or crystal items from the big French makers, such as **Baccarat** or **Lalique.** No, not stemware—silly you. These brands now make fashion statements and accessories, such as Lalique belts and stickpins. "Exotica" is the Lalique line of leather belts with smoky glass buckles; they run about 200€ ($230), but you can apply for a détaxe refund. Lalique's stickpins, named "Nerita," are also quite chic and cost a bit less. The newest product is a thin leather cuff bracelet on which you place a Lalique crystal slide; the two parts are sold separately and cost about 180€ ($207) for both.

- While we're on the subject of handbags, try the brand **Just Campagne,** which makes sporty bags in styles you've never seen in the U.S.—they'll make your friends drool and sigh. A large tote is about 200€ ($230).

Best Status Gifts Under $25

- **Hermès** soap, sold in the Saddle Shop.
- **Lanvin chocolates,** available in any grocery store.
- **Champagne.** In addition to the ones you've heard of, there are several good champagnes that aren't as well known in the U.S.—I swear by *nv* (nonvintage) Alain Thienot, found at Nicolas or Monoprix.
- Anything from **Diptyque,** the candle, soap, and scent maker. This luxury brand is not that well known in America (its first U.S. shop opened recently in Boston), but is a cult item among celebs and serious shoppers (p. 229). Also available at Au Printemps.

Best Gifts for $10 or Less

- Anything from **Sephora,** preferably the house brand of bath goodies. See above and p. 205.
- **Le String** is the French version of the thong—it has been banned in French high schools because local girls were doing a Monica Lewinsky with theirs. *Sacré tush!* Sloggi is a popular brand (it's Italian) although I buy the Sloggi wannabe, Scandy, because they make *elasticité extrême* (extreme stretch) in a microfiber string that is a dream for comfort and travel—it dries in hours. From Monoprix.
- **Hot-chocolate mix** (5€/$5.75) **from Angelina,** 226 rue de Rivoli, 1er (Métro: Tuileries), the most famous tea shop in Paris.

- A box of **Mère Poulard cookies** (1.40€/$1.60). These indescribably good butter cookies are imported from Mont St-Michel. Available in any grocery store.
- A bag of real French **coffee** (2.20€/$2.55). I buy Carte Noire, and there are other good brands; Grand Mère has a cute package, but is considered just a morning coffee by locals. Available in any grocery store.
- A jar of hard-to-find **flavored mustard** (2.20€/$2.55). I buy Maille brand, either cassis and red fruits or one named Provençale. Most fun when bought at Maille's own store, place de la Madeleine, 1er (Métro: Madeleine). Most grocery stores or gourmet markets have a large selection of unusual mustard tastes—even blueberry.
- A box or bag of **tea** . . . but nothing British or easily found in the U.S. We're talking about the famous mix of red fruits, or French herbs or flavors not known to the American palate. Grocery stores carry Elephant brand; Mariage Frères is a luxury brand with its own tearooms and distribution in department stores. My favorite is the Monoprix brand of *fruits rouge*.
- A bar of milled **soap,** from a made-in-France brand *(bien sûr),* teamed with *gant de toilette,* a French-style **washcloth.** The two pieces together don't have to cost more than 10€ ($12). I like Roger & Gallet soaps, especially the more unusual scents, such as the cherry-and-tomato combination.

Best Gifts for Kids

- **Monoprix,** a chain of "popular stores," is packed with items, ranging from a selection of books (Disney translations are nice) to LEGOS®. I also buy kids' clothes here.
- **Sephora** carries little animal-shaped bath-gel thingamabobs for .50€ (60¢) each. Each animal shape is a different scent, and there must be 20 of them in all.

Best Store for Teenage Girls

ETAM, CITE DE LA FEMME
73 rue de Rivoli, 1er (Métro: Pont Neuf).

An entire department store of style: fashion, beauty, even home touches and a cafe. It occupies a makeover of one of La Samaritaine's landmark buildings. Low prices.

RUNNERS-UP FOR TEENS & TWEENS

H&M
54 bd Haussmann, 9e (Métro: Havre Caumartin).

The Swedish phenomenon has copies of the latest looks for men, women, and children at affordable prices. This is the flagship; there are other, smaller branches around town.

LE SHOP
3 rue d'Argout, 2e (Métro: Etienne Marcel).

The music is too loud for me—but this is a great concept store (tons of boutiques inside one big store) and is very trendy, very with-it, and a must-do for anyone under 40.

Best Kitsch

It's not hard to find kitsch in Paris—just stroll the tourist traps along the rue de Rivoli.

Best Whimsy

MR. GAS
44 av. Etienne Marcel, 1er (Métro: Etienne Marcel).

Gas has been around for years: It's a teeny-tiny jewelry shop that sells colorful, creative whimsies. Now, "Mr. Gas" has added a clothing store next door. Funky, exotic, and hip. Large sizes need not apply.

Best Arts & Crafts

CREA
55 rue St-Placide, 6e (Métro: St-Placide).

If you think Arts and Crafts is a design period, you are not a do-it-yourself (DIY) kind of person. The crafty ones will fall into fits of glee when they step inside Crea.

Best Fashion Icon: Traditional

Blame it on Pablo Picasso or Coco Chanel, but the traditional striped fisherman's T-shirt has become an iconic fashion statement.

This time, the colors are not so traditional (although you'll have no trouble finding navy-and-white or red-and-white stripes). The wacky colors are usually sold in specialty stores. Brands to check out include **Le Phare de la Baleine,** passage l'Havre, 9e (Métro: St-Lazare), part of a small chain that specializes in marine looks from Brittany; **Amour Lux,** a line sold all over France (I buy mine at Galeries Lafayette) that makes the shirts in wild colors; and **St-James,** 13 rue de Rennes, 6e (Métro: St-Germain-des-Prés), which has free-standing stores and perhaps the best colors, but the highest prices. You may be shocked by the prices—often 40€ ($46) or more—but in this case, you're paying for quality (they wear forever) rather than *la mode.*

Best Fashion Icon: New Age

HERVE CHAPELIER
390 rue St-Honoré, 8e (Métro: Concorde).
1 rue du Vieux-Colombier, 6e (Métro: St-Germain-des-Prés).
3 rue Gustave Courbet, 16e (Métro: Victor Hugo).
53 bd de Courcelles, 8e (Métro: Courcelles).

Kate may be passé, so take a look at Hervé Chapelier, a French classic that makes brightly colored nylon tote bags. The major department stores stock a lousy selection, so head to the free-standing stores. The best location is the flagship, not far from the rue Royale in the heart of the best shopping in town. I use the large tote bag for my dog.

Best One-Trick Pony

The trick is the very French look of black and white teamed together for casual or dress-up. Both of these brands sell only white or black shirts, blouses, and tops.

ANNE FONTAINE
64 rue des Sts-Pères, 6e (Métro: Sèvres-Babylone).
50 rue Etienne Marcel, 2e (Métro: Etienne Marcel).
12 rue Francs-Bourgeois, 3e (Métro: St-Paul); and many more.

Ms. Anne has shops all over town and boutiques in the major department stores. She sells only two things: white blouses and black blouses. She also has shops in select U.S. cities and an outlet store at La Vallée.

RAYURE
8 rue Francs-Bourgeois, 3e (Métro: St-Paul).

Rayure is not as expensive as Anne Fontaine, and doesn't have as many stores (though the line is also sold in department stores). It carries more white shirts than black, but is competitive with Anne Fontaine in terms of styling.

Best New Department Store

LAFAYETTE MAISON
35 bd Haussmann, 9e (Métro: Opéra or Havre Caumartin).

You don't come across many new department stores anywhere in the world, so it's a great pleasure to welcome Lafayette Maison, in the space once occupied by Marks & Spencer, right across the street from the flagship Galeries Lafayette. This home store offers five floors of home style—I think the most interesting ones are the ground floor, which resembles a snazzy Target, and the lower level, for cooking demos.

Best New Retail Block

Get a look at the corner of **boulevard Malesherbes** and **rue Royale**—not the part that indents, but the real street part at the beginning of Malesherbes, in the 8e. Here you'll find three totally new buildings filled with wonderful things to see, sniff, and touch. The stores are **Sia** (home style), **Résonances** (gifts and novelties), and **Shiseido** (the Japanese beauty maven). The whole new energy that's come to this corner of Paris makes you think that U.S. marketing concepts can work on other shores. (Métro: Madeleine or Concorde.)

Block to Watch

Check out the two parallel streets rue St. Roch and rue du 29 Juillet in the 1er (Métro: Tuileries)—they are filling up with adorable tiny shops. To get my drift, pop into **Dominique Denaive**, 7 rue du 29 Juillet, 1er (© 01-42-61-78-22; www. denaive.com), for resin jewelry and accessories.

Best Marketing for Travelers

We shoppers are the winners here—despite the temporary loss of CDG airport terminal 2E and its fabulous shopping, there are many other new stores in Paris train stations, including a Monoprix in the **Gare du Nord** (for Eurostar shopping) and a brand-new Sephora in the **Gare de Lyon** (for trains heading to Provence and Côte d'Azur). These stores offer great last-minute gift shopping and browsing opportunities while you're waiting to depart.

Best Ethnic Fashion Store

MIA ZIA
4 rue Caumartin, 9e (Métro: Havre Caumartin).

Lest you forget that many parts of the U.S. were once French colonies, note that numerous stores throughout Paris reflect French roots in other parts of the world. Mia Zia sells clothes and home style with a touch of North Africa, which makes them great for resort wear without being costume-y. ✆ 01-44-51-94-45. www.miazia.com.

RUNNER-UP

R BY 45RPM
4 rue du Marché St-Honoré, 1er (Métro: Tuileries).

For an interesting runner-up, but with clothing from Japan (which, of course, was never under French protection), look inside this small shop. Here, jeans and clothes are made from block-printed Japanese fabrics and bandannas. ✆ 01-47-03-45-45. www.45rpm.fr.

Best French Brands for Large American Bodies

While I do not consider myself immense, let's face it, if you are larger than a size 6, you do not have a French body. Most French clothes are made up to size 44 (American size 12) and some go to size 46 (size 14), but they are cut small and, even if purportedly large enough, many don't fit. Do not panic. There's a report on plus sizes on p. 188, but here's my secret list of brands that have their own size system or go up to size 52—these are all available in the major department stores: Lilith, Weill, Weinberg, and Yohji Yamamoto.

For casual clothing, I often visit the men's department. *Warning:* A French men's XL in mass-market clothing may still be too small.

Most Hyped New Store in Paris

LOUIS VUITTON
101 av. des Champs-Elysées, 8e (Métro: Etoile or George V).

If I am dumbfounded and knocked speechless by this new space, that says it all. Just the outer-space walls with the old valises used as art forms are enough to make you realize you're not in Kansas anymore. This is almost a department store, with four full floors to gawk at. ℂ 01-53-57-24-00. www. louisvuitton.com.

Most Hyped Old Store in Paris

GROYARD
233 rue St-Honoré, 1er (Métro: Tuileries).

It's a coincidence that I list this store just after Louis Vuitton, because they're alike, yet totally different. Older than Vuitton, Groyard has long been the insider's preferred brand of luggage, steamer trunks, and travel gear. It, too, has a specific logo, but unlike Vuitton, it has remained a hidden source. Few people even knew of its store right behind the Hotel Meurice and near the famed boutique Colette. Although Groyard was first known for its luggage, the company now suddenly makes the must-have handbag or tote bag of the decade.

The venerable firm was bought in 1998 and old traditions were maintained while a new design team moved in. Suddenly, a small gimmick has been added and the skies turn bright, the sun shines, the band plays, and the waiting list is 6 months long. All that Groyard has done is to offer its regular pattern in bright colors, along with the additional service of monogramming its canvas in contrasting hues. You can also get a crown emblazoned. The result is so hot that you not only have to fork over a movie star's ransom, but you also must wait a long time. But, honey, *ooh-la-la*.

Insider's tip: Buy your bag in France, but have the monogram or printing done in the U.S. where the waiting line is only 3 months long. The line is sold at Bergdorf's and Neiman-Marcus; free-standing stores are opening in the U.S., including a new one just opened on Union Square in San Francisco. Expect to pay 1,044€ to 1,304€ ($1,200–$1,500) for the tote bag and another 348€ ($400) for the monogram.

AARON'S PICKS

Sneaker Tips

If the shoe fits, you do what? To me, that depends on the price and the novelty. Good shoes are everywhere and in places you're going to be visiting anyway: On the rue de Rivoli, there's a big **Adidas** store, and on the Champs-Elysées, a **Puma** store.

These flagships are visually stimulating and offer the widest array of gear for their respective labels, but patrons should expect to pay full retail price. Even in the unlikely event of a sale, you'll still do better elsewhere—or in the U.S. Only serious collectors or enthusiasts looking for rare, Euro-only editions should shop here.

For everyone else shopping for sneakers in Paris, look for **Sprint,** a chain of chic shoe shops with locations all over Paris and in most high-traffic districts. It carries all of the hot brands and, within those brands, all of the best styles. The shoes can be a bit pricey, but if you go in, you'll come out with a winner and won't end up wasting your time.

In the Pompidou area, check out these two notables: **Shoe Bizz,** which has a modest selection of shoes, but hosts Paris's most diverse selection of Golas, and **Johnny Guitar,** whose shoes are less hipster and more hip-hop. See the sneakers and dress shoes by Ecko, Diesel, and my favorite, Royal Elastics.

Guy Fashion

CENTRE HALLES
15 rue Pierre Lescot, 1er (Métro: Etienne Marcel); 92 & 75 rue de Turenne, 3e (Métro: St-Paul).

If you're going to dress like a bum (that is, in jeans, T-shirt, and sneakers), you might as well look like a bum who knows a thing or two about fashion. That's why Centre Halles is my absolute favorite clothing store in Paris. When it comes to the aforementioned big three of comfort, nobody in town carries more of the hottest labels.

Aaron's Five Best Buys in Paris

1. **Blue-gray denim Converse high-tops:** 65€ ($75) at Bathroom Graffiti, 4 rue de Sèvres, 6e.
2. **Burnt-denim G-Star jeans:** 110€ ($127) at Centre Halles, 92 rue de Turenne, 3e.
3. **Blueberry cheesecake:** 4€ ($4.60)—just wander the Marais.
4. **Leather wristband:** 11€ ($13) at Centre Halles, 92 rue de Turenne, 3e.
5. **Custom button-down shirts:** 35€ ($40) at Ray Club, 76 rue de Turenne, 3e.

You'll find a wide selection of denim, including Paul Smith, Miss Sixty/Energie, and G-Star, and the full line of the high-end Ringspun Allstar T-shirts. Centre Halles also has a sizable stock of limited-edition Converse and Onitsuka Tiger sneakers. These items generally have standard retail prices (read: pretty expensive), but there's also a rather decent sale rack and some excellent discounts. Looking like a chic bum has its own cachet.

RAY CLUB
76 rue de Turenne, 3e (Métro: St-Paul).

A string of stores on the rue de Turenne, at the edge of the Marais, offers discounted men's fashion and tailoring. Ray Club stands out as the best, the cheapest, and the most presidential: It offers beautiful custom shirts for only 35€ ($40)! If you don't want to take my word for it, just ask former U.S. president Bill Clinton, who is pictured on the wall, standing next to the owner and holding up a recently purchased button-down. Talk about the Comeback Kid.

JENNY'S PICKS

··

Favorite *Quartier*

THE MARAIS
3e–4e (Métro: St-Paul).

The Marais (which means "swamp") has been one of the city's most dubious districts for decades. It is ethnically more diverse than most parts of Paris; it was once considered the Jewish ghetto. Similar to what's been happening in Williamsburg, Brooklyn, what once was ghetto is now ghetto-fabulous.

This *quartier* is home to many of the hippest boutiques and designers in the city, and it's a great place for eats as well. Where else in Paris can you find cheesecake? The Marais also has two wonderful Jewish-style delis—on rue Rosier, right near the local temple. This is the only place in Paris where you're likely to see a bagel, but the French have a long way to go before fully realizing this culinary staple. In fact, their bagels are sort of fluffy—almost like a round croissant with poppy seeds. But who cares? They're still great.

Having nothing to do with religion and everything to do with tourists, the Marais is also open on Sundays, so this is the perfect place to have brunch and wander.

Best Gift Source

WHY?
41 rue Francs-Bourgeois, 4e (Métro: St-Paul).

For all your nonstop nonsense needs and gifts, you must visit Why? Why, you ask? Because this store is just plain fun and, more important, it reminds you that even the French like to be silly from time to time. The products here perhaps mirror the locals' indescribable penchant for the humor of Jerry Lewis.

Jenny's Five Best Buys in Paris

1. **Pinstripe bias-cut skirt:** 35€ ($40) at Etam, 73 rue de Rivoli, 1er.
2. **Wool track jacket:** 17€ ($20) at H&M, 54 bd Haussmann, 9e.
3. **Collapsible ashtray:** 6€ ($6.90) at Why?, 41 rue Francs-Bourgeois, 4e.
4. **Limited-edition European Pumas:** 65€ ($75), at Sprint.
5. **Sparkly white scarf:** 14€ ($16), at Etam, 73 rue de Rivoli, 1er.

Best Jeans

EMET
15 rue Francs-Bourgeois, 4e (Métro: St-Paul).

This Marais boutique has a great selection of young women's clothing, and it has reasonable prices, even to an American. In fact, when last I visited, it was having a denim sale and had brand-new Diesel jeans for 60€ ($69) or less—this being just short of a miracle. Strongly recommended, especially since you'll be browsing this part of Paris anyway. *Note:* Stores are open Sundays, but closed Mondays.

Best Vintage

PLANETE 70
147 rue St-Martin, 3e (Métro: Hôtel de Ville).

This is Paris's first legitimate vintage-clothing store and one of the only ones in the metropolitan area. It's very similar to the type of vintage store you might find in Greenwich Village:

cramped yet spacious, with racks overflowing with worn and torn clothing, from shoes to hats and everything in between. Prices vary, but are mostly reasonable. The buyer has a good eye for what's funky and what's junky.

Best Department Store

ETAM
73 rue de Rivoli, 1er (Métro: Pont Neuf).

Rue de Rivoli's Etam is by all accounts a teen/tween/20-something shopping mecca. This five-floor holy land of hot stuff puts to shame any American shopping mall. It is a massive structure able to accommodate even the most serious shoppers. For die-hard Levi Strauss fans, there is an entire half floor devoted to its denim clothing.

Chapter Two

....

PARIS DETAILS

WELCOME TO PARIS

Forget CNN, BBC, and FOX News. Forget anything you hear on TV or read in the papers about the French. Forget everything but Paris. Paris is fine. In fact, Paris is great.

Despite the crazy prices and oh-my politics, Paris is sizzling—Americans may as well throw in their chapeaus and join the fun. Sure, sometimes there are strikes or *manifs* (protest parades) but this is not new. They just make the news more often these days because they're more interesting than war and fear. I have been in Paris during these so-called times of strife and I can tell you with all honesty—c'mon in, the water's fine.

There are also lots of new stores and American touches, so French retail shopping is easier than ever to cope with. (That means you can sometimes return things!)

Also, note that the capital of luxe and deluxe has really cracked down on counterfeits. You can be arrested or fined if you so much as tote a fake brand-name handbag. I'm not talking about getting a ticket for jaywalking. The fine goes up to 300,000€ ($345,000) and you can get prison time if you attempt to sell counterfeits.

- **Monoprix,** my favorite store for general merchandise (that is, a dime store), has opened new and improved versions around town, including one in the Gare du Nord for those heading out or coming in from London and places via Eurostar, Thalys trains, and so on. The store at Opéra is downright *moderne* now.
- Meanwhile, at **Lafayette Gourmet** on Thursday nights, you can choose to carry a purple shopping basket, which signifies to the other shoppers that you're single and open to conversation . . . or a date.
- If you like that one, you may want to sign up for cook-dating—it's also on Thursday and costs 70€ ($81); make sure you book based on your sexual orientation. Call ℡ 01-40-29-46-04, or log on to www.latelierdefred.com.
- **Starbucks** has arrived with great success—they keep popping up everywhere. There's even one in the heart of the Left Bank at the Odéon Métro. *Mon Dieu!* **Niketown** (called NikeParis) has arrived. Watch out for those Americans; they're everywhere.

Note: Real estate prices are soaring and this means that alternative neighborhoods are getting hot. Suddenly the little streets between the rue de Rivoli and the rue St.-Honoré in the 1er are filled with cutie-pie little shops. New stores no longer choose to open in the 6e—it's too expensive. For less central locations, the 10e and 11e are still blossoming. See chapter 5 for the lowdown on all the neighborhoods.

Warning: As French retail expands and redefines itself, the stores are pursing the same war of the brands that stores in the U.S. have been enacting for several years now. The problem in France, however, is that the novelty brands tend to be American—especially in beauty. Don't buy in Europe what you can buy for less in the U.S. Also, note that L.A. (as in Los Angeles) is considered a design kingdom of its own in Europe these days—stores are touting merchandise from L.A.-based designers as if they had invented freedom fries.

On the other hand, there's still lots to see and be inspired by, there are different selections in those same old designer stores, and there are some items that are typically French or simply well priced . . . so you need not go home without a souvenir or two.

If you are returning to Paris, you'll notice that a lot has changed, much of it instigated by that cute little euro. Yes, the euro will make traveling within the European Union easier, but it sure has brought up prices in France. Dollars and euros are not at parity as we go to press, so the realities of translating prices have hit home and hit the wallet. But don't panic—I have many tricks up my sleeve.

Paris is, of course, one of the world's premier shopping cities. Even people who hate shopping enjoy it in Paris. What's not to like? The couture-influenced ready-to-wear? The street markets? The most extravagant kids' shops in the world? Jewelers nestled together in shimmering elegance? Fruits and vegetables piled in bins like more jewels? Antiques and collectibles that are literally the envy of kings? It's not hard to go wild with glee at your good luck and good sense for having chosen such a place to visit. If the prices are higher, well, you'll just have to be a little smarter.

ALYSE IN WONDERLAND

Before you shrug and say you can't afford to shop with the low dollar or there's nothing in Paris that you can't find in the U.S., I want to remind you of a few items I've found that will surely make you smile. Whether or not you buy them doesn't matter. The point is: No place has the *ooh-la-la* factor like Paris.

- **Biotherm,** the beauty treatment firm, has launched color cosmetics—not odd or surprising. However, the company claims that its powdered eye shadows have active thermal ingredients which, *bien sûr,* have an affinity for the skin and therefore stay in place longer. How can you argue with that? Science is part of the new beauty and, remember, it was Marie Curie who taught us what French women know about science.

- **Tupperware** has opened its own shop in a mall in the heart of Paris, where it offers products in French fashion colors. Tupperware parties are all the rage for those chic ladies with pearls at their necks and dogs at their heels.

- **Toilet paper** in my corner grocery store comes in peach, green, purple, and pink—not that these aren't fashion colors, but each signifies the scent blown into the tissue: *clementine, tilleul, lilas,* and *rose.*

- **Knee-highs,** what the French call *mi-bas,* can be bought with padded and quilted soles . . . how very Chanel. Meanwhile, the real fashion statement is a footie in black or white lace with ballet ties, from Monoprix, *bien sûr.*

- The French have finally accepted the fact that sun can be bad for the skin, but tans are still important to them. So now you can walk into a showerlike stall and *voilà:* be sprayed (then air-dried) with a fake tan. Or you can book a tanning massage at **Lancôme,** where fake tanning cream is rubbed in during the treatment.

- **Jean Paul Gaultier** has launched a blush-on type of powder rouge for men. In fact, every French firm now has skin care and treatments for men. There's even a spa in the 8e that's just for men, and no, it's not against the law in France.

KNOW BEFORE YOU GO

The French Government Tourist Office in the U.S. is an excellent source for visitor information and trip-planning advice. Go online to www.franceguide.com.

If you prefer, you can call one of the U.S. offices, in New York (✆ 212/315-0888), Chicago (✆ 312/337-6301), Dallas (✆ 214/720-4010), or Los Angeles (✆ 310/271-6665).

MORE INFORMATION, PLEASE

··

It's not hard to get information on Paris and France, but you'll find a few local publications to be very helpful. The main one is *Paris par Arrondissement,* a book of intricate maps. Mine fits in the palm of my hand and is so complete that I can look up an address in the front of the book, and then check a chart for the nearest Métro stop of that destination. The book comes in large format, too. For some reason, these babies are not available in the U.S., so buy yours at any bookstore in Paris; it's also sold at some street newspaper kiosks.

I also like *Paris par Autobus,* a map guide with bus routes listed by numbers. Bus travel is slower than the Métro, but I prefer it because you get to see more. Now then, in these days when every euro counts, it's my job to tell you that there are various editions of the bus book—some cost 11€ ($13) while others cost 6€ ($6.90)—so shop around a bit and see which format you prefer. There are at least three styles of these books; be sure you can read the tiny print!

If you want to know about immediate events once you get here, try *Where,* a freebie magazine given out in most hotels.

Le Figaro publishes a weekly insert, *Figaroscope,* about everything that's going on in the city, including special flea markets and shopping events. It appears in the newspaper every Wednesday.

My favorite of the regular weeklies is *Zurban,* which includes movie listings and information on cultural events. It's in French, but movie times (which use the 24-hr. clock) are easy enough to check. *Zurban* also lists special events, such as big flea markets. Buy it at any news kiosk. It costs .87€ ($1) because it is more graphically interesting than the other weekly magazines.

If you're staying in an apartment and your landlord has not left a television guide, you will need to buy one. TV guides are different from events guides and are always published 7 to 10 days in advance, making it difficult to find one for the current week. There is a free TV insert in each newspaper, either the Friday edition of *Le Parisien* or the weekend edition of *Le Figaro*.

Electronically Yours

The Internet is a fabulous source for researching your trip to France. Hotels, airlines, and travel agents all have their own websites. Most major brands also have websites, as do the French *grands magasins*—the big department stores. As we go to press, none of them offers international e-commerce, but it's on its way.

Getting online before you arrive and during your stay can help you with daily life—especially if there's a strike or you need something such as a train schedule (log on to www.sncf.fr). You can even order train tickets and print them out at home, if your French is good enough. (Any website that ends with ".fr" is likely to be in French.)

So many businesses have websites that it's impossible to give you a list. For everything you need in a one-stop site, I think the best English-language option is **Bonjour Paris** (www.bonjourparis.com). If you come to France often, you might want a subscription. For a quick look at what's happening in town, try **Time Out** (www.timeout.com), which has listings for many international cities.

Electronically Yours, Part 2

- **Wi-Fi** (Wireless Fidelity) is in vogue, just pronounce it the French way: Wee-*Fee*. You can now connect from just about anywhere in Paris. For more on Wi-Fi, see below.
- If you're going online via dial-up in your hotel room, but continually get cut off by **AOL,** don't curse AOL. It could be the phone line and the difference between digital and analog connections (don't ask). Take your laptop to the hotel's business center and tap into its T-line (the equivalent of an American T1 line). It saves the day for me every time.

- New or renovated hotels have in-room dataports; these may facilitate connections. I bought a French connector at FNAC that lets me insert my American phone plug into one side and insert the French end of the plug into the French wall. This may work better for you than connecting directly into your hotel phone. On the other hand, most hotels are Wi-Fi-enabled, so all this other stuff is outdated nonsense to most.

- There are **Internet cafes** and centers around town (p. 176). Hotels often have business centers or a cute little invention that enables you to buy a card and go online in the hotel lobby. Prices vary, but are often less expensive than hotel business centers—but more than Internet cafes. *Warning:* If you do use an Internet cafe, remember that the French use an AZERTY keyboard, not QWERTY, so your fingers will be messed up, as will your A's and Q's.

WI-FI "R" US

Since postcards and stamps are an expense you can spare, send e-mails from Paris—especially easy now that so much of the city has Wireless Fidelity, or Wi-Fi. This means you can be out and about, laptop in tow, and go online—anywhere from cafes and train stations to airports.

Obviously, your laptop, PDA, or TREO must have wireless capability (this wasn't so obvious to me), and then you need to find an area that's wired—and away you go! In some cases, you'll have to buy a Wi-Fi card (this is most common in cafes) for the airtime. Don't fret; the cards are pretty cheap: about 3€ ($3.45) for 30 minutes.

I recently stayed at a hotel that offered the loan of a Wi-Fi adapter—you pay for airtime with your own credit card—and it ended up costing about 9€ ($10) for 2 hours. Prices for airtime obviously vary.

Of the numerous hotels I stayed in while working on this revision, I had all sorts of differing Wi-Fi experiences. They ranged from free Internet connections to the ability to book a half-hour/an hour/a day to the outrageous possibility that you could only book a 24-hour session for $25. I dare say that Internet availability and cost could be a determining factor in hotel choice.

ABOUT THE PHONES

If you have a tri-band phone, it will work in Europe. Usually, you have to manually switch the band and then you're set. The phone will change to a local carrier. This means it costs you a fortune to receive calls, but you can make local calls at a decent rate.

Should your phone work on a system compatible with a SIM card, you can get a French SIM card and have a local number and pay as you go.

As for local phones, here's the system: All phone numbers in France have codes built into them. All cellphones begin with 06. Toll-free numbers are usually 08 or 0800 or something similar to the U.S.; they may also be called "green lines." Local phones in Paris and the greater Paris metro area begin with 01. All the phone numbers given in this book have the local numbers. The digits 02 to 05 depict other regions of France, so automatically I know that a phone number beginning with 04 is in the south of France. Since this is a Paris guide, there are no other regional codes in these pages.

Every now and then, you'll pick up a business card with an old-fashioned French phone number printed on it: It won't have 8 digits. To adapt this number to the current code, add 014.

For more on calling home, see p. 35.

GETTING TO PARIS BY PLANE

Flying from the U.S.

While getting to Paris may seem easy enough—after all, most of the major carriers fly there—I've got a few secrets that make getting there more fun and less expensive.

The cheapest airfares are always in winter. Furthermore, winter airfares often coincide with promotional gimmicks, such as: buy one ticket, get one at half-price; buy one ticket, bring along a companion for a discounted price; or kids fly free. Also during winter, airlines may reduce the number of frequent-flier miles you need to reach a particular destination. This seldom applies to Paris, but Brussels often goes "on sale."

Winter always brings airfare price wars; when Air France announced a $299 weekend fare to Paris last winter, I think half of New York tilted into the Atlantic in a mad rush for tickets. Friends from Houston (who had the exact same rate) called me immediately.

Don't forget online sales and online purchases—two different subjects. Most airlines allow you to register for e-mail announcements of bargains on your favorite routes. I just had a message from Delta telling me I could fly from New York to Nice for $458 round-trip.

Promotionally speaking, there's a more or less standing deal that if you buy a full-fare business-class ticket with your Platinum American Express card, you get a companion ticket for free. That might not be the least expensive way to get to Paris, but it's still a bargain.

Between the airlines' online specials, discounters' online fares, and airfare wars usually announced in the newspapers, you should be able to find a number of good deals.

Airfare-war trick: If you buy a ticket, and a price war then makes the same ticket available at a lower price, don't just sit there and stew. The airlines will rewrite your ticket, subject to a service charge. The charge is usually $100 to $150, but you may save money overall.

Another strategy: Buy a cheapie ticket, then pay the fee to change to different dates, which may not have been included during the price war.

Also, check out consolidators, which unload unsold tickets on scheduled flights at discount prices (which vary with the season, like regular prices). You might not earn frequent-flier miles, but these tickets are great for last-minute travelers who do not qualify for 21-day advance-purchase prices. You need only about 4 business days' notice.

Don't forget the big-time tour operators. Rates are lower if you book through French tour operators or wholesalers like **Nouvelles Frontières** (www.nouvelles-frontieres.fr), a major chain of French travel agents, which calls itself New Frontiers in the U.S.

Sometimes you will do better if you fly into a well-trafficked or promoted hub such as Amsterdam, London, or Frankfurt. The "Brussels Trick" is explained below.

Insider's tip: If you like to fly business class (who doesn't?) but can't afford the high prices, check with Air France. It often has a promotion whereby if you purchase your ticket 2 or 3 months in advance and accept it as nonrefundable, you'll get a business class fare of about $2,200.

Another tip: Should something go wrong in your connections within the U.S., and you miss your flight to Paris and are stranded in an East Coast airport, there's a good chance you'll get rerouted through London. You may have to layover in London for many hours. Smart travelers always have £50 ($91) in their travel wallets. Also see below.

Flying from the U.K.

If you think you'll just make a quick little hop from London to Paris on a whim, you may be shocked to realize that the regular airfare is outrageously high, depending on the day and time you fly. For a regular round-trip ticket, bought on a regular carrier at the last minute, you may have to pay £200 ($362) per person. There are ways to beat this, of course, but it takes practice . . . or luck.

If you need one-way transportation between London and Paris, but are keen on flying, an advance round-trip ticket that includes a Saturday night stay will be less expensive than a one-way ticket. Just throw away the unused portion. *C'est la vie.*

One of the best fare-savers is to fly round-trip from the U.S. to the U.K. and then take the train to Paris, if you can get a promotional train ticket. See p. 30.

Flying through Brussels

This is my famous "Brussels Trick." Don't look at me like that! Brussels is less than 1½ hours from Paris, thanks to speedy Thalys train lines. You can easily fly into Brussels and out of Paris (or vice versa), or even go to Paris for the weekend from Belgium. Sometimes, when there are airfare deals and promotions, all seats in and out of Paris are sold—so try Brussels for one leg and see if you can beat the system by being a little bit clever.

Flying through Amsterdam

With the recent financial merger of Air France and KLM, you may find some great deals to Paris simply by changing planes in Amsterdam.

Flying from Nice

Many people like to combine the south of France with Paris, especially because the Delta nonstop flight from New York makes it so easy. But getting to Paris can be complicated if you don't work it all out beforehand.

If you're flying Delta on the triangular route, so to speak, you will need a train, a car, or a plane ticket to get you to Paris. Or you can book with Air France. Since Air France has no direct flights from the U.S. to Nice, it offers an alternative that should be priced competitively when it includes Nice—you just want a layover between legs. Note that because Delta and Air France have merged many of their flights and services, you may be able to book a mixed ticket at a good price. The point of the game is to avoid overpaying for the Paris-Nice link.

GETTING THERE BY TRAIN

There are many, many train fares for travel to and from Paris. Several **BritRail USA** packages allow you to choose which method you'd like to use for getting from the U.K. to the Continent; the Continental Capitals Circuit connects London with Paris, Brussels, and Amsterdam.

Rail Europe (© 888/382-7245 in the U.S.) sells passes for travel in specific countries (such as the France pass) that enable you to save money on train fares. The price of some products includes an automatic discount (about 30%!) off a Eurostar (Chunnel train) ticket. Note that the Eurostar ticket is not part of any pass currently available; it must be bought as an add-on. Rail Europe also offers multiple-country train passes, as well as other train-drive promotions and products. It's a one-stop agency that can arrange everything, and you'll have the train pass in hand when you land in Europe. Note that if you travel on the fast TGV trains in France with a train pass, you will need an additional reservation. The price of a train reservation varies, but within France is usually 3€ ($3.45).

Rail Europe not only has tons of train passes, but also books transatlantic flights, hotels, car rentals—the works. One of the greatest things about its system is that there are different prices based on age (youth passes, seniors, and so forth), as well as on the number of people traveling together. Not just "the more the merrier"—the more the cheaper.

If you can get by in the French language and have a French address, you can go directly online and order your tickets from SNCF—Societé National Chemin de Fer, the French rail system; log on to www.sncf.fr.

ARRIVING IN PARIS

If you're arriving from the U.S., you'll fly into **Charles de Gaulle International Airport** (CDG; ✆ 01-48-62-22-80 for English language info on transport; www.ratp.fr).

Note: Flights to and from the U.S. no longer use Orly Airport.

A taxi to the 1er from CDG costs about 50€ ($58), including tip and the traditional surcharge for luggage. Most French taxis are small; if you have a lot of luggage, hold out for a Mercedes taxi. If you have a lot of passengers plus a lot of luggage, expect to take two taxis.

If you are arriving in Paris from Europe, there's a good chance your flight will come into **Orly.** Orly is also the airport of choice for low-cost carriers. The airport is now so much in demand that it has been totally renovated.

Speaking of low-cost carriers, a few of them like to use the Beauvais airport, which is well over an hour outside of Paris. If you use public transportation to get there, you must allow 3 to 4 hours before your flight departure to meet at the *rallye* point in Paris for the transfer.

To transfer into Paris from Orly and/or CDG, you can use bus service to and from Etoile (take a taxi to your hotel from there), and several other midcity drop-off points.

You can also take Roissy Rail, which lets you off in town at the Gare du Nord or Châtelet, although these are better for those who have easy-to-handle luggage.

For private car service, see p. 35.

GETTING AROUND PARIS

Paris is laid out in a system of zones called *arrondissements,* which spiral around from inside to outside. When France adopted postal codes, Parisians incorporated the arrondissement numbers into their codes as the last two digits. Codes for addresses in the city of Paris begin with 75; the last two digits match the arrondissement. For example, a code of 75016 means the address is in the 16th arrondissement (16e). The first arrondissement is written *1er;* for others, the number followed by a small "e" (2e, 3e, and so forth) signifies the arrondissement.

Knowing the proper arrondissement is essential to getting around easily in Paris. For many people, indicating the arrondissement is also a shorthand way of summing up everything a place can or may become—simply by where it is located, or by how far it is from something that is acceptably chic.

Think about arrondissements when planning your shopping expeditions, but check the map frequently: You may think that, say, 1er and 16e are far apart, but you can walk between them, and have a great time doing so. (Take the rue du Faubourg St-Honoré toward the Champs-Elysées and you even get a tour of the 8e.)

With its wonderful transportation system, Paris is a pretty easy city to navigate. Tourists are usually urged to ride the Métro, but buses can also be a treat—you can see where you're going and get a free tour along the way. *Paris par Arrondissement* usually includes bus routes, as well as a Métro map. Métro maps are available for free at hotels; keep one in your wallet at all times.

By Métro

There are many Métro ticket plans. If you can speak a little French and visit Paris often enough to take the time to do this, buy a **Carte Orange.** It is exactly what it sounds like: a small orange card, with a passport-type photo. (Bring a photo, or use the photo booth in the station.) The orange ID card is inserted into a plastic carrying case with a slot for a *coupon.* The coupon is good for 1 week and is good for the bus, RER within Paris, and Métro.

This option is not for everyone, as it covers an entire week, *from Monday to Monday*. (It is not for sale after Wed.) But the Carte Orange is only about half the price of the weekly tourist ticket, called **Sesame.** Bargain shopping begins at the Métro station, *mes amis*. However, the Carte Orange doesn't pay for itself if you don't use it a lot.

Note: You probably cannot get your first Carte Orange unless you speak enough French to negotiate the purchase and answer a few questions. Touristy tourists will be guided toward other, more expensive arrangements, such as the Sesame.

I ask the hotel concierge to write down everything I need, and then I slide the paper under the window at the ticket booth of the Concorde Métro station. Only a handful of stations process the Carte Orange for first-timers, and Concorde is one of them. Remember, you will need a passport photo. Also remember where you put the card when you return home; I keep mine with my passport.

Everything I've just told you is basic. Here's the new twist: Your Carte Orange can come in an electronic version called a **Navigo** card. I call it an Octopus because that's what it's called in Hong Kong, where I first saw the technology. Rather than feeding your coupon into the turnstile, you simply lay the carte packet on top of the turnstile, where it will be read electronically.

If you want individual tickets, you can buy a *carnet* at any station. The 10-ticket carnet costs 11€ ($13) and is good on both the Métro and the bus. An individual Métro ticket costs 1.40€ ($1.60), but with the carnet, the price drops to 1€ ($1.15). That's a pretty good savings. At some point in the near future, the carnet will be replaced with a chip-based card as well.

The **Paris Visite** transportation pass provides travel for 1, 2, 3, or 5 days; it even can include rides to the airport, outlying suburbs, and Versailles. It's an awfully good deal if you plan to use it. The pass comes in a black case in which you insert something that looks like the coupon used in a Carte Orange.

Passes are for sale at RATP stations (big Métro stations or RER stations—I look at the acronym and think "rapid transit"), SNCF (French national train) stations, and ADP (Aéroports de Paris) booths at both airports.

By RER

If you take RER trains within the city of Paris, you can use a regular Métro ticket; some Paris Visite coupons are valid on RER out of town, even as far as Versailles.

By Bus

Buses are much slower than the underground, but you get to see the sights. Paris buses accept the same coupons as the Métro, cash, and (soon) bank cards. The fare, if you are paying in cash, is currently 1.30€ ($1.50). If you use a ticket from your carnet, you save almost 30%. If you have a coupon or electronic pass, show it when you board the bus, but do not put it in the validating machine.

By Taxi

The taxi meter drops at 2€ ($2.30) and goes up, up, and away—extras for luggage, for extra people, for dogs. Taxi drivers may also take you on a scenic route in order to bring the fare up, blaming traffic. Sit back and enjoy it. Tip at least 1€ ($1.15) unless the cheat has been in violation of common sense.

By Car

If you plan to visit the countryside or Disneyland Paris, you may want to rent a car. As long as you avoid driving around the place de la Concorde, you'll be fine. As an added convenience, most major car-rental agencies will allow you to drop the car at a hotel, saving you the time and trouble of returning it yourself.

If you intend to drive around Paris (silly you), be sure you know the parking regulations and how to work the meters, which provide a ticket that proves you've paid. (Display it prominently in your windshield.) Just because you don't see a meter like we have in the U.S. doesn't mean that parking is free. Also, you may need a newfangled parking *carte* from a news kiosk to get the ticket.

If you prefer a car and driver, contact **Paris Millénium** (© **01-30-71-93-03;** fax 01-30-71-97-91); ask for Mathieu, who speaks perfect English. There are special Born to Shop rates for airport transfers and shopping tours.

E.T., PHONE MAISON

- When calling a phone number inside Paris, dial the entire number, including the "01." When dialing from outside of France, drop the "0." International calls to Paris all begin with "33-1."
- The most expensive way to phone home is direct dial from your hotel room.
- The least expensive way to call home is with a phone card, provided you can make such a call from your hotel room. Some allow it, some don't. *My rule of thumb:* The fancier the hotel, the less likely it is to allow use of phone cards. I usually buy a Tele2 international phone card for 7.50€ ($8.60)—this gives me about 200 minutes of chat time to the U.S. Honest.
- Using a pay phone is not particularly difficult, especially if you use a French Telecom *télécarte*. You can buy one at any newsstand. There are three different kinds of phone cards, so investigate—one is magnetic and used exclusively for pay phones *(cabines)*; one is for mobile phones; and one is for land lines.

- Another way to save is to use a direct-dialing service through your long-distance carrier at home. For **AT&T**, call © 08-00-99-00-11; for **MCI**, call © 08-00-99-00-19; for **Sprint**, call © 08-00-99-00-87. These systems are more expensive than I like, but many people pay for the convenience and like the well-advertised connect numbers.
- Renting a mobile phone, especially a tri-band, is a popular way to keep in touch. You can rent in the U.S. or France, often through your car-rental firm or hotel. If you rent the phone before leaving the U.S., you can give out your number in advance. Call **InTouchUSA** (© 800/872-7626).

ONLINE TIP

If you're doing research for your trip, note that sites that are dot.coms often have information in many language choices. Sites that end in ".fr" are usually in French.

E-MAILING HOME

If you do not normally travel with your computer, you can still use e-mail. Most luxury hotels have Web television, as well as a business center where you can log on. Paris also has tons of Internet cafes (p. 176).

POSTCARDS HOME

Postcards in Paris are as original and arty as the city itself. There are thousands of designs and styles to choose from, but watch out—many of them cost 1€ ($1.15) or more, especially the good ones. You can buy postcards for less if you shop carefully; you may even luck out and find 15 cards for 2€ ($2.30). Walk along the rue de Rivoli, where the TTs (tourist traps) are thick, checking prices as you go. The price per card drops as you head uptown (away from Concorde, toward the Louvre), and the bulk deals get better. Tourist traps near Notre Dame also sell postcards and often offer bulk deals.

You can buy stamps at a PTT (post office), at a tobacco shop, or from your hotel concierge. Postage to the U.S. (even for a postcard) is .95€ ($1.10); local postage, which includes other E.U. countries, is .50€ (58¢).

Traditionally, stamps in France do not have the price printed on them. They are color-coded: the orange stamp is for E.U. (including local) mail, and the gray or dark-blue stamp is for international and non-E.U. items.

SHOPPING HOURS

Shopping hours in Paris are extremely irregular and independent. Welcome to France. Thankfully, they are big-city hours, so you needn't worry about a lot of downtime, as in Italy or the French provinces. There are plenty of shopping opportunities, even on Sunday and Monday, along with some serious late-night shopping.

Generally speaking, *stores are open Monday, or part of Monday.* Stores that are closed on Monday morning—usually small establishments—open anytime from noon on, or sometimes from 1, 2, or even 3pm. Department stores and branches of the major chains are open on Monday morning, and so are about 50% of the stores in the prime shopping areas on the Left Bank.

During the rest of the week, most stores consider 10am to 7pm standard hours, but there are many exceptions to this rule, such as it is. Some stores open at 10am, except one day of the week, when they open at 9:30am. Some stores are open until 10pm on Thursday only. A few stores are open until 8 or 9pm every weekday, especially in high-traffic areas.

My favorite for idiosyncratic hours is Au Printemps, which opens, not at 9:30am, but at 9:35am! It's impossible to know or keep track of every store's hours. Other stores have a few weird twists to their hours, like Hermès—which closes for lunch on Monday and Saturday.

In summer, many stores close for lunch on Saturday, but stay open later in the evening. Some stores are open for lunch during the week, but close for lunch on Saturday.

France has about 15 bank holidays a year; stores may close on these holidays. Beware the month of May! Not only does May have about 10 holidays in it, but it's also hard to know when stores will be open. May 1 is a huge holiday, when everything is closed. May 8 is a less important holiday, and stores may or may not be open—check ads in *Le Figaro*. Your hotel concierge may not know. Also note that openings may be related to the part of town. On May 8, I was shut out in the 16th arrondissement, but found stores in most other neighborhoods open. Go figure.

Bastille Day, July 14, is a holiday, and stores are closed— but some small retailers open, if only for a few hours, to take advantage of the crowds in the streets.

The entire month of August may be unusual. Most of France closes down on August 15 for the Feast of the Assumption, but some stores close for the entire month, or just from August 14 to August 31.

Bonne chance, as we say!

SUNDAY IN THE PARK WITH GEORGES

Although traditional Parisian retail stores close on Sunday, there is still an enormous amount of shopping on offer. Aside from the flea-market business, which has always been hot on Sunday, nowadays entire neighborhoods are jumping. Check out:

- The **Louvre,** with the adjoining mall Carrousel du Louvre, the Antiquaires des Louvre, and all the touristy shops on rue de Rivoli.

- The **Marais,** including the retail street rue Francs-Bour-geois, where most stores are open.
- The **Champs-Elysées,** where most stores open on Sunday at noon (except Monoprix, which does not open on Sun).
- The **Ile St-Louis.**

Many stores that open on Sunday are closed on Monday.

Antiquing on Sunday is a national hobby; don't forget to check the newspapers, or ask your concierge about special week-end shows or events. From February through May, the week-ends are dense with special events, many of which highlight shows for antiques, *brocante* (used items, not necessarily antiques), or both.

When the weather is good, shops in the main flow of tourist traffic may open on Sunday to catch the extra business. Every now and then, a duty-free shop will open. Tourist traps near popular attractions are almost always open on Sunday after-noons. By 5pm on Sunday, though, it's hard to find any place that's open.

EXCEPTIONAL OPENINGS

The French government allows retailers five exceptional Sun-day openings during the year. These are most often taken around Christmas, but there's usually one in September or Octo-ber for back-to-school shopping. Often, openings on holidays in May are also known as exceptional. Exceptional openings are usually advertised in newspapers like *Le Figaro*.

SALE PERIODS

Officially, the French government sets the dates of the sales, and there are only two sales periods: one in winter (Jan) and one in summer (June–July). However, many retailers, strapped for cash, offer assorted promotions and discounts these days. A few, like Hermès, have special events held outside the stores. These events are advertised and listed in papers; check the page called *Le Carnet du Jour* in *Le Figaro* for sale ads.

The big department stores turn their sale promotions into mega-deals, with banners all over the storefronts and enticing titles. You don't need to speak French to get the picture—the ads and banners make it quite clear.

The thing that I find most frightening about these French promotional sales is that they last a set time and are then over. The sale merchandise does not stay marked down. I once fell in love with a tablecloth at a department store and decided to think about it. When I went back, the 3-day promotional sale was over and the price was up 25%.

PERSONAL NEEDS

Pharmacies are marked with a green neon cross; at least one in each neighborhood must be open on Sunday. When a pharmacy is closed, a sign in the window indicates the nearest open pharmacy.

Machines in all Métro stations and pharmacies sell condoms, often male and female versions in machines that are coded blue or pink. Honest.

Monoprix on the Champs Elysées is open until 10pm in winter and midnight in summer—it stocks any personal needs you can imagine, except books in English.

If you need a book in English, try **W. H. Smith**, 248 rue de Rivoli (Métro: Concorde), which sells American and British books and periodicals. Most luxury hotels sell daily or Sunday London newspapers. Or head to Left Bank bookstores/expat hangouts **Village Voice**, 6 rue Princesse (Métro: Mabillon) or **Tea & Tattered Pages**, 24 rue Mayet (Métro: Duroc).

Speaking of books, there is an amazing bookstore in Paris with more artistic offerings than simply a book to read on the plane: French publisher **Assouline** has its first free-standing store (35 rue Bonaparte, 6e; Métro: St- Germain-des-Prés).

AIRPORT SHOPPING

Both Orly and CDG have more than their share of shopping opportunities—in fact, the shopping is so brisk that the airports have their own shopping bags. Stores at CDG are fancier than those at Orly (which handles no U.S. international traffic), but you will have no trouble dropping a few, or a few hundred, euros at either.

Prices at the airport duty-free shops may be lower than at comparable retail stores in Paris, but the selection may not be the same. I priced Longchamp tote bags—80€ ($92) in stores in Paris and 60€ ($69) at the airport, a significant savings. However, the color selection was horrible at the airport.

Those in search of cosmetics and fragrance bargains should already have bought them in Paris at the duty-free shops that offer 20% to 40% savings. You will save only 13% at the duty-free stores at the airport. The selection at the airport may be better than the selection on your plane, but the airline's prices can be better.

It pays to take the duty-free price list from the plane when you arrive and save it for comparison when shopping at the airport at the end of your trip. I also keep a Saks Fifth Avenue price list in my wallet for each of the fragrances that I like. Saks prints them constantly in mailers, bill stuffers, ads, and so on. You'd be surprised how often an airport price can be the same as a department-store price.

Legally speaking, you may not buy duty-free goods if you're leaving for another E.U. destination. To be precise, you can buy them, but you will pay the full retail price.

If you are departing the E.U., you may buy at the duty-free price (13%–14% less than regular retail).

To learn what stores are represented at the airport, check out www.aeroportsdeparis.fr. Note that these shops are interspersed among several different terminals, so you must know which terminal you're using to accurately assess your future shopping adventures.

Chapter Three

······················

MONEY MATTERS

OUCH

···

The dollar and the euro have not had an easy-to-live-with relationship in the last few years, and the exchange rate has fluctuated drastically. At present, the euro/dollar ratio stands at about the same point as when the euro was officially unveiled: 1€ equals $1.15. In the best of times, we saw a 74¢ euro; in the worst of times, one euro cost $1.34. Obviously, these fluctuations will affect your shopping. They should also affect how you spend your money. So pay attention.

COIN OF THE REALM

···

Travelers will find that euro bills are the same throughout the zone, but the coins are minted locally—they have different art on them and are of differing weights. (This causes problems in highway toll machines, but shouldn't affect you in Paris.) If you have any old 10F pieces, they can be used in luggage trolleys at train stations.

There are a lot of coins in the new equation, so most Europeans use a change purse of some sort (they do come in masculine and feminine forms, if you think real guys don't carry change purses).

How to Sound Local

When in France, you might want to pronounce the word *euro* with the local accent, or people may not know what you're talking about. Say "uh-*roh*." If you speak enough French to add numbers to it, remember to slur the plurals—that is, since *euro* begins with a vowel, *deux euros* is pronounced "duh zuh-*roh*," *dix euros* is "dee zuh-*roh*," and so on.

Collectors note that coins with the portrait of Pope John Paul II are expected to be very valuable.

FAKES & FRAUDS

If you're worried about fake euros, you're not the only one, and, yes, they have been spotted. Some appeared *before* the launch of the euro. Talk about dumb. Here are some characteristics of the real thing:

- All bills are made with a cotton fiber blend, so you can feel the texture.
- The bills have an iridescent band that seems to dance in different colors in the right light.
- A hologram band within the strip has the amount printed on it.

ABOUT PRICE TAGS

Unlike in the U.S., the price on the tag is what you pay at the checkout counter. Your cash-register receipt may well be marked in French francs as well as euros, as some people still have trouble with the newfangled currency.

ALAS, MY DÉTAXE

One of the other goals of the E.U. is to bring value-added tax throughout member countries to the same 15%. Given the economic problems suffered by many member nations, it's unlikely this goal will be met in the near future.

French TVA (or VAT, value-added tax) is currently 19.6% for most goods. *But* (of course there's a but), when you file for a tax refund, you rarely get back 19.6%. Instead, expect 12% or maybe 13%.

For an explanation of détaxe, see "Détaxe Details," below.

CURRENCY EXCHANGE

ATMs

Sacré cash card! This is without doubt the easiest and possibly best way of exchanging money—*le bank machine*. You can use your ATM card from the U.S. to withdraw euros from French ATMs, which can be found everywhere, including at the airport (so you can have euros for your taxi into town). Just look for the Cirrus, PLUS, or NYCE logo (some bank cash machines are only for local bank cards). Also note that when you see several machines in a row, they may not be the same. Sometimes only some of the machines give money back; the others are for customers' transactions. Read the signs above each machine.

As much as I love ATMs, I find myself betwixt and between on the fee-versus-safety issue. If you try to save the $5 fee that your bank at home will probably charge each time you use an ATM, you may end up with a lot of cash in your wallet and feel nervous.

My assistant Jenny has a U.S. bank card that does not charge a fee for international withdrawals! Find out about yours; consider changing bank cards.

Amex & Visa

Card members can draw on their American Express cards for cash advances or to cash personal checks. (Never travel without your checkbook.)

It's relatively simple: You write a personal check at a special desk and show your card, have it approved, and then go to another desk to get the money in the currency you request. Allow about a half-hour for the whole process, unless there are long lines. The same desk usually handles cash advances.

Some Visa cards allow you to take cash loans from your bank while you are in a foreign destination. With some types of cards, you can write a check in dollars at a hotel and get back euros.

Note that all bank cards now charge an additional conversion rate when flipping rates.

Cambios vs. Banks

If you're silly enough to have a big fat wad of dollars in your fist and want to change them into euros, you may be wondering if you should go to one of those change places dotted all over Paris or to a bank instead. A bank is not a sure thing in terms of a better rate; shop around for a good *cambio*, and you just may do slightly better.

Traveler's Checks

You can buy traveler's checks in euros, which will be good for later trips to other destinations—but this does lock in the rate, which can be good news or bad news.

I still think they're great, and I *love* having "free money" for my next trip if I didn't use all the checks I bought. I used to get mine through AAA, so I didn't have to pay a fee. On the other hand, there are some downsides.

In recent years, I've had more and more trouble cashing traveler's checks in stores—first, there's the explanation that yes, this check is in euros (not dollars). Then there's the cashier who doesn't know how to put it into the register (as cash is the answer, but will anyone listen to you?). And finally, there's more and more insistence on behalf of stores that the traveler's check be for no more than double the purchase price of your goods. That means the old trick of buying a tube of toothpaste and cashing a 100€ ($115) check no longer works. The final insult? A bank in London charged me a fee for cashing a traveler's check that was already in sterling.

DEBIT CARDS

U.S. and French debit cards work on different formats. You will probably use your U.S. debit card more like a credit card for your end of the transaction in France, although the payment will be automatically deducted from your debit account. You will probably have to sign a paper, however. *Note:* I got a notice from my U.S. bank saying that my U.S. debit card could be used internationally only six times. Check your bank's policy.

TIPS ON TIPPING

For tipping, forget your old trick of handing out U.S. dollars. These days, no one wants them. What they really want is a 2€ ($2.30) coin.

Tipping in Paris can also be confusing because all restaurant and hotel bills include a service charge and many guidebooks tell you not to add an additional tip. While you do not have to add a tip to a restaurant check, it's often done—simply round up the bill or plunk down an extra euro or two or five. It's all the waiter will see of your real tip; think 5% of the total.

Also note that tipping has suffered with the loss of the 10F coin, which used to be the perfect tip. If you are cheap, tip in dollars. If you are going French style, substitute 2€ ($2.30) for 10F and just suck it up.

That Was No Tip

So my girlfriend Dorrie and I go to the flea market at Vanves, and stop at one of the cafes on the main drag when the market is about over. Tourists speaking many different languages fill the cafe. We have lunch and speak French. The bill is 26€ ($30). We put 31€ ($36) on the tray and wait for change. We wait and wait. Up to that point, we had planned to leave 2€ ($2.30) as a tip.

Finally we ask, "Where's the change, dude?" . . . and the waiter says, "Change? I thought that was the tip for my colleague and myself."

Tourists, beware. And don't be bullied.

You may, however, do some rounding up—say 3€ ($3.45) for two pieces of luggage to the bellboy. The hotel doorman can get 1€ ($1.15) for calling a taxi, or you can leave an envelope at the end of your stay at the hotel with a total of 5€ to 10€ (about $6–$12) for the doormen.

Insider's tip: The French mourn the loss of the 10F coin, which was an excellent tip amount worth approximately $1.75. Now that you are forced to tip in euros, some tend to round down to 1€. Please round up to 2€. There will be fewer strikes in France if you do this.

SEND MONEY

If necessary, you can have money sent from home, a process that usually takes about 2 days. Money can be wired through **Western Union** (© 800/325-6000 in the U.S.). Someone brings cash or a certified check to the office, and Western Union does the rest—this may take up to a week. You can also get cash with an international money order, which is cleared by telex through the bank where you cash it. Money can be wired from bank to bank, but this works only when your American bank has branches in Europe or a relationship with a French bank. Banks usually charge a large fee for doing you this favor.

In addition, American Express (© 800/543-4080 in the U.S.) can arrange for a Money Gram, a check for up to $500 that family or friends at home can send. You cash it at the American Express office in Paris.

DÉTAXE DETAILS

Détaxe is the refund you get on TVA, the 19.6% value-added tax on all goods sold in France (except goods needed for home repairs, which carry a 5.5% tax). TVA is similar to sales tax in the U.S. The French pay it automatically. Tourists can get a refund on it.

There are more and more ways of getting that refund. The basic détaxe system—the process of getting a refund on this tax—works pretty much like this:

You are shopping in a store with prices marked on the merchandise. This is the true price that any tourist or any national must pay. If you are a French national, you pay the price without thinking twice. If you are a tourist who plans to leave the country within 6 months, you may qualify for a détaxe refund. Currently, the minimum by French law for a détaxe refund is 175€ ($201) for a person spending this amount (or more) in one store on a single day. Each store has the right to establish the amount over 175€ ($201) you must spend to qualify for the refund.

You may no longer save up receipts over a period of time. To qualify for a tax refund, you must spend the money in the same store on the same day. For this reason, planning one big haul at one of the department stores is your best bet.

If you go for the détaxe refund, budget your time to allow for the paperwork. It takes about 15 minutes to fill out each store's forms, and may take 20 to 60 minutes for you to receive the forms back, because the store must process them. But you never know—I've zipped through the line in less than 5 minutes. Allow more time than you need, just in case.

My secret? Return to the department store the moment it opens, and head directly to the détaxe desk.

You will need your passport number (but not necessarily the passport itself) to fill out the paperwork. The space that asks for your address is asking for the name of your hotel. You do not need to provide its address. After the papers are filled out, they will be given back to you with an envelope, usually addressed to the store. Sometimes the envelope has a stamp on it; sometimes it is blank (if the latter, you must affix a stamp to it before you leave the country). At other times, it has a special government frank that serves as a stamp. If you don't understand what's on your envelope, ask.

At the airport, go to the Customs official who processes the détaxe papers. Do this before you clear regular Customs or part with your luggage. There are two ways to do this: 1) Check your luggage, but keep your purchases separate and carry them onboard with you, or 2) wheel your packed luggage to the Customs office and be prepared to unpack the items.

The Customs officer has the right to ask you to show the merchandise you bought and are taking out of the country. Whether the officer sees your purchases or not, he or she will stamp the papers, keeping a set (which will be processed) and giving you another set. Place this set in the envelope and mail it to the shop where you made your purchases. (Sometimes the Customs officer keeps the specially franked envelopes. Don't worry, they'll be mailed.)

Note: Since unification in 1993, you claim your détaxe when you leave your final E.U. destination to return to the U.S. For example, if you are going on to Belgium from France, you claim everything as you exit Belgium and process your paperwork there. You'll get the French laws and the French discounts, but the paperwork itself is done at Belgian Customs. Ditto for Britain, Italy, and elsewhere in the E.U.

When the papers get back to the shop and the government has notified the shop that its set of papers has been registered, the store will grant you the discount through a refund. This can be done on your credit card (the shop will have made a dual pressing) or through a personal check, which will come in the mail (see below).

So that's how the system works.

Now, here are the fine points: *The way in which you get your discount is somewhat negotiable!* At the time of purchase, discuss your options for the refund with the retailer. Depending on how much you have bought, how big a store it is, or how cute you are, you may get a more favorable situation. This has become more complicated in the last year or two since Global Refund is taking over most of the refund business and insists you take a cash refund from them at the airport. Whenever possible, you want your refund applied to a bank card.

Here are the two most popular ways to get your refund, in order of preference to the tourist:

- The retailer sells you the merchandise at the cheapest price possible, including the tax refund, and takes a loss on the income until the government reimburses him or her. For example: The bottle of fragrance you want costs 50€ ($58). The détaxe is about 9€ ($10). The best possible deal is for the retailer to charge you 41€ ($47), give you the détaxe papers, and explain that he will not get the rest of his money unless you process the papers properly. Being as honorable as you are, of course you process the papers. This is "instant détaxe," and is the practice in some name-brand stores and most *parfumeries*.
- You pay for the purchase, at the regular retail price, with a major credit card. The clerk makes a second imprint of your card for a refund slip, marked for the amount of the détaxe. You sign both slips. When the papers come back to the retailer, the shop puts through the credit slip. The credit may appear on the same monthly statement as the original bill, or on a subsequent bill. Just remember to check that the credit goes through.

With the old-fashioned and most basic method, you pay the regular retail price with cash, traveler's check, or credit card. You take the forms and go through the refund process described above, get on your plane, and go home. Several (usually about 2) months later, you get a check for the refund amount in the mail.

This check is in euros and will have to be converted to dollars, a process for which your bank may charge you a percentage or a fee (yes, the fee can be more than the refund). Or you can go to a currency broker and get the money in euros for your next trip to that country. Either way, it's a pain in the neck— and you lose money.

Again, the best way to take the refund is on your credit card! Then you do nothing, yet still receive the maximum amount of funds due you.

Remember: While it's more and more popular to offer you a cash-back return at the airport (in the currency of your choice), don't be blinded by this opportunity. You will lose money on the conversion.

Money, Money Everywhere

So, if the department stores and boutiques are "making" about 7% off each refund, you can begin to figure that this refund business is hot stuff. Add to that the fact that it's confusing to beginners, time-consuming, and possibly annoying. Enter the professional refund services, which will happily help you through the process. *Phew,* you are thinking. For a fee, of course. Well, that seems fair enough, you say—nothing is free. Usually, it's a hidden fee or even a double fee in the guise of fee plus exchange rate.

Repeat: The smartest way to get your détaxe refund is as a credit applied to your charge or bank card. Even if you paid for the purchase with cash, you can still have the refund applied to a credit card. Even if you are issued a "refund chèque," you can endorse it on the back to be refunded to your credit card.

Détaxe on Trains, Boats & Ferries

If you leave Paris by train (such as the overnight train to Istanbul), you may be in a panic about your détaxe refund. Not to worry. As mentioned above, you now apply for the refund as you leave the E.U. If your train is taking you to another E.U. country, you do not even have to think about filing for your détaxe refund in France.

If your train (or ferry) is taking you to a non-E.U. country, you will need to do the paperwork onboard. No problem. Shortly after you board the international train, the conductor for your car will poke his head into your cabin, introduce himself (he speaks many languages), ask for your passport, and give you the Customs papers for the crossing of international borders. If you are on the sleeper, he handles the paperwork in the middle of the night while you snooze.

If you are catching the *QM2* in France, transiting to Southampton (U.K.) before a transatlantic crossing, you do the détaxe at the port when you leave France. At check-in for the ship (which is on land, not onboard), ask where the Customs agents are so you can have your paperwork stamped.

U.S. CUSTOMS & DUTIES

To make your reentry into the U.S. as smooth as possible, follow these tips:

- Know the rules and stick to them.
- Don't try to smuggle anything.
- Be polite and cooperative (up until the point when they ask you to strip, anyway).

Also, remember the following:

- You are allowed to bring in $800 worth of merchandise per person, duty-free. (Books, which are duty-free, are not included.) Each member of the family, including infants, is entitled to the deduction.

- Currently, you pay a flat 10% duty on the next $1,000 worth of merchandise.
- Duties thereafter are based on the type of product and vary tremendously.
- The "head of the family" can make a joint declaration for all family members. Whoever is the head of the family should take responsibility for answering Customs officers' questions. Answer honestly, firmly, and politely. Have receipts ready, and make sure they match the information on the landing card. Don't be forced into a story that won't wash under questioning. If you tell a little lie, you'll be labeled a fibber, and they'll tear your luggage apart.
- Have the Customs registration slips for your personal goods in your wallet or otherwise easily accessible. If you wear a Cartier watch, be able to produce the registration slip. If you cannot prove that you took a foreign-made item out of the U.S. with you, you may be forced to pay duty on it. If you own such items but have no registration or sales slips, take photos or Polaroids of the goods and have them notarized in the U.S. before you depart. The notary seal and date will prove you had the goods in the U.S. before you left the country.
- The unsolicited gifts you mailed from abroad do not count in the per-person rate. If the value of the gift is more than $50, you pay duty when the package comes into the country. Remember, it's only one unsolicited gift per person. Don't mail to yourself.
- Do not attempt to bring in any illegal food items—dairy products, meats, fruits, or vegetables. Generally speaking, if it's alive, it's forbidden. Coffee is okay. Any creamy French cheese is illegal, but a hard or cured cheese is legal as long as it has aged 60 days.
- Elephant ivory is illegal to import. Antique ivory pieces may be brought into the country if you have papers stating their provenance.

- Antiques must be 100 years old to be duty-free. Provenance papers will help, as will permission to export the antiquity, since it could be an item of national cultural significance. Any bona fide work of art is duty-free, whether it was painted 50 years ago or yesterday; the artist need not be famous.
- Dress for success. People who look like "hippies" get stopped at Customs more than average folks. But women who look like a million dollars (sporting fur coats, first-class baggage tags, and Gucci handbags) and declare that they've bought nothing are equally suspicious.

Chapter Four

....

SLEEPING IN PARIS

ARE YOU SLEEPING?

Some of the world's best hotels are in Paris; thankfully, they are cheaper than those in London. But the really fancy ones have gotten a lot fancier in recent years—and more expensive. Even midpriced hotels can be expensive; furthermore, you can stay in a fabulous hotel or in a terrible hotel for the same amount of money. That's why I do so much hotel research and keep looking for the best buys (for some of my secret finds, see p. 66).

The kind of trip you have is very much related to the hotel you book. Take time to research value and make sure you don't get burned. Also, remember that often a more expensive hotel—or a slightly higher package rate—turns out to be cheaper, if you add in the extras. Sometimes you have to spend a little more to save a lot more.

When pricing hotels, especially during promotions, be sure to read the fine print. Some hotels require a minimum stay of 2 nights for you to qualify for a bargain price. Some "deals" are good only on weekends. Bear in mind that prices may be per person or per room.

July and August are high season for airfare, but low season in terms of hotel rooms in Paris. Some of the best deals of the year can be made during this time.

Other secrets:

- **Think winter.** The rack rate, or official room rate, at a midrange luxury hotel in Paris is 400€ ($460) and up. For multistar luxury in the lowest category, you are generally asked to pay about 600€ ($690). It can go up (easily). Avoid Paris when it's most fully booked (and, therefore, most expensive) in May, June, September, and October. Think December. Think January. Even February.
- **Think tragedy.** It's terrible, but it's true. In times of war and sorrow, when no one is traveling, there are airfare and hotel deals galore.
- **Think opening day . . . or reopening day.** New and newly renovated hotels introduce themselves and woo back regular clients with amazing deals and perks. When Inter-Continental reopened the Grand after 2 years of serious renovations, there were many good deals to lure back lost customers. Perhaps the best deal in Paris was the Discovery Package offered by the new Hilton Arc de Triomphe. *Note:* Specifically ask your travel agent about new openings.
- **Go down a notch (or more) in hotel choice.** Yes, we'd all like to stay at the Four Seasons, but other hotels abound. Best of all, there are hotels you've never heard of that you will enjoy. It's okay if you don't stay in a palace.
- **Try a less chic neighborhood.** There are wonderful hotels in Montmartre (18e) or Bastille (12e) that you will really like (I promise), and they cost less because they are not in the Marais or the 6e, the 1er, the 8e, or the 16e. Branch out a little.
- **Use associations and memberships to your advantage.** AAA, AARP, and American Express card members get deals on prices, upgrades, or even gifts.
- **Work with hotel associations and chains.** Most hotels are members of associations or chains that have blanket promotions. Leading Hotels of the World offers a fabulous corporate rate. Most hotels have rates frozen in U.S. dollars

for at least a portion of the year, especially when they are in a promotional period, but often in summer. These invariably have to be booked in the United States, but usually offer incredible value. Some hotels offer special rates for certain months; others offer these rates year-round!

- **Never assume that all hotels in a chain are equal.** Even if you're talking about big American chains, such as Hilton or Sheraton, you will find hotels in every category of style and price within the same chain.
- **Learn the French chains.** Americans may know the Sofitel brand, but they possibly have not heard of Libertel—a great chain of three- and four-star hotels. You may know Best Western from the U.S., but the France Best Western group has different ownership and better hotels. Not all French chains are equal, but whenever I hear of someone staying in a Libertel, I am impressed by that person's travel savvy.
- **Compare apples to apples.** Get the best price you can from one or two luxury or palace hotels, and use that as your baseline so that you can figure out what you are really getting with other hotel offers.
- **Think package tours.** Airlines and tour operators often offer you the same trip you could plan for yourself with the kinds of hotels you really want to stay at, but for less money. Check them out. Beware, however: On a package tour, you may not get as good a room as you would on your own, and your chances of being upgraded are lower.
- **Think competition.** When the George V closed to transform itself into the Four Seasons, two neighboring hotels—the deluxe Prince de Galles and the Queen Elizabeth—enjoyed increased business. With the Four Seasons now open, try these hotels, which may try to lure you with price cuts.
- **Don't forget online deals.** The hotels themselves as well as hotel discounters and specialty websites often offer great deals online. Spend time on this research, as websites can offer a variety of deals, often at the same hotel. I like Hotels.com. Remember, some discounters' websites charge for booking

and do not let you cancel. When I find an attractive deal through a hotel broker, I call the reservations desk and ask them to match it on a personal basis.

- **Consider the grab-and-run technique.** I have a friend who came to Paris with a reservation for 3 nights at one hotel, but a plane ticket for a 10-day stay. She went online and checked hotel deals from a cybercafe in Paris and moved every few days, chasing the best deals and testing different hotels and neighborhoods.
- **Check out www.bonjourparis.com.** This site has tons of info on Paris (and all of France), as well as hotel deals. When booking with any online source, if you're considering a hotel you do not know, check out not only photos, but also your own map. A hotel with buzzwords such as Tour Eiffel or Arc de Triomphe may not be very close to these landmarks, no matter what the name implies.
- **Rent an apartment.** If there are more than two in your group, you can get more of the feel of living in Paris—while saving money to boot—by renting an apartment. Go to www. VBRO.com or any of a zillion other sites. An apartment might give you a lot more space (and flexibility) for the same rate as a hotel room. You also have the option to cook or eat a few meals in the apartment.

HIDDEN DEALS

Find a few websites you like and check them regularly, even if they're in French—or especially if they're in French. For example, I totally by accident discovered a promotion that offered a room in any of 99 European Hilton hotels for 99€ ($114) per *room*—not per person—including breakfast for two. The offer was an Easter special, available only for a 2-week period.

Now, you might not have wanted to stay in a Hilton, and you might not have been traveling to Paris during those 2 weeks . . . but for a rate that low, a person can learn to be flexible. Because I regularly check the site (www.hilton.com),

I found the special. Otherwise, I would have missed it. Many of the best deals are quickies that you have to be actively researching in order to profit from.

COMPARING PALACE HOTELS

FOUR SEASONS GEORGE V
31 av. George V, 8e (Métro: George V).

I hang out at the Four Seasons a lot and love it for a visit; actually, I insist you visit while in Paris. Although it's incredibly luxurious, the hotel does not feel very French and could be a Four Seasons anywhere in the world, but that isn't bad. Although this hotel has been open for 7 years, I just stayed here for the first time and, I must say, I've never, ever, been pampered like this. Everyone in the hotel knew my name. (I am certain they have photo drills each night.) While the Internet service in the room was priced at $25 per 24-hour period, guests are granted one half-hour a day of free Internet access in the business center. The price of local phone calls was obscene; the price of room service was moderate. There is a phone *cabine* in the lobby so that you can easily retreat there to use your phone card.

Rates: You can get a room for $650, but the rack rate is higher—in season, a lot higher.

Celebrities: Movie-star heaven. No names, please.

Beauty: The pool is gorgeous, as is the entire spa area. There's a wide variety of treatments, including one with chocolate. Bulgari bathroom amenities are freely stocked.

Eats: The three-star Le Cinq is famous, but La Galerie is a good place to eat and just stare at the flowers and the crowd. You'll pay $29 for a burger, but it's worth it considering the theater involved. I ordered pasta from room service, since I was concerned about price—it wasn't great.

Packages: This hotel has various promotions that include a lot—such as a free spa treatment or dinner in the three-star restaurant.

For reservations from the U.S., call © **800/819-5053,** or 01-49-52-70-00 locally; or log on to www.fourseasons.com.

HÔTEL DE CRILLON
10 place de la Concorde, 8e (Métro: Concorde).

One of the most famous palace hotels in Paris, the Crillon has just refurbished most of its rooms and suites and has added a fancy health club and a Guerlain spa. This hotel is expected to change a lot now that Starwood has bought the brand, so keep an eye on it.

Rates: Officially begin at $600.

Celebrities: Presidents, heads of state, Madonna.

Beauty: Guerlain spa (see p. 214 for details).

Eats: The restaurant is one of the most famous in Paris. Its chef, Jean-François Piège, was Number Two to Alain Ducasse before coming to the Crillon; the hotel was proud to "poach" him. While Les Ambassadeurs is the fancy restaurant, a well-known trick is to eat in the more casual L'Obélisque in the rear of the hotel—you get the same chef for less money.

Packages: The Crillon offers a number of packages and promotions with dollar rates, which can make the hotel almost affordable. In addition, there are weekend and honeymoon specials; one includes dinner and breaks down to be a good value. There's also a shopping package that includes limo time. Dogs stay free and receive a tag that says, "If I am lost, return me to the Hôtel de Crillon." I wish I had a tag like that.

For reservations from the U.S., call © **800/888-4747,** or 01-44-71-15-00 locally, or fax 01-44-71-15-02. The Crillon is a member of Leading Hotels of the World (© 800/223-6800) and Relais & Châteaux (© 212/856-0115). Log on to www. crillon.com.

HÔTEL MEURICE
228 rue de Rivoli, 1er (Métro: Concorde or Tuileries).

The sultan of Brunei bought this hotel and merged it into the Dorchester Group (with London's Dorchester and Paris's Plaza Athénée). After extensive renovation, the Meurice has emerged fancier than before—and more expensive. On the other hand, it's essentially a palace hotel in all senses of the words: they don't make 'em like this anymore and you definitely don't have one of these back home. Furthermore, you get the most amenities for free of any of the palace hotels, including free Internet access in your room.

Rates: Officially begin at $750.

Celebrities: More European in its celebrity net, the hotel attracts a lot of fashion and publishing people, and royalty.

Beauty: The health club boasts the only Paris location of Le Source de Caudalie, the wine spa from Bordeaux that creates treatments from the anti-aging pepins of grapes from the château. Bathroom amenities are from Penhaligon.

Eats: The chef, Yannick Alléno, has three stars and offers up a creative *carte;* one of the best deals in town is the $55 lunch. The dining room is as gorgeous as the food. My recent dinner here was one of the most memorable meals of my life—it began with celery mousse over foie gras and went on and on. Don't forget the fixed-price dinner in Le Jardin d'Hiver, for $55 per person. Note that the famed tearoom Angélina is next door.

Packages: The variety of packages can make the high prices more attractive; for example, the "Just Between Us" package provides shopping addresses, a private shopping tour, and various perks at luxury stores. Reservations for this package must be made at least 3 weeks before arrival (to line up your tour) and are based on double or triple occupancy—perfect if a bunch of girls want to go together on a Paris shopping spree and can share a room.

For reservations from the U.S., call Leading Hotels of the World (© **800/223-6800**, or 01-44-58-10-10 locally; fax 01-44-58-10-15).

NOT QUITE PALACES

If you love your luxury hotel, but prefer to pay under $400 a night for a room, you'll find that the above hotels are out of your budget. In fact, it's pretty hard to find a deluxe hotel that combines amenities with price. Here are a few suggestions that get my vote.

HILTON ARC DE TRIOMPHE
51–57 rue de Courcelles, 8e (Métro: Courcelles).

I am really not a Hilton kind of gal, but this hotel is so spectacular and well priced that it's my duty to tell all. But first, important information: Make sure you are getting a deal. I was recently upgraded to a suite in this hotel, yet the price on the door was the exact same as a suite at the Meurice. This is not an apples to apples comparison, believe me.

You stay at the Hilton because you are getting a deal. You do not stay at the Hilton if you aren't ready to give up some of the palace hotel touches. It's not that the Hilton is in any way lacking. The only downside is that the place has 512 units, so if you want small and *intime*, it isn't for you. Also note, the folks who stay here—or the ones I see in the lobby, anyway—tend to be more casually dressed than the guests at the Four Seasons or the Meurice. There seem to be a lot of groups, too. This hotel is the single most popular destination for bookings with mileage points.

That said, may I please start to drool over this place? This hotel opened in May 2004 and is like no other Hilton in the world. The hotel bought the rights to the Emile-Jacques Ruhlmann estate, so the Art Deco theme more than permeates the space—it's a total movie set combining genuine signed pieces with reproductions from the original drawings. (Yes, you can buy the furniture.)

The location seems odd at first—this is essentially a residential area—but you're within walking distance of all major streets and can enjoy the hidden charms of the rue Courcelles (with one of the best resale shops in Paris). The first Carita spa is here, called Mosaics. The no. 84 bus, right outside the front door, connects the hotel to all of Paris if you aren't walking or taking the nearby Métro.

The rate is usually around $345, which, if you get a promotional deal, can include breakfast for two. Breakfast is a very comprehensive buffet. Call © **800-HILTONS** in the U.S., or 01-58-36-17-17 locally, or log on to www.hilton.com.

HOTEL DE SERS
41 av. Pierre 1er de Serbie, 8e (Métro: George-V or Alma-Marceau).

Let's start with the name, address, and pronunciations: There was an actual Marquis de Sers, and you so say the last "s." So don't say "Le Sers" or "La Sers," as you could end up at a very expensive restaurant. To say the address, say "Pierre Premier de Serbie."

I mention our friend the marquis because this hotel has been created from his family mansion and is now totally redone in the newfangled *moderne* style begun by the Costes Brothers. This is the next generation, which means the hotel is Costes-like, but warm while mixing the baroque with the Starck.

The atrium, which uses a projector to change the colors of light, thus affecting the mood and ambience, is a nice touch; the concierge service sent me a printout to confirm all bookings and a map with walking instructions. The attention to details was seductive. The clients were very hip—the kind of travelers who always wear black.

The hotel is smack-dab in the middle of the luxury 8e shopping district, around the corner from the Four Seasons George V. There is an Internet station in the lobby or free access in your room, if you have your computer with you.

Best yet, while my room had a price tag of $633 inside the closet, I had booked with Yellin Hotels (www.yellinhotels) and was paying $335, a rate that included continental breakfast. I'd return in a heartbeat. The local phone number is © 01-53-23-75-75. Or log on to www.hoteldesers.com.

HOTEL PONT ROYAL
7 rue Montalembert, 7e (Métro: Rue du Bac).

This is one of those hidden-in-plain-sight finds that you might overlook because it isn't flashy. The hotel has one of the best shopping locations in Paris, especially if you love the Left Bank—it's more or less at the corner of rue du Bac and boulevard St-Germain. There are buses and the Métro out the door and you can walk easily to the major museums. If you are a foodie, you already know that Atelier de Joel Robuchon is in the hotel and Pierre Gagnier's new Gaya is across the street.

The hotel itself is a little bit British in feel, in an old, French aristocratic manner. The lobby is paneled in wood; the furnishings throughout are *moderne*. It's a homey little palace, not one that makes you nervous. The hotel is known for its place in literary circles and is also a registered landmark. Note that it is a member of a small chain, HRR (Hotel et Residence Roy)—the other hotels are hidden jewels as well—although not always at bargain prices.

The hotel website had a number of promotions and fair deals with prices beginning just under $300. A good offer through Yellin Hotels: bed-and-breakfast with all taxes and everything included, in high season, with upgrade, for $335. The local phone number is © 01-42-84-70-00, or check www.hotel-pont-royal.com or www.yellinhotels.com.

SUZY'S SECRET THREE-STAR FINDS

....

HOTEL DE L'ELYSEE
12 rue Saussaies, 8e (Métro: Clemenceau or Miromesnil).

If I had a hotel like this in every city, I'd be a happy traveler. I am even reluctant to share it now, lest it fill up beyond capacity, since it is already in demand. But I digress. Let me start at the beginning.

This is a small, three-star, family-owned hotel 1 block from the rue du Faubourg St. Honoré. It's charming and well priced— expect to pay $161 to $173. Continental breakfast is $12 more. Rooms are not huge, but the decor is comfy and great for the price. Some bathrooms have tubs; some do not. TVs do have CNN; there is an Internet station in the lobby. The local phone number is © 01-42-65-29-25.

HOTEL SAINT GERMAIN
88 rue du Bac, 7e (Métro: Rue du Bac).

This is also a three-star hotel; I have not stayed here, but the location is great (Left Bank, wonderful street of small boutiques, near Bon Marché), and the price is fabulous. Prices are based on room size, number of beds, and whether or not there is a bathtub versus a shower. The lowest price rooms do not have tubs. There are 29 rooms, and this hotel books up quickly. Rooms are about $200 per night. You pay the first night in advance; cancellations are accepted up to 48 hours before arrival date. Local phone © 01-49-54-70-00. www.hotel-saint-germain.fr.

VALUE LUXURY HOTELS

....

The following are a few of the four-star properties from the **Concorde Hotels,** which was sold to **Starwood.** I like these hotels a lot, no matter who owns them, so try tracking them down to see what is offered.

Note: The hotels are nice, but often are visited by groups. Since their rack rates are some $460 a night (no one pays rack rate!), I've decided to call them "luxury." They are fancier than my finds (listed above), but not as fancy as the demi-palaces.

HOTEL DU LOUVRE
Place André Malraux, 1er (Métro: Palais-Royal).

This hotel hosts some of the fashion shows during the spring and fall collections. It is directly across the street from the Louvre and Palais Royale. Local phone: ✆ 01-44-58-38-38.

But wait! There are other hotel chains that have fabulous hotels with deals galore. I have just rediscovered Millennium, part of the Millennium-Copthorpe Group.

HOTEL ST-LAZARE
108 rue St-Lazare, 8e (Métro: St-Lazare).

Rooms here are uneven. When you pick a hotel based on price, make sure you're getting a good value, and don't be shy if you don't like your room—ask to see others. The hotel itself is a landmark building and has the wonderful location of being next to the St-Lazare train station and a block from major department stores. Local phone: ✆ 01-40-08-44-44.

MILLENNIUM OPERA
12 bd Haussmann, 9e (Métro: Chaussée-d'Antin).

This hotel just came back into my life after friends found it online and queried me. This used to be a grand dame hotel named the Commodore; then it became the Millennium Commodore when it was bought and totally gutted—and I mean right down to the historic walls—and renovated. Some marketing genius decided to change the name to Millennium Opéra to make the hotel a little sexier or give you a hint of the area where it is located. Do not be fooled into thinking this hotel is next door to the Garnier Opéra, although it is nearby.

In addition, this could be the insider's find of the day. Located 2 blocks east of Galeries Lafayette (and yes, the Garnier Opéra) the hotel is grand, chic, and seemingly unknown. Therefore, it offers incredible rates. I found it on Expedia for under $200 a night; my friends used the hotel site and got an even better rate—and for high season! The location takes a little bit of getting used to, but at these prices, you're going to love it. Upgrade yourself to a club floor and get many perks. Call © 01-49-49-16-00 locally, or log on to www.millennium hotels.com.

STREET OF DREAM HOTELS

If you are more of a neighborhood person and are looking for charm over convenience, the main drag through the Ile St-Louis is jampacked with adorable three-star hotels. It can be hard to find a taxi and you have to schlep a bit for the Métro, but you may not care. Rates in these hotels usually begin around $173. The most convenient Métro is probably Pont Marie, but Cité is also doable. Try:

HOTEL DU JEU DE PAUME
54 rue St-Louis en l'Ile, 4e.

Call © 01-40-46-02-76 for more information.

HOTEL ST-LOUIS
75 rue St-Louis en l'Ile, 4e.

Call © 01-46-34-04-80 for more information.

Chapter Five

······················

SHOPPING *QUARTIERS* IN PARIS

THE BASTILLE IS UP

···

Paris is a city of neighborhoods. The word *arrondissement* is not synonymous with "neighborhood"—each arrondissement contains many neighborhoods, or *quartiers*. Some quartiers straddle portions of two arrondissements.

Now, a few words about orientation. I tend to categorize sections of arrondissements by their landmarks and stores. The Bronx may not be up and the Battery may not be down, but the way I look at it, the Bastille is uptown and the Arc de Triomphe is downtown. From the Right Bank, it's "crosstown" to the Left Bank.

As a tourist, you'll probably stick to a dozen or so must-see neighborhoods to which you'll want to return someday. Some areas you visit only for shopping, but for the most part, you wander to take in everything—sights, shopping, dining, and more. Certain streets will fulfill all your fantasies of what Paris should be. While the city limits sprawl all the way to the highway loop Périphérique (and beyond), my parts of town are compact and easy to manage.

The Left Bank

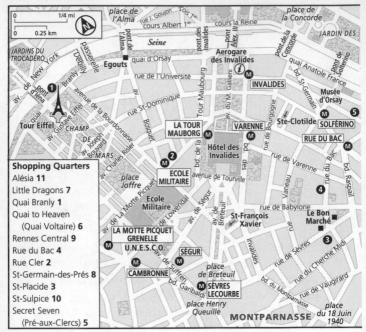

Shopping Quarters
Alésia **11**
Little Dragons **7**
Quai Branly **1**
Quai to Heaven
(Quai Voltaire) **6**
Rennes Central **9**
Rue du Bac **4**
Rue Cler **2**
St-Germain-des-Prés **8**
St-Placide **3**
St-Sulpice **10**
Secret Seven
(Pré-aux-Clercs) **5**

LEFT BANK ARRONDISSEMENTS

To many, the essence of Paris is *le Rive Gauche*. I see it as several villages, all with different personalities. If you're the type who just likes to wander, go to the 6e and spend the day, or even the week. If you're tired of the best-known parts, learn your way around the hidden sections of the district.

The Fifth (5e)

Okay, I plead the Fifth. I love parts of it (try the market at place Monge) and would like to move here, but don't think I can afford it. As a tourist, you may not ever make it to my favorite parts and will end up staying in the more congested areas instead.

The 5e is the famous **Latin Quarter,** or student quarter, also called Panthéon. Filled with little cafes and restaurants, it's also paradise for book hunters. Shops sell *fripes* (non-designer

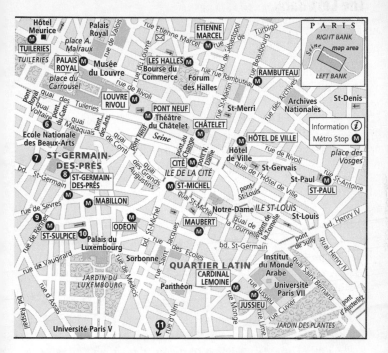

used clothing from the 1970s) and jeans, which seem to be all that people wear around here. This is the funkiest part of the Left Bank, just above the chic part of the boulevard St-Germain.

If you are not a student, you might not end up shopping in the 5e. But wait, there are a few good stores in the 5e—if you're a **Diptyque** (p. 229) candle, soap, and scent freak, you can find the store here.

The Sixth (6e)

This is one of the most Parisian arrondissements for tourists and shoppers. It's often called Luxembourg because the **Jardin du Luxembourg** is here, or **St-Germain-des-Prés** because of the church and boulevard of the same name. Let's just call it heaven and be done with it.

This district has everything. On the **rue de Buci** and the **rue du Seine** is a street market piled high with fruits, vegetables, and flowers (great for picnic supplies). Prices tend to be higher than at other street markets because of the number of tourists who shop here, but it's so luscious, who cares? The antiques business is also clustered here, and there are a number of one-of-a-kind boutiques. But the area is no longer small and funky. Led by **Sonia Rykiel,** who arrived years ago, a herd of major designers—**Louis Vuitton, Hermès, Christian Dior**—have moved into this prime real estate. Their shops are tasteful (and then some!) and respectful to the soul of the neighborhood.

The Seventh (7e)

Difficult to get around because of its lack of Métro connections, the 7e is a mostly wealthy residential area, with just a handful of shopping destinations. The real story here is for foodies: the **rue Cler,** a 2-block street filled with food stores, and a street food market on Sunday morning.

The portion of the 7e next to the 6e forms an invisible barrier (much like that between the 1er and the 8e on the Right Bank); it is impossible to know where one begins and the other ends. The closer you get to the 6e, the farther you go into an enclave of hidden good taste.

The best part is the **rue du Bac,** which lies in the 7e alongside the 6e. It is crammed with wonderful shops for the neighborhood's rich residents—everything from fancy pastry shops and linen stores to fashion boutiques and tabletop temples. More chic still is the 1-block **rue du Pré-aux-Clercs,** which took me years to discover. Some of the best talent in the world lines both sides of the street. Shhh, don't tell the tourists.

There are also some hidden finds on rue Bellechasse and even over on rue Bourgogne, where **Loulou de la Falaise** has opened her first shop in a tony area right behind the Assemblée Nationale. With this kind of shopping, you might not buy anything, but will still enjoy looking in the windows, watching the people, and feeling like you belong to this very private little world.

The Thirteenth (13e)

One of the largest arrondissements, the 13e is mostly residential and of little interest to tourists. Its districts are Italie, Gobelins, and Austerlitz. Part of it is known as the **French Chinatown,** with a giant Chinese emporium called **Tang Frères.**

However, the 13e is large and has a few other tricks up its sleeves—there's been much speculation about the parts of this arrondissement around the library (Bibliothèque de France, also named Bibliothèque Mitterand) and along the Seine.

Those interested in architecture and urban planning might want to check out **MK2,** a movie cineplex that is best known around town for having love seats for couples, rather than single seats. This is more for the architecturally curious than the shopping maven, but it's an area that will find its feet in the next few years. There are places to eat here and a promise of more pizazz to come. The entire complex is scheduled to be completed in 2007; at that time, the MK2 portion (also called **Bibliothèque Nationale,** or BN) will link with the gallery street rue Louise Weiss.

There are some artists' lofts in the 13e and some wild nightclubs—not that I would know anything about wild clubs. But at last, 13 is considered a lucky number. For those who want to wander and see what's happening, start at the rue Louise Weiss to find the new gallery district. There's also a bookstore called **Editions Modernes** that specializes in art books.

The Fourteenth (14e)

Looking for a Sonia Rykiel outlet store? Step this way. There are two of them now. The 14e is home to the **rue d'Alésia,** a street of several bargain shops, including both of the Sonia Rykiel outlets, both called **SR.**

There's a great weekend flea market, **porte de Vanves,** on the other side of the 14e.

The Fifteenth (15e)

The 15e is the largest arrondissement. A piece of the 15e touches the back of the Eiffel Tower. A small, very chic area forms the boundary between the 15e and the 7e. After that, chic ends rather quickly.

Rue de la Convention is a main drag. The porte de Versailles is just beyond, and there are tons of commercial streets all around this portion of the neighborhood. There are a few outlet stores near porte de Versailles.

I happen to like the area around the Monoprix and the rue Motte-Piquet simply as a fun residential area with neighborhood shopping, but there is no reason for a tourist to venture forth.

LEFT BANK SHOPPING QUARTIERS

When it comes to shopping in Paris, you must decide if you are just looking or if you actually want to buy something. Do you want a fantasy experience or a real-people experience? Do you mind crowds of tourists, or would you prefer to be surrounded by the people whose home you have invaded? Is your time so limited that you just want the one address that will give you the most value? Please answer these questions for yourself as you read up on my favorite shopping districts and browsing treats. *Allons-y.*

The St-Germain-des-Prés Métro stop works for all the main touristy and tony shopping areas on the Left Bank, except for the far-flung ones, which by definition aren't the touristy ones.

If you have no particular plan, but want to browse the best of the Left Bank, look at a map, pinpoint convenient Métro stops, and decide where you want to be around noon. I often arrange my patterns of exploration so that I end up leaving the Left Bank through the Sèvres-Babylone or the Rue du Bac Métro stop (because then I don't have to change trains). At the end of a hard day's shopping, especially if you are laden with packages, you might want to forgo a long, complicated journey on the Métro. Look at bus route maps to adjust to your own digs.

If you prefer a taxi, flagging one can be difficult in this area. Go to the Lutétia or to the taxi rank in front of Café Lipp near Emporio Armani on boulevard St-Germain. Note that the traffic on the boulevard St-Germain moves one-way in what I call the "uptown" direction. The traffic along the Seine goes one-way in the "downtown" direction.

St-Germain-des-Prés, 6e

Métro: St-Germain-des-Prés.

Shopping Scene: Does anyone here speak French? Young, hip, and busy, but very touristy.

Profile: To many visitors, this is the core of their Paris. They don't even care that more and more designer stores are moving in. They just want to sit at a cafe and feel like they're part of this world.

St-Germain-des-Prés is the main drag of the Left Bank and the center of the universe. Take the Métro or have a taxi drop you at the church, and you'll be at the center of the action, ready to hunt down the stores and the shoppers.

You can begin the day with breakfast (coffee and croissants) at any number of famous cafes, like **Les Deux Magots** or **Café de Flore.** Sure, a cup of espresso costs 4€ ($4.60) and fancy coffee or hot chocolate costs up to 6€ ($6.90), but this is the greatest show on earth. You can sit for hours and watch the passing parade. By the way, Café de Flore has the best hot chocolate in Paris.

Stores that can afford the rent on the boulevard cluster around here. In addition to **Etro, Emporio Armani,** and other big names, there's **Sonia Rykiel,** at no. 175, and **Shu Uemura,** a fabulous Japanese cosmetics firm, at no. 176.

Note that the boulevard St-Germain-des-Prés is awfully long. Some of it is somewhat boring, some of it has furniture and lighting showrooms, and some of it marches right into the 5e, which is a "far piece" (as we say in Texas) from the church at the heart of it all. Consider the church as the center of the shopper's world, and then wander into other areas.

Note: On the surface, this area is very touristy, but as you get closer to the Seine and into the design showrooms and fancy antiques shops, the air changes—as does the attitude. These stores and dealers are very closed; they prefer their own company or rich French speakers who know their stuff. There are plenty of snobby and status-y places back here that tourists never visit or find.

Rennes Central, 6e & 14e

Métro: St-Germain-des-Prés or St-Sulpice.

Shopping Scene: Real-people Montparnasse (14e) leads to touristy Left Bank.

Profile: At one of the major intersections of the Left Bank, two streets converge in a V—the rue de Rennes and the rue Bonaparte. Bonaparte runs behind the church as well; Rennes does not.

Rue de Rennes is the central drag of this trading area. It's a pretty big street with a lot of retail stores; the farther it goes from St-Germain, the less fancy the stores become. Rue de Rennes has a big-city feel, so it isn't exactly the charming Left Bank scene you may have expected.

Closer to boulevard St-Germain, rue de Rennes holds many big-name designer shops, from **Celine** to **Habitat,** as well as the **Gap, Stefanel, Kenzo,** and **Burberry.** Also here are a number of hotshot boutiques, such as **Loft,** and trendsetters like **Estéban** (home scents).

As you move away from the boulevard St-Germain, there's still plenty to enjoy, but fewer designer stores. Teens can have **Morgan;** I'll take **Geneviève Lethu,** 95 rue de Rennes, for tabletop and fresh fabric ideas.

Little Dragons, 6e

Métro: Sèvres-Babylone or St-Germain-des-Prés.

Shopping Scene: Shoe freaks.

Profile: West of Rennes Central (see previous listing) are several very small, narrow streets crammed with good things to eat and to wear. They are epitomized by the **rue du Dragon,** which is why I call this neighborhood Little Dragons. The bus stop calls it Croix Rouge.

You'll want to check out rue de Grenelle and rue des Sts-Pères and this part of the rue du Cherche-Midi. Just wander— get lost, get found. This whole warren of streets abounds with great shops, many belonging to designers of fame.

The area is sandwiched between the Sèvres-Babylone Métro stop and the neighborhood I call Rennes Central. To one side is **Le Bon Marché,** one of Paris's biggest and most famous department stores. You can also easily walk to St-Placide from here (see below).

St-Sulpice, 6e

Métro: Mabillon, St-Sulpice, or St-Germain-des-Prés.

Shopping Scene: Chic, in the know.

Profile: The core of this area lies between rue Bonaparte and place St-Sulpice. It comes complete with a gorgeous church, a park, several designer shops (**Castelbajac, YSL**), and the new **Shanghai Tang** (inside Maison de la Chine). Also here is the jewel-box pastry shop of Paris's most famous pastry chef, **Pierre Hermé,** 72 rue Bonaparte.

This area stretches behind the park and *place,* over to the rue Tournon and the rue de Seine, and includes the American-style mall **Marché St-Germain.** The side streets are full of small designer shops, some with names you've heard of—like **Souleiado** and **Les Olivades**—but many more that are largely unknown to Americans and exciting to discover.

Along the rue St-Sulpice, before you get to the park, you'll find all the kinds of shops you came to Paris to visit.

Quai to Heaven, 5e

Métro: St-Michel, then walk west along the river to the Louvre. If you head toward St-Michel and go east, it's a total zoo.

Shopping Scene: Insiderish, quiet, and private.

Profile: Most of the serious antiques dealers on the Left Bank lie between the river and the boulevard St-Germain, from the quai des Augustins to the quai Voltaire. If you continue along the river and just shop the quais, you will pass the stalls that sell old books, ephemera, and junk. This is a tourist scene, and fun to do once or twice as you get to know Paris. The real antiques scene is much more hidden. It's best to make appointments in advance, even. While some browsing occurs, it is generally by locals who continually visit the dealers, know them by name, poke around, chat, pat the dog, and then peek in the back room.

Rue Cler, 7e

Métro: Ecole Militaire or Motte-Picquet.

Shopping Scene: Foodies.

Profile: The Sunday-morning market on the rue Cler, in the 7e adjoining the 15e, is one of my favorite Sunday treats. Some consider it just another Paris food market. I consider it a religious experience. There is a market every day except Monday. Sunday is simply the most fun.

Quai Branly, 15e

Métro: RER C: Champs de Mars.

Shopping Scene: Hidden, residential, upper-middle-class.

Profile: Aside from the obvious **Eiffel Tower** business (very little shopping, even for souvenirs), none of the shopping here is immediately obvious. But the highlights are infectious: The **quai Branly** sometimes has an art or antiques show, and the **Village Suisse,** a village of antiques shops, is 2 blocks from the Paris Hilton.

Just 2 blocks from there is a nice street market underneath the elevated rail track at La Motte Piquet. I promise you, there are very few tourists here. This market is on Wednesday and Sunday only, from 8:30am until 1pm. Although it's mostly a food market, there are some sellers of tablecloths from Provence, olive oils, and such.

Rue du Bac, 7e

Métro: Sèvres-Babylone or Rue du Bac.

Shopping Scene: Left Bank snobbish.

Profile: As a residential neighborhood, you can't beat the 7e—not even in the 16e. As a shopping neighborhood, you can't beat the **rue du Bac**, especially if you like looking at the lifestyles of the rich and Parisienne.

You can get here by the easy method or the longer, more complicated, but more fun method. For the former, take the Métro to the Rue du Bac stop and walk away from the river on rue du Bac. For the latter, begin on the Right Bank, cross the bridge at the Louvre (see that bright golden statue of Jeanne d'Arc?), and hit the quai at rue du Bac. Walk toward the Rue du Bac Métro stop and away from the river. You get 3 or 4 more blocks of shopping this way. While it's not the best part of the rue du Bac, it's great fun. The street twists a bit, but just wander, following the street signs. You will quit rue du Bac only when you get to **Le Bon Marché.**

Pré-aux-Clercs ("Secret Seven"), 7e

Métro: Rue du Bac.

Shopping Scene: Privately chic. You came with the car and driver, didn't you?

Profile: This is just a 2-block stroll in another world, a world inhabited by very rich and chic women. This walk takes you along the rue du Pré-aux-Clercs, which lies between boulevard St-Germain and the river.

LEFT BANK DISCOUNT NEIGHBORHOODS
··

Alésia, 14e

Métro: Alésia.

Shopping Scene: Discount heaven.

Profile: This is one of the city's major discount districts. Prices in some places may not be the lowest, but there are a good half-dozen shops to choose from. Not every store in this area is a discount house, so ask if you are confused. Don't make any assumptions!

Most of the discount houses have the word *stock* in their name, which means they sell overruns. Some shops bear a designer's name plus the word *stock;* others have store names, without alluding to what is inside. **Stock 2,** a spacious space at 92 rue d'Alésia, sells men's, women's, and kids' designer clothes at discount prices. Most of it is from **Daniel Hechter,** but there are other brands as well.

Don't miss **Cacharel Stock** (no. 114), with fabulous baby and kids' clothes. It carries some men's and women's things, but I've never found anything worthwhile here that wasn't for children.

The stock shop of **Diapositive,** a big, hip line, is at no. 74. But the highlight of the block is undoubtedly **SR** (no. 64), which stands for—shout it out, folks—**Sonia Rykiel.** The clothes here are old, but they are true-blue Sonia.

When you shop this area, keep store hours in mind. Stores generally don't open until 2pm on Monday; many close for the entire month of August. And, again, remember that not all of the stores are discount; they just want you to think they are.

St-Placide, 7e

Métro: St-Placide or Sèvres-Babylone.

Shopping Scene: St-Placide abuts the chichi department store Bon Marché and feeds into fancy rue du Bac, but its style is a million miles away. This is a street of discounters and jobbers—tons of fun, if you like down-market shopping.

Profile: This area is not particularly near Alésia (although you can walk from one to the other), but mentally the two are sisters—homes of the discount shop, the stock shop, the great bargain.

There are maybe 10 stock shops in this 2-block stretch. They are not inviting from the outside—you must be the kind of person who likes to rifle through racks and bins. The most exciting shops are **Vidya**, the Nitya outlet; **Crea**, an arts-and-crafts store that has nothing to do with discounts; and the local branch of **Le Mouton à 5 Pattes**. St-Placide feels a bit seedy and isn't as attractive as Alésia—but there's nothing wrong with the neighborhood, and it is safe. Not every store offers discounts, but many do.

RIGHT BANK ARRONDISSEMENTS

The First (1er)

The 1er is a prime shopping area, with several high-rent neighborhoods. You'll find the city's fanciest designer boutiques on the **rue du Faubourg St-Honoré** (which crosses into the 8e), and some wonderful boutiques on the **rue St-Honoré** (an extension of the Faubourg St-Honoré that begins after the rue Royale). The 1er is also where you'll find tourist-trap heaven (the **rue de Rivoli**), some of the city's best museum shops, and the **Louvre** and its many shopping opportunities. The best secret of the 1er? The **Jardin du Palais Royal**, with fabulous shopping and strolling.

The Second (2e)

The 2e, known as **Bourse**, consists of the business district—basically the Wall Street of Paris—with some border areas for shoppers. Years ago, if you were in the 2e, it was because you were doing business, or you had the heart of a *garmento* and wanted to visit the **Sentier** (garment center).

There used to be tons of little wholesale-only shops in the Sentier, but the area is becoming more and more residential. A handful of famous restaurateurs have opened, including Alain Ducasse at **Aux Lyonnais** and Philippe Starck at **Bon II**.

The Right Bank

Shopping Quarters

Avenue Montaigne **5**
Bastille **25**
Batignolles **14**
Bercy **26**
Canal St-Martin **22**
Champs-Elysées **4**
Department-Store Heaven **6**
George V **3**
Hidden Madeleine **9**
The Islands **27**

Les Halles/Midtown-
  Beaubourg **21**
Madeleine **8**
Marais/Place des Vosges **23**
Montmartre **15**
Montorgueil **20**
The New Madeleine **7**
Oberkampf/Charonne **24**
Opéra **13**
Palais Royal & Victoires **18**
Passy **1**

Information ⓘ
Métro Stop Ⓜ

For shopping, the **Galerie Vivienne** is in the 2e; one of the most famous *passages* in Paris, it sits at the edge of place des Victoires. There are also a few hidden upscale treasures in and around here. Victoires is on the border of the 1er and 2e, and its designer and avant-garde shops make it one of the highlights of Paris.

The Third (3e)

To most visitors, the 3e *is* the **place des Vosges**—not just the square itself, but the tiny, curvy streets, arcades, shops, and off-beat finds all around it, which make up the **Marais**. It's everything you've dreamed Paris would be. To be totally accurate, the **Picasso Museum** is in the 3e and the place des Vosges is in the 4e, but the spirit that connects them allows most visitors to lump them together. The 3e has several yummy museums in it and much historical perspective; it also has some funky edges.

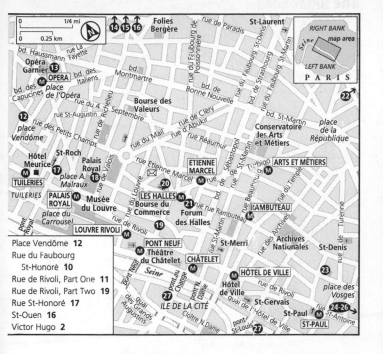

The Fourth (4e)

This neighborhood backs up on the Marais. The **Village St-Paul** (antiques galore) is in this *quartier,* and you are a stone's throw from Bastille and the new opera house. Once you cross the boulevard Bourdon at the canal, you are in the 12e, but never mind, you are now in an area of town considered very *branché* (with it).

The 4e also encompasses the **Ile St-Louis,** whose local church is the **Cathédrale de Nôtre-Dame.** There is some pleasant tourist shopping near the church. You'll find touristy, but fun shopping on the Ile St-Louis's main thoroughfare, rue St-Louis en l'Ile, which begins almost immediately after you cross the tiny bridge from the rear of the Nôtre-Dame onto the Ile St-Louis.

The Eighth (8e)

The 8e, nestled between the 1er and the 16e, connects the **rue du Faubourg St-Honoré** with the **Champs-Elysées,** stretching across some of the best shopping areas in the world. To me, the real soul of the 8e lies directly behind the Hôtel de Crillon, where you have not only the rue du Faubourg St-Honoré, but also the boulevard de la Madeleine and the tiny rue Boissy d'Anglas, which abounds with great stores. The 8e is probably the single most shopping-dense district in Paris.

The Ninth (9e)

The 9e sits on the far side of the 2e and the back end of the 8e; it is famous to most of the world as the location of some big department stores, including the French icons **Au Printemps** and **Galeries Lafayette.** Originally, the 9e owed its fame to the St-Lazare train station, which brought shoppers to the department stores on boulevard Haussmann.

The Tenth (10e)

Wholesale? Did you say you like wholesale? The 10e is one of the city's many wholesale neighborhoods. It's known for its fur, glass, china, and coiffure suppliers, but also for its hookers, hoods, and dealers, particularly around St-Denis. It has a strong ethnic mix as well. But wait, this part of town is losing the hookers and getting the good lookers.

Call me irresponsible, but I adore this area, having just discovered it when I needed professional hair supplies. I take the Métro to Château d'Eau, then walk south to Passage de l'Industrie & Commerce, where the hair suppliers are all in a row. I go to **Delorme,** 17–19 Passage de l'Industrie. *Note:* While the brands may be the same ones you know from professional hair suppliers in the U.S., the shades are different.

At the corner, before I pop into the Métro (Strasbourg–St-Denis), I hit the **Monoprix** (mostly a grocery store, sorry) and the various stores selling low-cost but legal DVDs.

If you remember this area as the home of the Baccarat factory and the crystal dealers on rue Paradis, note that Baccarat has moved to the 16e and many of the crystal dealers have moved out.

A little farther east is **République,** a formerly boring neighborhood that is now getting to be part of the popular new-chic (the New Republic?). Around the big square, you have the usual suspects, stores like **Habitat** and **Go Sports,** and even a Holiday Inn. But heading off to the east by just a few blocks, you arrive at a neighborhood in the works, where those who specialize in the cutting edge go out of their way to shop. The hip stores are dotted around, but the ones that get hyped the most are on quai de Valmy, alongside the **Canal St-Martin.** Rollerblades optional.

The Eleventh (11e)

Yes, yes, yes—those who like the funky neighborhoods, the original retailers, the not-yet-overtaken-by-the-mall feel will like to explore here and in the area that jumps between the 11e and 12e. It's happening on the rue Oberkampf—just don't wear fur. If you want to give this area a few years to really get going, that's fine, too.

The Twelfth (12e)

This is the arrondissement of the moment, gathering no moss as it rolls across Paris from the far side of Bastille, past Gare de Lyon, toward **Bercy Village.**

Le Viaduc des Arts is a long stretch of street under an elevated train track that has been turned into boutiques and artisans' workshops. Not far away is the **place d'Aligre,** with a great food market and a small, funky flea market. You can walk between the two; by the time you get to place d'Aligre, however, you are in the funky part of the district. Watch your handbag.

Leading away from the Bastille Opéra is the area's main thoroughfare, **rue du Fauborg St-Antoine,** which is now so popular that most of the artists have moved out and the big-name brands representing mass shopping have moved in. **Habitat** is opening soon.

The Sixteenth (16e)

Rue de Passy is a terrific find for someone who wants to shop and see a specific version of the real Paris, as experienced by the BCBG *(bon chic, bon genre)* crowd that hangs out in this district . . . and doesn't care to know about funky. The well-heeled residents of the 16e have their own park, the **Bois de Boulogne,** and living close to the park is considered very chic. More important, the 16e has lots of resale shops, since this crowd likes brands (the more famous, the better). To demonstrate how tony this area is, it has its own luxury department store, **Franck et Fils.**

The Seventeenth (17e)

This is another fashionable district, at least in parts. The acceptable neighborhoods for the BCBG set are Péreire, Ternes, and Monceau. The shopping is rather neighborhoody, but there are two great street markets: **rue des Levis** (Métro: Villiers) and **Poncelet** (Métro: Ternes). Additionally, the flower market at place de Ternes is lovely. I look, but don't buy—I think it's expensive.

The avenue Niel and the rue des Ternes are the big local shopping thoroughfares, although they are not as packed with name brands as, say, avenue Victor Hugo. But wait—this is a great eating district.

Also note that the Convention Center at Porte Maillot has a small mall with a great grocery store that is open on Sunday. Nearby, **L'Espace Champeret** (Métro: Champeret) has food and antiques specialty markets that are announced in magazines.

Finally, although the new **Hilton Arc de Triomphe** is in the 8e, it sits at the edge of the 17e and is a good place to launch a shopping expedition along the rue de Courcelles (walk north), which offers a peek into a wealthy residential shopping district and a very good resale shop, **Dépôts-Ventes 17e**.

The Eighteenth (18e)

You've heard of the 18e because it includes **Montmartre**. This is a scenic area that tourists like to visit in order to confirm their fantasies of Paris or check up on scenes from the movie *Amélie*. It is also the site of some of the fabric markets that are haunted by design students.

In reality, Montmartre is divided into two halves of the hill, the north side being less touristy. The south side has the Moulin Rouge, the fabric markets, the jobbers selling discounted clothing from bins, and the station for the cable car up to **Sacré-Coeur**. At the top of the hill is the place de Tertre, where the artists will paint your portrait. (Sociological report: Most of the artists are now immigrants; they are no longer French.)

The edge of the north side of the 18e is home to the famous flea markets of **St-Ouen**.

The Nineteenth (19e)

This is really getting out of the swing of things for tourists, except when you get to La Villette park. Although there's no shopping reason to visit here, it is part of the residential renaissance of Eastern Paris; lots of young people live here.

The Twentieth (20e)

Maurice Chevalier made this area famous when he sang about Ménilmontant, but other than that, there isn't too much shopping action in this booming residential neighborhood. To say you live in **Belleville** tells the rest of the world you're a filmmaker or struggling *artiste*.

The famous **Père-Lachaise** cemetery is here; the only piece of retailing advice I can offer is to make sure you buy a map of the gravestones—otherwise, you'll never find Jim Morrison's. And, yes, shops near the cemetery sell flowers and Doors posters.

RIGHT BANK SHOPPING QUARTIERS

The neighborhoods below are listed in roughly geographic order, starting in the west with the 16e and working to the east.

Passy, 16e

Métro: Passy or La Muette.

Shopping Scene: Rich casual, with a black-velvet headband and pearls.

Profile: Passy is the main commercial street in one of the nicest districts in one of the nicest arrondissements. It has a little of everything and is convenient to other neighborhoods. You can visit Passy on your way to the Eiffel Tower, Trocadéro, or the resale shops of the 16e, or you can catch the Métro and be anywhere else in minutes. If possible, visit Passy on a Saturday morning—then you will really be French.

The street has been booming ever since the opening of **Passy Plaza,** an American-style mall with that number-one American tenant, the Gap. Go to Passy Plaza for a lesson in French yuppie sociology. Shop the supermarket in the lower level, the various branches of American and British big names, and the French candy store.

Franck et Fils, a small department store formerly for blue-haired old ladies with apricot poodles, has been redone. Now, somewhat in the style of a smaller Bon Marché, it is very chic.

Shopper's tip: When you get to the end of Passy (at the **Max Mara** shop), you'll find a back street, **rue Paul-Doumer.** If you love home furnishings and good design, you'll find a few good shops along this tiny street. Forget about shopping in this neighborhood on Monday until at least the afternoon, when stores begin to reopen.

Victor Hugo, 16e

Métro: Victor Hugo.

Shopping Scene: Chic, French, and rich . . . with well-groomed dogs.

Profile: This uptown residential neighborhood is still where the big money shops. Victor Hugo is one of the fanciest shopping streets in Paris. Years ago, many big-name international designers had shops here. Most of them have moved, giving the neighborhood a more intimate feel. Today, most shoppers appear to be regulars who live nearby. This isn't the kind of street tourists normally visit to actually shop; you come here to get a feel for a certain part of Paris, to experience a lifestyle that is totally unknown in America, and to pretend you're a French aristocrat.

Batignolles, 17e

Métro: Rome.

Shopping Scene: Stopped in time, yet friendly and French.

Profile: Small-town Great Neck on the main street (rue des Batignolles), but otherwise simply village-y with nooks and crannies all around. This is not a touristy area, but it gives you a wonderful feel for village life. Cross streets like rue des Moines, rue Legendre, and rue Brochant in the low numbers are filling up with cute small shops.

George V, 8e

Métro: George V or Alma Marceau.

Shopping Scene: Between two Métro stops, this area is hidden in plain sight; it's a "secret" district of small boutiques where the staffs know shoppers—and their dogs—by name. There are some name-brand stores, but most are either in the cult league (**Creed** perfumes) or tiny branches (**Hermès**).

Profile: This nugget centers on avenue Pierre 1er de Serbie, between Alma-Marceau (and av. Montaigne) and the

Champs-Elysées. The Four Seasons George V is at the heart of this area and its surrounding shops.

Champs-Elysées, 8e

Métro: Franklin D. Roosevelt.

Shopping Scene: Outdoor mall.

Profile: The tourist mobs and shopping-cinema-cafe ratio make this one of the most crowded parts of Paris. The stores go from the ridiculous to the sublime. In a single block, there's Virgin Megastore, the Disney Store, and Monoprix. At the far end, closer to the Arc de Triomphe, is the newly reopened Le Drugstore; across the street is a brand-new branch of Cartier. Someone thinks the neighborhood is on the way up.

Along the way, you'll see numerous car showrooms, parfumeries, drugstores, movie theaters, airline offices, cafes, and change booths. A few big-name designers have stores here. The **Galerie du Claridge** minimall has two levels (go downstairs, too) and the best selection of the kinds of shops you want to see; most of them are big names.

If time is precious, you might want to make sure you've paid homage at **Monoprix**, 109 rue de la Boétie, and popped into **Paris St. Germain,** where you can have football shirts imprinted with the name of your choice. Go to the cinema in English and eat at a car showroom—check out the cafe in the **Renault** showroom for a snack, lunch, or dinner.

In the past few years, the Champs-Elysées has changed a lot, and some of it has been changing for a long time: the **Disney Store, Virgin Megastore,** and flagship **Sephora** brought new life to the most famous street in Paris. Then came the tearoom **Ladurée, Louis Vuitton** (where Japanese visitors may beg you to stand in line for them), and the **Gap** flagship. There are also branches of French chains like **Lacoste, Petit Bateau,** and the French equivalent of Gap, **Celio,** as well as a spurt of luxury brands at the top end, such as **Cartier** and **Montblanc.**

Note: Hours and opening days are odd. Monoprix is open until midnight in season and 10pm in winter, but closed on

Sunday. However, many of the other stores (Virgin, Disney, Sephora) are open on Sunday.

Avenue Montaigne, 8e

Métro: Franklin D. Roosevelt or Alma-Marceau.

Shopping Scene: The internationally rich, chic, and bored.

Profile: Landmark shoppers. The avenue Montaigne has become a monument to itself. **Dior** and **Ricci** have always been here. For years, the **Chanel** boutique was a secret jealously guarded by those in the know. Then, Montaigne became the mega-address it is now. Of course, the Italians also came: **Krizia, Ferragamo, Max Mara,** and **Dolce & Gabbana.**

One stroll down the short street's 2 blocks of retail stores will give you a look at those famous names, as well as **Loewe, Thierry Mugler, Ungaro, Porthault, Celine, Christian Lacroix,** and **Valentino.**

Some of the other places are old-fashioned French shops that deserve a visit just to soak up the atmosphere. Try **Au Duc de Praslin** (for candy and nuts) and **Parfums Caron,** with its giant glass bottles filled with scents not carried in department stores in Paris, let alone America.

Rue du Faubourg St-Honoré, 8e

Métro: Concorde.

Shopping Scene: Rich regulars from out of town.

Profile: This used to be the fanciest retail therapy in town. Now there are some multiples (chain stores) and some wannabe big names. **Façonnable** has moved in, but so have **La Perla** (jazzy lingerie and bathing suits), **Tod's,** and even **Lolita Lempicka.** Old standbys range from **Hermès** to **Sonia Rykiel,** with international big names (**Bottega Veneta, Ferragamo**) thrown in.

Madeleine, 8e

Métro: Madeleine.

Shopping Scene: Upscale international, plus foodie heaven.

Profile: Scads of food specialty shops cluster here. The heart of the area is a string of famous food shops almost in a row— **Hédiard, Fauchon, Nicolas** (the wine shop), **Maison de la Truffe,** and more. Fauchon has all but gutted itself and started over, and now has an extremely interesting tea department.

Stretching away from the church on rue Royale, there's **Polo/ Ralph Lauren** and the glass-and-porcelain showrooms that give way to the name-brand shopping on **Faubourg St-Honoré.**

Hidden behind rue Royale are a few passages that lead to the **rue Boissy d'Anglas,** the narrow street that runs behind the Hôtel de Crillon, from the place de la Concorde, past **Hermès,** down to the place de la Madeleine. It doesn't see many tourists. What it does see are a lot of chic fashion editors and in-the-know types who pop in and out of their favorite stores, secure in the thought that the tourists are on the Faubourg and haven't caught on.

If you cut through the passage de la Madeleine, just off the place de la Madeleine, it leads to the chic part of the rue Boissy d'Anglas. Walk toward Concorde, to your left. Don't stop until you get to the passage Royale, which will lead you to tea at **Bernardaud.**

But wait—there's more here, in another direction. Mentally, go back to "start," at the Madeleine Métro side of the church. On the corner is a department store for men called **Le Madelois.** Also here are branches of **Kenzo, Weill, Chacok, Body Shop, Marina Rinaldi, Burma, Dorothée Bis, Agatha, Mondi, Georges Rech, Rodier Homme,** and **Stephane Kélian.**

This area, and the warren of tiny streets between the mall and rue Royale, has become the new headquarters for home design and tabletop shops. **Le Cèdre Rouge,** sort of the French version of Pottery Barn, is here, as are other stores that specialize in affordable home style, like **Conran** and **Habitat.** Search out the first free-standing **Le Jacquard Français** store, near Le Cèdre Rouge, where fabulous multicolored French table linen is sold.

The New Madeleine, 8e

The newest addition to the Paris "must-do" list is a single block on the Baccarat (west) side of the Madeleine church. Boulevard Malesherbes has long been home to Baccarat and Burberry. Now there are three new stores in a row: **Sia, Shiseido,** and **Résonances.**

Hidden Madeleine, 8e

Métro: Madeleine or Concorde.

Shopping Scene: Real people who know what they are doing and where they are going.

Profile: I've nicknamed **rue Vignon** "Honey Street" because it's the home of the **Maison de Miel,** one of the leading specialists in French honey. This street runs on the other side of **Fauchon** (just as the rue Boissy d'Anglas runs behind Hédiard). Vignon holds a few smaller clothing shops, as well as other places I like to explore. It's chic without being touristy. This is one of my favorite streets in Paris, and I often use it as my route for cutting over to *les grands magasins.* There are now a number of soap stores, and since the French invented the process that created triple-milled soap, this is a good place to get souvenirs.

Department-Store Heaven, 9e

Métro: Havre-Caumartin or Chaussée d'Antin.

Shopping Scene: In summer, a zoo. At other times, middle- to upper-middle-class French suburbanites and out-of-towners mix with an international crowd.

Profile: This 3-block-long, 2-block-deep jumble of merchandise, pushcarts, strollers, and shoppers is a central trading area. You need to see it now because of the brand-new Lafayette Maison store. Go early (9:30am), when you're feeling strong and the crowds aren't in full swing. Winter is far less zoolike than summer.

The two major department stores are reinventing themselves in front of our very eyes. Both **Au Printemps** and **Galeries Lafayette** have redone their various buildings. Furthermore, Galeries has opened another store called **Lafayette Maison,** for home style; it will knock your socks off. Also check out **Lafayette Gourmet,** the grocery store—it's fabulous, with a new wine library and much more to make you dizzy with delight. You can enter the new area from the rue de Provence.

Speaking of rue de Provence, this is a great street (although it's more like an alley) to know about. Printemps has three buildings in a cluster here and has also opened **Citadium,** an architectural wonder of a French version of the Nike store.

Where the rue de Provence crosses the pedestrian rue de Caumartin, you can pop into **Monoprix** (downstairs, below the Citadium) or walk north to **Passage le Havre,** half a block away. This is an American-style mall, with **FNAC, Sephora,** and many branches of popular midlevel French clothing chains.

Rue de Rivoli, Part One, 1er

Métro: Concorde or Tuileries.

Shopping Scene: International tourists on their way somewhere.

Profile: The rue de Rivoli is the main drag that runs along the back side of the Louvre. The Louvre was once a fortress, which is why it seems to go on forever. They just don't build 'em like that anymore. Exit the Métro at Concorde and face away from the Eiffel Tower. Now you're ready to walk.

I call this part of the street "Part One" because it is the main tourist area (see p. 99 for the scoop on Part Two). The rue de Rivoli continues after the Louvre, but has an entirely different character. Part One has a few chic shops toward the Hôtel de Crillon end, but soon becomes a good street for bookstores, such as **W. H. Smith.** As you get closer to the Louvre, the stores get more touristy. Here you'll find tons of tourist traps, all in a row.

Opéra, 1er

Métro: Opéra.

Shopping Scene: Touristy.

Profile: Transition City. The avenue de l'Opéra, running between the Garnier Opéra and the Palais Royal, has always been a big commercial street with little of interest except for a lot of airline offices. Now things are looking up: The first **Starbucks** in Paris opened in the middle of the block (Métro: Pyramides), and more and more nice stores are coming onboard.

Old standbys include **Brentano's** bookstore and **Monoprix.** Along with the reopening of the Inter-Continental Grand and the redone **Café de la Paix,** there's also a **Benetton** store in the next block and a newly redone **Lancel** across the street. The well-known duty-free cosmetics firms **Michel Swiss** and **Raoul et Curly** are both on avenue de l'Opéra.

Place Vendôme, 1er

Métro: Tuileries or Opéra.

Shopping Scene: Hidden, quiet, discreet.

Profile: Ritzy. The far side of the place Vendôme is the rue de la Paix, which dead-ends 2 blocks later into place de l'Opéra. There are more jewelers here (including **Tiffany & Co.**) than on West 47th Street in New York. Well, sort of. It seems Paris is living through the War of the Couture Jewelers. It's not enough that every fancy jewelry shop has always been represented here— **Chanel** decided to move in with its own real-jewelry store (none of that costume stuff, please). To up the ante, **Dior** opened a real-jewelry store nearby. Is it hot here, or what? Maybe these diamonds just make me sweaty.

Don't confuse **Charvet** (a men's store) with **Chaumet,** a jeweler. There are several men's haberdashers on this street— everyone from **Alain** (Figaret) to **Zegna,** with lots of storefronts now taken over by **Alfred Dunhill.** Figaret is not quite as famous as others in the neighborhood, but is a local hero for shirt making for both men and women. There's also a range of **Armani,** from the high-end store on your left (with Opéra to your rear) to **Emporio** on your right.

Rue St-Honoré, 1er

Métro: Concorde, Tuileries, Madeleine, or Opéra.

Shopping Scene: In the know.

Profile: This is a district I think of as "Behind the Meurice." It includes not only the rue St-Honoré, which begins at the rue Royale, but lots of side streets and hidden shopping venues, such as the Marché St-Honoré. The district also includes the rue Castiglione. Packed with designer shops of known and unknown reputations (**Jacqueline Peres, Annick Goutal, Guerlain, Payot, Hans Stern**), rue Castiglione is the connecting street from the Tuileries to the place Vendôme and rue de la Paix.

Okay, so here's the inside scoop: The Faubourg St-Honoré got the reputation, but in truth, the big-name designer shops do not end where the Faubourg St-Honoré changes names and becomes plain old rue St-Honoré, which happens once you cross the rue Royale.

On the plain old rue St-Honoré, there are branches or flagship stores of everyone from **Joseph** (British stylemeister, with cafe) to **Grès** (as in Madame), including names we would follow anywhere, like **Longchamp, Hervé Chapelier,** and **Nitya.** As you move uptown toward the Palais Royal, you find **Goyard,** a luggage brand that is older than Louis Vuitton; **Colette** the infamous; and the teeny-weeny **Atelier de Villette.**

Palais Royal, Victoires & Beyond, 1er & 2e

Métro: Palais-Royal.

Shopping Scene: Trendsetters.

Profile: If you want your shopping experience very French, upscale, and special, this is it. The **Jardin du Palais Royal** is my single best Paris shopping experience. (It's good for non-shopping husbands who can appreciate the park, the history, and much style.) The Jardin du Palais Royal and the area around Victoires have seen a good bit of turnover. The don't-miss it retailer is the gardening shop **Le Prince Jardinier,** which is next door to **Shiseido**'s perfume shop—an older must-do if there ever was one. Note that the brand has launched a dozen new scents. Across the way is the new **Marc Jacobs** boutique, which leaves me cold. Give me **Didier Ludot** and his resale wonders any day.

You'll find the place des Victoires nestled behind the Jardin du Palais Royal, where the 1er and the 2e connect. Facing it is a circle of hotels; the ground floor of each holds retail space. Wonderful shops fill the streets that radiate from the *place*.

The main drag is the **rue Etienne Marcel,** which has long housed some of the big *créateurs* (designers). You can save this area for last, and depart the neighborhood by browsing this street before heading toward the Forum des Halles or the Beaubourg. Or you can start your stroll from the Etienne-Marcel Métro stop and work backward.

The rue Etienne Marcel is important in the lexicon of high style because so many cutting-edge designers, many of them Japanese, are here. There has also been an influx of stores for women who wear very tight jeans, such as **Diesel Style Lab** (35 rue Etienne Marcel), **Miss Sixty** (49 rue Etienne Marcel), and **Replay** (36 rue Etienne Marcel). Peep into **Kokon To Zai** (48 rue Tiquetonne), which also has a branch in London.

If you care, note that one side of Etienne Marcel is in the 1er and the other is in the 2e. The extension, **rue Tiquetonne** (which has a ton of good stores), is also in the 2e. Don't forget to check your trusty map before you leave Victoires—you can continue in any number of directions. You can easily walk to the Forum des Halles or Opéra, or to the boulevard Haussmann and the big department stores, or to the rue de Rivoli and the Louvre. The world starts at Victoires, and it's a magnificent world.

Hidden Passages, 1er

Métro: Palais-Royal.

Shopping Scene: Funky chic.

Profile: This area is hidden in plain sight. You would never find it unless you came upon it by accident or with an insider tip. Between the **Louvre des Antiquaires** and the place des Victoires, this little area includes the old-fashioned *passage* **Véro-Dodat** (where there's a **By Terry** makeup shop) and some retailers who are known by their reputation. They include **Why?** for funny novelties, and **L'Oeil du Pelican**, 13 rue Jean-Jacques Rousseau, the kind of antiques shop that sells what are called *curiosités*— neat little things. Rue Jean-Jacques Rousseau is only 2 blocks long and leads from the Louvre right to the mall **Forum des Halles**.

For those who have to trade in francs, the main branch of the **Banque de France** is in this area, too.

Montorgueil, 1er & 2e

If it's good enough for Queen Elizabeth II, then it might interest you, too. This is a small pedestrian area, tucked next to Les Halles and famous for its food markets and vendors. It's especially bustling on a weekend and offers up that real-Paris feel that will make you want to move in. There are several restaurants and many historic storefronts—some shops have no numbers and possibly no names. Just take it all in, hungrily.

Les Halles, 1er/Midtown-Beaubourg, 3e

Métro: Les Halles or Rambuteau.

Shopping Scene: Funky; teen- and tourist-oriented.

Profile: Two landmarks dominate this area: the American-style mall at **Les Halles** (which replaced the famed food halls) and the **Centre Georges Pompidou,** the art museum. Surrounding them are all sorts of shopping styles, from museum stores to vintage-clothing shops to those that sell videos and posters and books and faience. (Don't ask me why the **Quimper** people opened a store in this district, at 15 rue St-Martin.)

While a mall may not be your idea of how you want to shop in Paris, if it's raining, remember that Les Halles is large and filled with branches of all the big names in international retail. It's mobbed on Saturdays.

Rue de Rivoli, Part Two, 1er & 4e

Métro: Pont Neuf or Hôtel de Ville.

Shopping Scene: Real, with some emphasis on teens, tweens, and real-people budgets.

Profile: The rue de Rivoli changes names to become the rue St-Antoine, leading directly to the Bastille. Along the way are some junk shops and discounters, as well as the path to the place des Vosges and the Village St-Paul.

I like this part of the rue de Rivoli—a zoo on Saturday, by the way—because it packs in a lot, and the stores are not too expensive. It's changed a lot and now has a lot of well-priced shops. They might not offer couture, but they have stuff to look at and things real people can afford to buy.

Etam, Cité de la Femme, has made a huge impact by opening an enormous department store, not like the dinky Etam branches all over Europe. I like **C&A,** the Dutch department store that is not known for upscale shoppers or chic fashions. It carries copies of fashion looks, big sizes (by French standards), and washable clothes (who can afford dry cleaning?), and nothing costs more than 50€ ($58).

Marais/Place des Vosges, 3e & 4e

Métro: St-Paul.

Shopping Scene: Fabulous, funky fun; Sunday afternoon "in" scene.

Profile: The rebirth of the Marais is no longer news, but new shops continue to open, making it a pleasurable area to explore every time you visit Paris. From the Métro, follow the signs toward place des Vosges. Or take a taxi to the **Musée Picasso** and wander until you end up at the place des Vosges. (This is difficult wandering; you will need a map if you start at the Picasso Museum.)

The area between the church of St-Paul and the Seine holds the **Village St-Paul** (for antiques). The Marais lies across rue St-Antoine and is hidden from view as you emerge from the Métro. You may be disoriented; I've gotten lost a number of times. That's why taking a taxi here is a good idea. There's also no hint of charm until you reach the Marais.

While the heart of the neighborhood is the place des Vosges, this is a pretty big neighborhood with lots of tiny, meandering streets to wander. Take in the arcade that surrounds the *place*. The side streets are dense with opportunities, from the chic charm of **Romeo Gigli** to the American country looks of **Chevignon.**

The main shopping drag is **rue Francs-Bourgeois;** look for it on a map when you're at the Picasso Museum, as the medieval streets tend to get you turned around. This street has a few cafes, a few stores that sell used family silverware by weight, and many branches of high-style stores, such as **Ventilo** for ethnic gloss and the newest branch of scent-master **Estéban.**

Between the well-known areas, a bunch of little streets house funky shops that sell everything from high-end hats to vintage clothing. Check out antiques at **Les Deux Orphelines,** 21 place des Vosges, and contemporary housewares and style at **Villa Marais,** 40 rue Francs-Bourgeois. Adjacent to all this is the Jewish ghetto, with stores that sell Judaica; check out the rue des Rosiers. There is talk about turning the rue des Rosiers into a pedestrian area, but shopkeepers are currently in revolt, not wanting construction work to slow down their business.

Because most stores are open on Sunday afternoon, the entire area is dead on Monday.

If you are sick of this area or find it too touristy, move over slightly within the upper 3e and check out **rue Charlot,** which is becoming the "in" destination for cutting-edge shops and fashion editors who look for the next word. The store **Food** has gotten a lot of the press in this area, but the whole street is filled with shops and eats.

The Islands, 4e

Métro: Pont Neuf or Cité; RER C: St-Michel.

Shopping Scene: Touristy, but charming—the tourists who think they know something or have found the real Paris.

Profile: There are two islands out there in the Seine, joined by a little footbridge in the rear of Nôtre-Dame. Ile St-Louis is the more famous; Nôtre-Dame is on the Ile de la Cité. There's tourist shopping near Nôtre-Dame, and a flower and bird market near the police station, but the real fun is on the Ile St-Louis. The rue St-Louis en l'Ile has many cute shops, cafes, and ice-cream stands, all of which are open on Sunday.

Canal St-Martin, 10e

Métro: République.

Shopping Scene: You're wearing black, right?

Profile: Don't look now, but the heretofore déclassé 10e is becoming chic, led by the area surrounding the Canal St-Martin. Overlooking a canal of the Seine, it has plenty of cafes, lots of in-line skating on weekends, and quite a few funky stores, with more along the side streets. The main action is on the **quai Valmy** and the **quai de Jemmapes** on the other side—all Paris quais change names every few blocks and on both sides of the water.

When you exit the Métro, use a map to guide you to the canal. Or take a taxi to the **Hôtel du Nord,** 102 quai de Jemmapes, and explore from there. The hottest store is **Antoine et Lilli,** 95 quai de Valmy, which sells fashion and kitsch. There's a cafe, so you can sip and soak up the area while staring at the patrons. Other with-it cafes: **Chez Prune** and **Café Purple.**

Oberkampf/Charrone, 11e

Métro: Ledru Rollin.

Shopping Scene: Don't trust anyone over 20.

Profile: The neighborhood is divided into two camps: movers and shakers who have decided that the time has come to gentrify and shop-ify this area, and locals who want it to stay out of the eyes of tourists and shoppers. If the district were so cute that it would break your heart to see it change, I'd be the first to say so. But you can't ignore it, either—or ignore the fact that trends are happening here. To explore, move away from avenue Ledru-Rollin and onto Charrone; you will transverse the 11e and 12e. While you're here, segue over to Métro Faidherbe, a corner of the 11e with more funky shops.

Bastille, 4e & 12e

Métro: St-Paul or Bastille.

Shopping Scene: Hip, moving to mass-market.

Profile: Dare I say it? People are losing their heads over this up-and-coming neighborhood. I wanted to move to this part of Paris, but my friend told me I was too old to live here.

Indeed, Bastille is benefiting from the rebirth of the nearby Marais, one arrondissement over, and the ugly but renowned new opera house. The artists have moved in; so have the Americans (to live, not to set up shop). Long known for its home-furnishings stores, the district is gaining some galleries and interior-design shops of note. Branch stores of the big names in French retail are here, as is the Gap. Yet it's also still home to the funky **Marché Aligre,** where I recently took a group of American journalists who all hated it. If you have no ethnic funk in your soul, stick to the **rue St-Antoine** and maybe the **Viaduc des Arts.**

The contrasts in the neighborhood are part of the fun. Jean Paul Gaultier's flagship shop, **Galerie Gaultier,** is at 30 rue St-Antoine. It's a new concept that has all sorts of designs (clothing and products for the home) in one space; there are similar stores in London and Tokyo. The area should be all stores like this, but unfortunately there are a lot of multiples as well. For some more outrageous stuff, look to the fringes. The rue de Reuilly has design ateliers and large decorator showrooms; try

Maison Soubrier, 14 rue de Reuilly. There's also some funky stuff in what is technically the 11e, on the north side of the rue du Faubourg St-Antoine, along rue Charonne, rue Keller, and rue de la Roquette—these streets form a circle that leads back to the place de la Bastille.

Bercy, 12e

Métro: Cour St-Emilion.

Shopping Scene: Local yuppies.

Profile: This is the new Paris, not anything old-fashioned. I'm not sure if the most fun is in riding the new Meteor train (no. 14 line of the Métro), seeing the rehab of the old wine warehouses, or just laughing at how American this area has become.

Bercy was out of it for centuries, before the government moved in with several buildings and Bercy became French slang for the Ministry of Finance. Now there's a terrific mall, **Bercy Village,** a modern high-rise with movie theaters, food halls, and *hypermarchés* (giant supermarkets), and everyone wants to hop onboard and see what it's all about.

I adore the Bercy Village mall, but then, I like to see American ideas catching on abroad. Nothing could be more charming in my sight than wine warehouses turned into stores. Many retailers tested ideas here and then branched out. They include **Résonances,** a gift shop, and **Truffaut,** a florist and gardening store. Sephora has tested its **White Store** (Sephora Blanc) concept here as well, although it now sells products that aren't just white. There's also an **Oliviers & Co.,** which carries Mediterranean olive oils; there are branches of this store all over Paris, so this one is more for locals in a part of town that has been late to discover disposable income and designer olive oil.

Montmartre, 18e

Métro: Les Abbesses.

Shopping Scene: Uphill, it's touristy as you get into Montmartre and near Sacré-Coeur. Down by the Métro Anvers, it's discount heaven, but very déclassé.

Profile: Tourists mix with locals in search of a bargain at the fabric and discount sources nestled into one side of the hill. The most famous discount icon in Paris, **Tati,** is in this area. You've got to be strong, but this is fun for some.

Warning: *Mon dieu,* what a schlep! I investigated the famous place du Tertre in Montmartre, where the artists supposedly hang out, and was royally ripped off—and breathless from the walk up the hill. I'm not certain which facet of the adventure came closer to giving me a heart attack—the number of stairs I climbed to get to the church, or the fact that the portrait artists run price scams. However, the fabric markets are great fun and there are some junk stores that sell overstock from bins. If you can stand the jumble, you might love it here.

Edge of Town/St-Ouen

Métro: Porte de Clignancourt.

Shopping Scene: Largest flea market in Paris.

Profile: Before we get into what's going on in this part of Paris, let me offer a few warnings and explanations so you don't get lost or confused.

Transportation: If you're going to the flea market, you want the Métro stop Porte de Clignancourt, although the market is in the town of St-Ouen. Ignore other addresses, Métros, or bus stops with St-Ouen in their names.

Shopping: From the Métro (or bus) stop, you'll walk through a junky flea market that sells new items and wonder what is going on. No, this is not the famous flea market. You must get to the other side of all this junk.

Lunch: Since you will undoubtedly have a meal out here, note that the market contains several fast-food stalls (crepes, frites, and the like), as well as bistros and restaurants. The real talk of the town, however, is a restaurant a block from the market, **Le Soleil,** 109 av. Michelet (© 01-40-10-08-08). It's a terrific bistro, the owner speaks English (and eight other languages), and the crowd has mostly been sent by Patricia Wells, who has written extensively about the place. Make a reservation, especially for weekend lunch.

The market itself actually consists of many small markets, each with its own personality. For a full description and a map, turn to p. 261.

Chapter Six

....

BARGAIN SHOPPING

SHOPPER'S SMARTS

Prices in Paris are not low (especially if you're spending U.S. dollars), so to sniff out the bargains, you're going to need some background information and insider tips.

- If you have favorite designers or acquisition targets, shop the major department stores and U.S.-based boutiques for comparison prices. Don't assume you will get a bargain on French brands—or any brands. Many international designers and retailers set prices that are virtually the same around the world; many are less expensive in the U.S.
- If you do not live in a city that has a lot of European merchandise, do some research through *Vogue* or *Harper's Bazaar*. In the ads for the designer boutiques, you'll find phone numbers and websites. Check on prices; call boutiques in major U.S. cities for info.
- Read French magazines to get familiar with the French look and the hottest shops. These magazines can cost a fortune (sometimes $14 in the U.S.), but many libraries and hairdressers have them. Most good newsstands sell them; I buy mine at Blockbuster. You can also get a coffee at any Barnes & Noble (with an in-store Starbucks) and leaf through the magazines without buying them. Hey, times are tough.

- Carefully go through the airline magazines that are given away free on the plane. Often they have advertisements and coupons with deals and promotional codes. I just tore an American Express insert from an airline magazine that had such diverse bargains as 10% off on department store purchases or a free dessert from Michel Rostang, the two-star chef. You could also get 10% off and an upgrade on Europcar (www.europcar.com) or a parity deal where dollars and euros are equal at Sofitel Accor Hotels (www.sofitel.com).

- Understand the licensing process. Designers sell the rights to their names, and often their designs, to various makers around the world. Two men's suits may bear a well-known French designer's label, but fit differently because they are manufactured differently. You may be dreaming of merchandise that isn't even made by your favorite designer.

- Don't assume a perfume bargain. Know prices before you leave home.

- Don't be fooled into thinking that merchandise with foreign-sounding names is made in Europe, or is French, or offers a bargain. Because Americans are so taken with European names, many American-made products have foreign—especially French—names. Furthermore, there are a few French clothing designers who didn't make it in France, moved to the U.S. and became famous, and then opened stores in Paris to stick it to the French.

- Don't buy an American brand in France unless you have a very good reason. Clothes from Gap, for instance, may cost more in France than the U.S., but may also come in colors not available in the U.S.

- French merchandise that might not sell well in the U.S. could be discounted in your hometown or unloaded at an off-pricer. At Marshall's in Los Angeles, I saw scads of French brands at way-low prices. At Loehmann's in Manhattan, I bought French brands at outrageously low prices—esoteric French brands that I'm certain few Americans have ever heard of.

- Yes, the French now have outlet malls, too, and you can save money by shopping at them. See p. 131.

SHOPPER'S SURPRISES

Now that I have finished telling you all that stuff, and you are about to read a chapter pretty much devoted to alternative retail and bargain hunting, let me stress that there are big bargains, many savings, and yes *(oui)*, savings on name-brand merchandise. They are out there, almost lying in the streets of France, often where you least expect them.

Follow this story, *s'il vous plaît*. Meredith Lahey, age 25, tells her mom Sarah (news director of Born to Shop) that she doesn't want any junk from Asia, but does want a real (no fakes, Mom) Longchamp folding tote bag, with long shoulder straps, in a pretty blue color. Sarah proceeds to hunt all through the duty-free stores of Asia and finds that across-the-board, the desired tote costs $115 to $125.

I suggest that the girls wait until I get to Paris.

Once in Paris, I pop into a regular Longchamp boutique and see the exact bag that I know Meredith wants. It is priced at 70€ ($81), which means that I won't get détaxe. I weigh taking the perfect bag or holding out for the airport. I remember the Moscow Rule of Shopping and buy the bag. I have to put it on my U.S. credit card, which means I will pay an additional fee for the transaction, but I feel confident that I am doing the right thing.

At CDG, in the duty-free shop, the same style tote bag does cost less—it's 60€ ($70)—but get this, they have no blue, no pastels, no yummy colors, only beige and rust and puce.

The triumphant bag goes to Meredith and Sarah goes to Saks to see if they have the same blue shade. (We are nothing if not thorough). Indeed! The exact same bag, same color, same style, same size, is available at Saks for a retail price of $136, which does not include sales tax. All told, the bag would cost $150 in the U.S.

In short, at regular retail, this designer item was almost half-price in Paris.

How to know?

There's no exact rule, but my rule of thumb is that French goods are less expensive in France.

BEST BUYS

PERFUMES, COSMETICS & HAIR CARE   Perfume in France may not involve savings. Know your U.S. prices and understand that new French laws have been passed recently, so what you paid or how discounts were handled during your last visit could be very different now.

But wait, let's talk about my wrinkles and the fact that there are still bargains to be found on some brands and some products. (Also see chapter 8, which is all about beauty products.)

I swear by Sisleya, which costs $300 a pot in the U.S. and can be yours for a mere (!) 150€ ($173) in Paris if you take advantage of all the discounts. See, what you save on four jars pays for your airfare.

If you are even more flexible on brand-name beauty creams, it may be time to visit a *parapharmacie*. These stores carry drugstore brands—no Chanel or Yves Saint Laurent—at a 20% discount. This is the place to load up on fancy hair-care products, skin creams, bath products, and possibly even face powder. Barneys New York has made T. LeClerc all the rage; now it's everywhere in Paris.

HERMES   Prices in Paris (with the détaxe refund) are definitely lower than in the U.S. In addition, you can frequently find Hermès bargains at airport duty-free shops and in airline duty-free catalogs and they're even better than Paris retail prices.

BACCARAT   All French glassware can be dramatically less expensive in France, but the cost of shipping it abroad voids the savings. However, have you seen the Baccarat crystal medallions and butterflies that hang from a silk cord? They are drop-dead chic and cost approximately $135 in the U.S. Get onto an airplane that has Baccarat in its duty-free catalog, and lo and behold, the same trinket sells for about $60.

Less-Than-Stellar Buys

Some things are simply not a bargain in any sense:

- **Non-French-Made Goods:** Unless you're desperate, avoid buying American-made goods, whether they be designer items (such as a Ralph Lauren jacket) or mass-market items (like a Gap T-shirt or a pair of Levi's). Ditto for British goods (Aquascutum, Hilditch & Key, and so on), men's business attire, electrical goods (wrong voltage), and Coca-Cola at bars, cafes, or hotels.

- **Souvenirs:** Postcards priced at 1€ ($1.15) or more are no bargain (see p. 36 for how you can do better), and neither are massive amounts of Disneyland Paris souvenirs. Kitschy souvenirs vary in price—shop around.

- **Cheapie Fashion:** The French simply don't do cheap very well. That's why H&M, the Swedish firm, was invented. Although, let me eat my *chapeau:* Etam has good cheap chic for young women—and Monoprix, the dime store, is good fun. But the fashion rule of thumb is that the French make luxe brands and good clothes; don't buy junk from them.

CANDIES, CHOCOLATES & FOODSTUFFS These make great gifts, especially when wrapped in the distinctive packaging of one of Paris's premier food palaces. I buy Maille's tomato soup–colored Provençale mustard in grocery stores (no fancy wrap for me, thanks) and give it to foodies around the world—it's unique and special. I haven't found it in any U.S. specialty stores yet. Some Maille flavors are available in the U.S. (and the U.K.), but not this one. Maille has a shop at place de la Madeleine (Métro: Madeleine).

ANTIQUE JUNK It's pretty hard to give advice about the ever-changing collectibles market, but things that have caught my eye have all turned out to be bargains when I compared prices at American flea markets (why didn't I buy more?). I bought an empty postcard album—probably from the turn of the 20th century—at the flea market in Vanves, in perfect condition, for 10€ ($12). I saw a similar one at a dealers' show in Greenwich, Connecticut, for $150. Museum-quality antiques offer few bargains, but fun junk is fun—and modestly priced, even now.

ONLINE ANSWERS

If you are the meticulous type, you may want to go online to compare prices on items in France and the U.S. Of course, the biggest issue is that it's often hard to match up apples to apples (the exact same styles) but with some items, this can be done and you can decide if it's wise to pounce or to wait.

CHEAPIE POSTCARDS

Now that I have a computer with me, I send online postcards rather than old-fashioned ones. But still, it's nice to know that you can send out postcards. I buy cards at Jeanne d'Arc, a TT (tourist trap) at 188 rue de Rivoli, 1er (℡ 01-42-60-62-91; Métro: Louvre). It costs almost .87€ ($1) for postage to the U.S. from France.

SWEAT EQUITY

If you were not born to shop or don't thrill to the chase, you may not enjoy all this comparison shopping. You should also be sure to factor in: the amount of time it takes you to find a trophy, taxi fares if you would not take a taxi but are forced to because of the size and weight of the shopping bags, overweight or excess baggage fees, and U.S. duties. Truly, sometimes it doesn't pay to buy that item abroad. Go to the Louvre and talk to da Vinci.

SAVING GRACES

....

These are tricks that give you more bang for your euro, helping you save on transportation, meals, and more. Combine your luxury hotel room with some down-and-dirty consumer facts, and enjoy the best of both worlds:

- Buy Cokes and mineral water at the grocery store and keep them in your minibar. Every chic Frenchwoman carries a large tote bag with a bottle of mineral water. If you really want to save money, avoid drinking Coke completely—it's expensive everywhere in Europe. One cafe or minibar Coke costs as much as an entire six-pack in the market.

- Drink tap water. In a restaurant, merely order *un carafe d'eau*—this is also called *eau Chirac,* or it is until the next presidential election. Tap water in France is perfectly safe to drink. I often fill an empty water bottle with tap water.

- Buy food from fresh markets (one of Paris's most beautiful natural resources), supermarkets, and *traiteurs* (stores that sell prepared gourmet meals, hot or cold). You can eat a fabulous French meal for 4€ to 9€ ($4.60–$10) per person this way. An entire rotisserie chicken, which feeds four, costs no more than 8€ ($9.20), depending on the size of the chicken. Pizza is another good buy.

- Eat your fancy meals at starred Michelin restaurants that offer fixed-price meals, usually at lunch.

- Get into the hotel dining-room game. Lately, it's become trendy for hotels to bring in a one-star (or more) Michelin chef to attract guests and locals. These hotel restaurants compete so fiercely with each other that they watch their prices carefully.

- Do your gift shopping in duty-free stores (not at the airport; see the beauty chapter for examples), *parapharmacies,* flea markets, or *hypermarchés.* Don't scorn those tacky tourist traps for great 3€ to 6€ ($3.45–$6.90) gift items. You can also find small gifts at Monoprix—even at Métro stops.

Actually, I buy a large percentage of my clothes and under-garments at Monoprix and have always bought baby and kids' clothes there.

DEPARTMENT-STORE DISCOUNTS & DEALS

The two major department stores in Paris, **Galeries Lafayette** and **Au Printemps,** offer a flat 10% discount to tourists on all non-food items that are not marked with a red dot. You gain the discount by flashing your special tourist card at the cash register before you pay. Don't get all sweaty in the palms: The big brand names all display a red dot.

In order to get the discount, you need a coupon for the card. These coupons are given away in most hotels and even through U.S. travel agents; they are also available at the Paris Tourist Office on the Champs-Elysées. Or go to the Welcome Desk of either store and simply ask for the coupon or discount card.

Do not be surprised if you are asked to pay for each purchase at a central cashier rather than the nearest cashier; this has to do with the discount card and the store's accounting process. It's a pain, but nothing in life is free.

Note: This discount card has nothing to do with détaxe.

MASS MARKET

If you are looking for some French style and some fair prices, don't rule out shopping at the dime store (Monoprix, *mon amour!*) or even the grocery store. In terms of the grocery store, the real fashion finds are in *hypermarchés* that are outside of Paris and in the provinces, so you may not find anything in your average day. (There's an Auchan in La Défense, see below.)

Clothing here is not inexpensive—I pay 27€ ($31) for a bra I like at Monoprix and I consider that a wild extravagance.

AUCHAN
Centre Commercial Quat'r Temps, La Défense
(RER: La Défense).
Centre Commercial Val d'Europe (RER: Val d'Europe).

Should you be staying at a hotel in La Défense, there on business or simply curious, Quat'r Temps is a giant regional mall with every store you can imagine, and it has a *hypermarché,* Auchan. There is another Auchan out near La Vallée outlet mall.

For the uninitiated, Auchan is a *hypermarché*—a grocery store that sells food, clothes, health and beauty aids, jewelry, office supplies, car supplies, electronics, home appliances, home styles, tabletop items, bed linens, beds, garden supplies, swimming-pool accessories, luggage, pet supplies, and more. You get the drift.

The clerks wear roller skates. Honest.

While the big brand British grocery stores now have branded clothing lines for sale, at press time, Auchan does not. It soon will, I am sure. I buy all sorts of clothes here—it's particularly great for children's clothing and baby gifts. The quality is what you might expect from Wal-Mart.

MONOPRIX
All arrondissements of Paris.

Not all Monoprix were created equal and many are being renovated, so expect changes. As we go to press, **Monoprix Opéra** (Métro: Pyramid or Palais-Royal) has just been redone and is a smash. Traditionally, **Monoprix Saint Augustin** (Métro: St-Augustin) is one of the flagships, as is **Monoprix Rennes** in the heart of the Left Bank (Métro: St-Germain-des-Prés). **Monoprix Champs Elysées** (Métro: Franklin D. Roosevelt) is pennies more expensive than other branches and is not that attractive, due to a strange and cramped layout, but it's open late at night.

The Monoprix located directly behind the department store Au Printemps is not worth your time.

FIDELITY CARDS

Fidelity cards are used all over the world, but seem to be particularly popular in France, especially in midrange designer shops, *parapharmacies,* and even some restaurants. The fidelity card is a small card, like a credit card, that is stamped or punched every time you make a purchase. Make a certain number of purchases or reach a total euro value, and you'll receive a discount or a gift. You get the card simply by asking for *une carte fidélité.* No, department stores do not have them.

GETTING TO KNOW YOU

Personal relationships are very important in France. People continue to do business with the same people—indeed, the same salesperson—in the same stores and markets for years, even generations. This is cultural, but it also helps the customer make sure he or she is not cheated.

When you find stores you like, spend the time to develop a personal relationship. Reinforce the connection with faxes or little notes during the year, announcing when you will return to Paris. Go so far as to make an appointment, if you feel this is warranted. The better you are known—and this truly takes years of repeat business—the better chance you'll have of getting a discount or a family price and extra perks.

DUTY-FREE SHOPPING STRATEGIES

Few shops use the word "discount." The proper name to hide behind is "duty-free." Paris is famous for its duty-free shops. It is one of the few cities in the world with a lot of duty-free–style shopping, not just at the airport but also on city streets. These shops take on a whole new importance now that duty-free between E.U. destinations has been outlawed and airport shopping has begun to change focus.

Most non-airport duty-free shops sell makeup, fragrances, and deluxe gift items—designer earrings, scarves, ties, and even pens. Some of the accessories have been created specifically for the enormous duty-free business and are not sold through the designer boutiques. Duty-free stores like to tell you that they give a 40% discount. In reality, expect to get a 20% discount without too much trouble, a 25% discount if you're lucky, and no further discount unless you qualify for a détaxe refund, which is another 12% if you have spent 175€ ($201).

SPECIAL-EVENT RETAILING

Paris abounds with special shopping events. Ask your concierge for details and the exact dates; events are also advertised in magazines and papers. (I know you read *Madame Figaro* when you're in town, so you probably know it all anyway.)

Hermès has twice-yearly sales that can be described only as world-class sporting events. They take place in March and October (the exact dates are revealed only moments before, in newspaper ads). The sales have become such events that they are no longer held at the store. The average wait in line is 4 hours before admission; items are marked down to just about half-price. Unfortunately, a code is worked into your purchase that tells the world your item was bought on sale. It is not obvious, but look for a teeny-tiny s in a scarf.

The latest trend comes from the New York sample sales. There are several shopping clubs in Paris; some require membership, others are free but you have to sign up. These are often categorized as *vente privée* (private sales) which I don't find accurate—it's not like these events take place in someone's home or are organized on a personal level. You join up and you get an invite to the event. It's that simple.

My favorite is Catherine Max, who offers up **Espace Catherine Max,** 17 rue Raymond Poincaré, 16e (Métro: Trocadéro), where she unloads designer this and that at unbelievably low prices.

The catch is that in order to know the sale dates, you have to have a membership that costs 18€ ($21) per year, then you get a postcard in the mail. **Born to Shop** readers may gain one-time entrance without membership by showing a copy of this book and paying 10€ ($12) at the door. To get sale dates or current sale information, call © **01-53-70-67-47** or go to www. espacecatherinemax.com.

I have never shopped with anyone except Catherine Max, but I do know she has competition. The one I have heard about is called **Espace NGR.** This one costs slightly less than Catherine Max and I hear it has good brands, but more bridge lines than luxe; check it out at www.espace-ngr.fr. Or call © **01-45-27-32-42.**

Note: Any website ending in an "fr" designation is bound to be in French only.

SPECIAL EVENTS: ANTIQUES

For antiques lovers, the event you really want to catch is the **Biennale Internationale des Antiquaires,** the single biggest, most important antiques event in the world. It's held only in even-numbered years, usually in September, at the Grand Palais, roughly halfway between the place de la Concorde and the Rond Point. Check the design trade magazines for the actual dates or ask your concierge. You need not be a designer to attend; it's open to the public.

A number of antiques shows take place at the same time every year and become special events to plan trips around. April or May in Paris means only one thing: time for the **Brocante à la Bastille.** Celebrated outside, in stalls planted around the canal at Bastille, it is truly magical. For more information, see "Brocante Shows" on p. 258.

For information on big shopping events, look in *Allo Paris, Figaroscope, Zurban,* or antiques journals such as *Antiques, Alladin,* or *Chiner.* The **French Government Tourist Office** in New York (© **212/315-0888**) can supply the dates of special events, or you can do some online research at **www.bonjour paris.com**.

PRE-SALE SALES

As discussed, sale dates (Jan and June–July) are set by the government and announced in the papers a few weeks beforehand. What is not announced, or even discussed, is that regular customers can get the sale price a few days before the sale starts or can set aside merchandise to be held for the markdown.

PROMOTIONAL SALES

If there are only two sale periods during the year, how do you get a break? Well, you wait for the big promotional events. The department stores run them at least twice a year and give them very silly names such as "The Three Days" (which lasts 10 days), "The Days of Gold," or whatever. Note that like most promotional sales, much of the merchandise is brought in to be sold at the sale price.

RESALE & VINTAGE

The French pride themselves on being practical people. They rarely throw anything away; they buy only the best quality and use it forever; they hate waste of any sort. But if someone in the family dies or if someone falls on hard times, they can sell his fine possessions at a *dépôt-vent*. Or, knowing that good merchandise is being sold, they will frequent a *dépôt-vent*. No one in Paris is ever ashamed to be seen buying used items. They think it's smart. I do, too.

Do note that designer clothing that you may not consider purchasing at regular retail can be sale-priced at the end of a season at virtually the same price you might pay at a *dépôt-vent*. A *dépôt-vent* traditionally sells used clothing of current styles, while a vintage shop sells older clothing. These days, with so many retro looks in vogue, it's hard to tell one from the other. The two big flea markets, St-Ouen and Vanves, each have dealers who sell vintage clothing. The term *fripes* generally refers to non-designer used clothing from the 1970s—not vintage Chanel or Balenciaga.

COME ON EILEEN
16 rue des Taillandiers, 11e (Métro: Bastille or Ledru Rollin).

My young friend Ruthie found this source. Ruthie works for Chanel in NY and often buys vintage Chanel when in Paris. She fell in love with a pair of shoes here and warned me that it took the store almost a week to find the second shoe of the pair, so patience can be a virtue. The store doesn't open until 11:30am each day, so don't plan on giving them an early start at finding anything. The store is open on Sunday late afternoons from 4 to 8pm.

Note that this neighborhood is convenient for tourists and shoppers. Call ✆ 01-43-38-12-11.

DÉPÔT-VENT DIX-SEPTIEME
109 rue Courcelles, 17e (Métro: Courcelles).

This is the best resale shop in Paris, and the only chic one. It carries men's and women's clothing and a few home items, all in one shop. The prices are sometimes a tad high—I paid about 350€ ($403) for a used Chanel handbag. Some Chanel bags are 500€ to 600€ ($575–$690), or more. You'll see designer costume jewelry, a large selection of Chanel suits, and a little bit of everything else. Sales take place during the regular sale periods. No détaxe. Open Monday at 2pm; otherwise, from 10:30am to 7pm. ✆ 01-40-53-80-82.

DÉPÔT-VENT PASSY
14 & 25 rue de la Tour, 16e (Métro: Passy).

Another contender in the used-designer-clothing wars. Catherine Baril has two shops with top-drawer stuff—YSL, Chanel, the works. One shop is for women, the other for men. They are a few yards from each other. Both carry a fair number of samples. On my last visit, I found tons of Chanel straight from the runway. The prices were generally high, but I found a few bargains. A summer-weight Chanel suit for 930€ ($1,070) seemed like a good buy, whereas a Chanel camisole for 175€ ($201) was overpriced, at least to me.

The best part about this shop is its location. You can easily combine a stroll along the rue de Passy with a shopping spree here and have a fabulous time. It's open Monday from 2 to 7pm and Tuesday through Saturday from 10am to 7pm. In July, it's open Monday through Saturday from 2 to 7pm. Call © 01-45-20-95-21.

DIDIER LUDOT
24 passage de la galerie Montpensier, Jardin du Palais Royal, 1er (Métro: Palais-Royal).

Ludot tries to sell only top-of-the-line used designer goods, specializing in Hermès, Celine, and Chanel. You may find Hermès bags from the 1930s, as well as vintage Vuitton luggage. This store is a standout for old-clothes junkies. Prices are high for quality items, but not unfair. I saw a Pucci in perfect condition and a wool Chanel suit with a matching blouse—both hard-to-find items.

This shop is not easy to find, so have patience and remember that it is on the gallery side of the building, not the street side. Leaving the Métro, zig to the right into the open arcade, then hug the left-hand side of the arcade (where it is covered). Shops line the walkway; Ludot is among them. Do not confuse the vintage clothing with his new Little Black Dress line. Call © **01-42-96-06-56** or 01-40-15-01-04.

RÉCIPROQUE
89, 92, 95, 97, 101 & 123 rue de la Pompe, 16e (Métro: Pompe).

Réciproque has grown at an alarming rate—there are now more storefronts bearing this store's name along rue de la Pompe than ever before. The main shop, at no. 89, has two floors; don't forget to go downstairs.

There are racks and racks of clothes, all of which are clean. You'll find separates, shoes, evening wear, and complete ensembles. You must look through the racks carefully and know your merchandise, although the labels are always in the clothes. Not everything is used or seriously used—many designers sell samples here. Every big name is represented; this is the best single resource for used couture clothing. Prices are not dirt-cheap— a Chanel suit will cost over 2,000€ ($2,300).

There's a shop for men's clothing; there are accessories, furs, and things for the home. There are sales, too. It can be overwhelming—you need patience as well as a good eye. Call © **01-47-04-30-28** or 01-47-27-93-52.

SCARLETT
10 rue Clement-Marot, 8e (Métro: Alma-Marceau).

Scarlett was once a fixture at the flea market at Vanves, but now she has her own shop. Her store carries gently worn clothing and accessories, mostly from Hermès, Chanel, and Vuitton. They aren't funky vintage and may only be a season old. Other items are, of course, older—but are classical enough to be used without implying a retro look. © **01-56-89-03-00.**

BRAND-OWNED STOCK SHOPS

As the word *stock* implies, these stores sell overruns or excess stock. They are located in Paris and are stand-alone stores; the rue d'Alésia has several such stores in a 2-block area. Most of the stores in this section are in areas that are easy to reach on the Métro; many are in neighborhoods where a tourist would want to go strolling anyway. Alésia is out-of-the-way, but makes up for it with the number of outlets in one place, and it's certainly worth it if you're a Sonia Rykiel freak. Start at Sonia's first store and walk south to the second one; along the way, there are 2 blocks full of stock shops. Explore at will.

Note that later in this chapter, I have listed outlet malls that are just outside Paris—these have a much wider selection of brand-name stores.

ANNE FONTAINE
22 rue de Passy, 16e (Métro: Passy).

This is a store that sells leftover stock; it's not a true outlet such as the one out in La Vallée. Nonetheless, you may score with a slight discount—since the merchandise is very classical, there's no worry as to what season it is. ✆ **01-42-24-80-20.** www.annefontaine.com.

APCG
45 rue Madame, 6e (Métro: St-Germain-des-Prés).

Funky, fabulous line, very trendy and Hollywood—even the discounted prices are not dirt-cheap, but if you like this line, you will find prices moderately better than at regular retail. Expect prices to begin at 87€ ($100). The store is only open in the afternoons, from 1 to 7pm, and is closed on Sundays. ✆ **01-45-48-43-71.**

BLEU BLANC
83 rue de Prony, 17e (Métro: Péreire).

This shop is near the *dépôt-ventes* of the 17e, so you can combine them on one visit. The Bleu Blanc line of men's and women's clothing and outerwear is of the best French quality, offering sportswear with a nautical twist—a shade more trendy than preppy. There are also promotional sales; you can get on the mailing list if you have a local address.

CACHAREL STOCK
114 rue d'Alésia, 14e (Métro: Alésia).

Men's, women's and children's clothing in a well-stocked stock shop.

ET VOUS STOCK
15 rue de Turbigo, 12e (Métro: Etienne Marcel).

Et Vous is a youngish line, a little more hip than Ann Taylor. Career clothes, but no serious bargains.

GR STOCK/GEORGES RECH
100 rue d'Alésia, 14e (Métro: Alésia).

Well-tailored clothing, no matter how old it is. A great brand for women who work and want classic clothes for the office with a twist of fashion but nothing *outre*. © 01-45-40-87-73.

KOOKAI
82 rue Réaumur, 2e (Métro: Réaumur-Sébastopol).

Kookai is a young brand, great for teens and tweens. The sizes run small. This location is pretty handy for a tourist. I also often find Kookai at **Sympa** stores in Montmartre (p. 130). © 01-45-08-93-69.

LILITH/FREE
66 rue Parmentier, 10e (Métro: Goncourt).

Lilith is not for everyone—although I have seen short women wear it and look chic. The clothes are often made with lots of fabric that floats or flits, the colors are soft, and the style is droopy. There are many no-waist or elastic-waist styles of which I am fond. This outlet shop is a tad off the beaten track, but well worth a special trip for Lilith fans.

MAX MARA/RAMA
7 rue Bisconnet, 12e (Métro: Bastille).

Go up one flight to this store that specializes in all the various lines made by Max Mara, which includes the less-well-known Penny Black, and others. There are also plus-size brands, including Elena Miro and Marina Rinaldi. Prices can be less at other jobbers in Paris, but you have to get lucky to find the brand at all. At this outlet, 100€ ($115) can get you into play, although most items cost more like 120€ to 150€ ($138–$173). This is still half the regular retail price. ✆ 01-43-07-37-66.

PLEIN SUD STOCK
51 rue Servan, 11e (Métro: St-Maur).

Very trendy line; older clothes are reduced by 50%.

P'TIT BATEAU (PULL'SION)
32 rue St-Placide, 6e (Métro: Sèvres-Babylone).

This may look like just another sweaters or knits store and it carries a few other lines besides Petit Bateau, but since it is mainly PB, I have listed it here. This is not an official stock shop, but since more than half the merchandise available comes from the PB factory and since I get a lot of mail from readers who want PB deals, *voilà*. Kids' sizes, baby clothes, and adult tees are about 40% off. Color choices can be iffy. ✆ 01-45-44-89-20.

REGINA RUBENS
88 rue d'Alésia, 14e (Métro: Alésia).

This is a very nice line with a feminine look; clothes here can be older than one season, but are fairly priced.

SCALP
102 rue St-Charles, 15e (Métro: Charles-Michel).

Scalp is the lower-priced line made by Weill, so don't think they're out to scalp you. This line isn't enormously trendy, but it fits larger-size women, with clothes up to size 52. The store is open on Mondays, but not until 11am. On other days, it opens at 10am; closed on Sunday. ✆ 01-45-77-13-09.

SR/SONIA RYKIEL STOCK
64 and 112 rue d'Alésia, 14e (Métro: Alésia).

Don't look now, but the best store in the 'hood—and the reason you schlepped over to the 14e in the first place—just got better by adding on another shop. The SR shop at no. 112 is very large and sells all of the Rykiel line, including men's, women's, and kids' things. The best way to attack is to prowl on rue d'Alésia at the first Sonia shop, then survey the other stores in the next 2 blocks and make your way to the shop at no. 64. Then you can decide what's what. ✆ 01-43-95-06-13 or 01-45-43-80-86.

VIDNA
9 rue St-Placide, 6e (Métro: Sèvres-Babylone).

This is one of the many discount and stock shops on the rue St-Placide (see "Left Bank Discount Neighborhoods" on p. 79). I specifically point out this one so you don't just walk past it, since nothing about it draws attention to the wonders within.

This is the stock shop for the brand **Nitya,** a chic line with stores all over Europe, including one at 327 rue St-Honoré, 8e. The look is slightly ethnic, but monochromatic and easy for all figures to wear. Don't go by the sizes; try everything on. I'm a 42 here (sometimes) and a 46 in real life. Okay, okay, so sometimes I wear a 48. Clothes are usually 2 years old, but the look is classic enough that it doesn't matter. Call ✆ 01-45-48-95-75.

ZADIG & VOLTAIRE STOCK
22 rue du Bourg-Tibourg, 4e (Métro: St-Paul or Hotel de Ville).

More hip than preppy, but not too weird or too very hip—some house designs and some big-name designer goods. The hours are unusual: the store is closed on Mondays. It is open on Tuesdays from 1 to 7pm, then from 12:30 to 7:30pm the rest of the week. Finally, there are Sunday hours, from 2 to 7:30pm. ✆ 01-44-59-39-62.

BARGAIN BASEMENTS

....

I call stores that sell many brands at lower-than-average prices "bargain basements," and list the best ones in this section.

(For stores that concentrate on one brand, see "Brand-Owned Stock Shops," above. See "Resale & Vintage" on p. 118 for resale shops, which can offer bargains on pre-owned designer clothing. Also check out "Left Bank Discount Neighborhoods" on p. 79.)

Paris has seen a lot of stock and so-called discount stores open in the past few years. Some even call themselves outlet stores. Often they are regular mom-and-pop stores that carry name brands, but cut their profit to appeal to shoppers who are disgusted by the high regular retail prices in France.

I don't need to give you the lecture about the nature of bargain shops, but I will say that on my last research trip I noticed two new addresses in popular tourist magazines (no names, please). I eagerly went off to these sources—each in the heart of Paris's best shopping district and convenient for any visitor. Maybe I hit a bad day; maybe I am too big of a snob. I hated both of them so much that I refuse to list them in this book. On the other hand, that doesn't mean that the sources I have listed are going to be super on the day you visit. Bargain hunting in Paris is even harder than in America, so think about how much time you want to invest in this pursuit. Good luck.

Finally, a word about sizes—if you are larger than a size 12 (U.S.), you may not find a fit . . . or should trade yourself over to full-figure sizes: lines made up to size 52. Since I am an American size 14 or 16, the brands I look for are Weill, Elena Miro, Marina Rinaldi, and Weinberg. (When I splurge, I buy Yohji at Galeries Lafayette with my tourist discount card.)

ANNA LOWE
104 rue du Faubourg St-Honoré, 8e (Métro: Miromesnil).

If you're looking for me in Paris, step into my parlor. I have a resident's permit on the sofa here at Anna Lowe, where I take a coffee break just about every day I'm in Paris. But enough about me.

This is a fun store because the owner has an eye for glitz and glamour and has connections with big-name designer shops (yes, Chanel) to get unsold stocks. Her genius is to mix regular retail with designer discount—there is always a sale rack in the rear. The regular stock is especially good on suits, but there are furs, dress-up clothes and gowns, and then the sparkle-plenty kind of clothes that work best on the Riviera. Call ✆ **01-42-66-11-32**.

ANNEXE DES CRÉATEURS
19 rue Godot-de-Mauroy, 9e (Métro: Madeleine).

This crowded shop lacks charm, but is crammed with clothes and bolts of fabric. It carries sizes up to 44 (size 12 U.S.). You won't have to make a special trip; it's close to many places in every woman's journey through Paris—halfway between boulevard Madeleine and the big department stores on boulevard Haussmann.

GRIFFE DE MODE
17 rue de la Boétie, 8e (Métro: Miromesnil or St. Augustin).

Before I get into this listing, let me get you here. The street is pronounced "boh-eh-*see*." The first Métro stop I have listed is pronounced "mee-roh-meh-*nee*." Yeah, I know all about it.

Now then, I am an expert on this store above all others because it is very close to my flat in Paris and when I go to the grocery store at Monoprix at St. Augustin, I am forced to stop here to see what's new. The store is very junky and may not be for everyone. You really have to wade through the stuff . . . but what stuff! There are shoes, lingerie, hosiery, accessories, bed linens, kids' clothes, and women's fashions. There's a men's clothing store two doors away, at no. 23.

Almost everything sold here is from a major brand. Stock varies quickly. Note that the main store has a few salons, so keep walking toward the rear.

I do especially well when they have Marina Rinaldi, and yes, I pay from 45€ to 100€ ($52–$115) per dress. On my last visit, I got three pieces for 300€, which appeared on my U.S. credit card as $345, and then there was the usual surcharge for converting. Since one of the items could have cost this same amount, I was over the moon with delight. Call ✆ 01-49-24-08-81.

Le Stock
66 rue de la Chausée-d'Antin & 9 rue Scribe, 9e
(Métro: Opéra or Chaussée-d'Antin).

I have never done very well in either of these shops and I've been checking them out for years. That said, note that the locations of these two outlets are so handy (next to Galeries Lafayette), that you'd be nuts to ignore them. Also, I'm a hard size to fit and a smaller person could be much luckier. Big names appear. ✆ 01-40-16-06-00 or 01-40-07-10-20.

Moda di Andrea
79 rue de la Victoire, 9e (Métro: Chaussée-d'Antin).

Before you don't recognize the address and ignore this listing, let me confess that this is one of my best sources in Paris. You'd be foolish to miss it. The store is also right behind Galeries Lafayette, so it's not hard to find.

Moda sells brand-name shoes for men, women, and children, plus some handbags. By brand name, I mean basics like Prada, Chanel, YSL, Tod's, and Hogan—for about half the regular European price. We are talking about putting down a hunk of money for shoes, and chances are great that you can't stop with just one pair. The selection can make you dizzy, and yes, they do have large sizes in some things.

I recently bought a pair of Hogan's linen trainers for 150€ ($173), which I saw advertised in a U.S. fashion magazine for $365. I thought what I paid was steep, but I got the shoes at almost half-price.

The shop takes credit cards, but does not give détaxe refunds. It's open mornings at 10:30am and closed on Sunday and Monday. Call ✆ **01-48-74-48-89**.

Note: If you're off to Biarritz, there's Moda di Victoria, with two stores.

MOUTON À CINQ PATTES
8 & 18 rue St-Placide, 7e (Métro: Sèvres-Babylone).
138 bd St-Germain (Métro: Odéon).

This is a small chain of stock shops; I have always called it "The Lamb Chop Store." Actually the name means "a lamb with five paws." I guess that's the kind of misfits it sells or considers itself to be, because of the unusual savings. You will find big names here.

I shopped at the St-Placide store for about 20 years and was never very impressed; then suddenly I hit pay dirt. In the last 3 years, I've gone nuts with good buys, so you just never know.

So what did I get recently? How about a fully lined, very well-made men's blazer for 49€ ($56)? Or a collection of Japanese fashions to wear en suite: a big twirly skirt, baggy long-sleeved top, and strange pleated white cotton vest. The total for the whole three-piece outfit was 240€ ($276). The Japanese-y outfit was not from a name I knew nor was it low-cost, but I got a great look at decent value—the store offers a lot of that philosophy.

The St-Placide locations are handy to Le Bon Marché department store (✆ **01-45-48-86-26**). The St. Germain location (✆ **01-43-26-49-25**) is not as good as St. Placide, so don't judge the system by this store—stop in only after you've scored on St-Placide.

STOCK DE MARQUES
190 rue de Rivoli, 1er (Métro: Louvre).

So it's a Sunday late afternoon in Paris and I am walking with my girlfriend Pascale-Agnes from the Louvre toward my hotel, the Meurice. Mostly we pass TT's and postcard/poster stores, but then we see a stock shop and feel it is our duty to investigate.

Oh my! Or *mon dieu* as we say in French. Major, major names in menswear and women's wear and accessories. Leonard scarves for 50€ ($58). Is there a better way to spend a Sunday afternoon? Now then, the day we were here, the men's was better than the women's; the women's was mostly in small sizes and very old merchandise. Like all these sorts of things, it's just how you hit it. The store is open daily from 11am until 7:30pm. Call ℂ 01-42-96-62-76.

SYMPA

18 rue d'Orsel, 18e (Métro: Anvers or Barbès-Rochechouart).

Hmmm, where to begin with this? Sympa actually has several storefronts and they move around a bit, but they dominate this area, so the given address above is just to get you started. There are usually several stores on rue Stalingrad, which runs perpendicular to rue d'Orsel.

Now then, Sympa is so about bins and piles, heaps and no sizes, stuff falling off hangers and sometimes damaged goods, that you really have to like this kind of shopping just to attempt it.

Finally, this location is sublime for a true shopper as you are smack-dab into the Marché St-Pierre (p. 152) for fabrics and on the north side of Montmartre—if you want to combine some tourism efforts, you can take the cable car right up the hill from this store.

But let's shop. You'll find all sorts of brands, often big brands but not big-name designers. I often see Kookai. I have seen Superga shoes from Italy. We're talking battle conditions and low prices. Call ℂ 01-42-62-22-73.

VINCY

9 bis rue St-Placide, 6e (Métro: Sèvres-Babylone).

Located on the rue St-Placide in the midst of many *dégriffé* (without the label) stores, this is a shoe store that has some name brands for men and women. In fact, I couldn't help but think of O. J. Simpson when I saw what was here. Prices are in the 44€ to 87€ ($50–$100) a pair range, worth a look. Expect classical styles. ✆ 01-42-22-58-96.

FACTORY-OUTLET MALLS

By definition, factory outlets lie outside of major metropolitan areas. As the outlet-mall craze grows in Europe, more and more are opening closer to Paris. A few are within an hour of the city, although only **La Vallée** was created with public transportation in mind. Others may advertise how close they are to transportation, but are really for those with cars.

La Vallée Village

I have very mixed feelings about this idea—after all, you've come to Paris and the point is to be in Paris. On the other hand, if you want to do a lot of shopping in one big power shopping trip, and if you have a car or a spirit of adventure, this outlet mall is handy to know about. It is also open on Sundays.

La Vallée Village is the fanciest and most chic outlet center in all of France. It's in the American format of a fake village with a pedestrian main street, with each shop along the walkway. *Resident's alert: You cannot bring your dog!* La Vallée was built alongside a regular mall (**Centre Commercial Val d'Europe**), so curious shoppers can have the best of all worlds (although the outlet center has much more liberal hours than the regular mall) and do some discount, as well as regular, shopping. See below for more on **Auchan,** the famed *hypermarché* that is part of the Val d'Europe mall.

La Vallée is excellent on brand-name fashion and so-so on home style. Among the brands with outlet shops here are Armani, Anne Fontaine, Kenzo, Ferragamo, Muriella Burani, Charles Jourdan, Max Mara, Nitya (one of my faves, see p. 125),

Camper (Spanish shoe brand for casual shoes), and Ventilo. There's also Bleu Blanc, Burberry, Mandarina Duck, Molton Brown, Ralph Lauren, Zadig & Voltaire and—get this—Starbucks.

In terms of home, there is a **Bodum** outlet, **Lagostina** (Italian cookware), **Villeroy & Boch,** and an **Anne de Solene** shop that sells bed linen.

I am assuming you know most of these brands or can look them up in the index of this book. There is a fair mix here of French, Italian, and British lines with the odd American brand (Ralph Lauren and Starbucks). There aren't a lot of surprises—but note that **Samsonite** is an Italian brand: It does sell the luggage you expect, but it also has clothes and shoes.

As mentioned, the regular mall has a branch of **Auchan,** which is my favorite *hypermarché* in France. *Note:* Auchan is not open on Sunday and the outlet mall is, so if Auchan is important to you, organize yourself accordingly. As you can imagine, a *hypermarché* is jammed on Saturdays, so the best day to do this is from Monday to Thursday.

If you're staying in a hotel or traveling by train, you may find it too hard to schlep purchases from a *hypermarché*. However, I like their low-cost fashions and home styles and think you'll have fun poking around here while you're in the neighborhood.

Note: If you're driving a rental car, you may want to gas up here—Auchan has the best gas prices in the area. *Further note:* The automatic machines will not take U.S. credit cards.

Hours are Monday through Saturday from 10am to 8pm, Sunday from 11am to 7pm. For information, call © 01-60-42-35-00 or go to www.lavalleevillage.com.

To get there, I would allow an hour of travel time.

- By car, take the autoroute A4 east in the direction of Nancy; look for exit 12, marked VAL D'EUROPE. Yes, I would consider renting a car for this adventure. The drive is easy and if there are several people along, you can share the rental cost, fill up on gas at the pumps near Auchan (pumps are open Sun), and drive back to Paris.

- By bus, a Cityrama shuttle bus from Paris runs every Tuesday, Thursday, and Sunday (call © **01-44-55-60-00** for reservations).
- By train, take the RER line A4 direct to Val d'Europe in the Disneyland direction. Go out through the mall (Centre Commercial Val d'Europe) to the outlet center on the far side. It is a hike.

Paris Nord 2/Usines Center X

You will pass this 120-shop center (© **01-48-63-20-72**) as you drive between Paris and CDG Airport in Roissy. It's about 40 minutes from Paris. I wouldn't send anyone here, unless you've lived in Paris for years and are curious or bored with life. However, it is alongside an Ikea and a Castorama, so locals and expats may find it useful.

Open Monday through Friday from 11am to 7pm, Saturday and Sunday from 10am to 8pm. From the A1 autoroute in the direction of Roissy, take exit ZI (Zone Industriel) Paris Nord 2.

Troyes

Troyes is a city, not an outlet center, and is home to two large outlet malls. The one owned by **McArthur Glen** is called Troyes Pont Marie because it's in a suburb of Troyes named, you got it, Pont Marie. This mall offers Saturday bus service (© **08-00-80-92-43**; www.eva-voyages.com). The round-trip fare for the 90-minute trip is 15€ ($17) per person. It departs at 10am from the place de la Bastille in front of the Opéra (Métro: Bastille) and returns back to Paris at 7pm. You can go to www.mcarthurglen.fr for further information, as well as promotions and exceptional opening dates (some Sun).

The mall situation at Troyes has changed enormously. It's much more built up than in past years, there are a lot of choices for young people and young couples, and it's not as chic as La Vallée or even as clean as you'd like it to be. You may get lost if you drive, but that can/will happen all over France.

All that said, the **Armani** at McArthur Glen had so many incredible deals that you could weep. Other tenants at this mall include: **Burberry, Georges Rech, Ralph Lauren, Ventilo, Weill, and Rodier.** There are stores for men, women, children, home style, and baggage.

Chapter Seven

....

PARIS RESOURCES A TO Z

ACCESSORIES

....

Paris department stores have very good accessories departments, and buying from them makes good use of your tourist discount card (10% off the top)—and goes toward your 175€ ($201) spending requirement for a détaxe refund that gives another 12% discount.

Likewise, many of the so-called duty-free shops sell some accessories—handbags, hair ornaments, gloves, and scarves. In fact, I think the single best $100 handbags in town come from **Catherine,** a perfume shop (p. 217).

Also note that most museum shops have pretty good accessories. You may not want a scarf that's a reproduction of the Mona Lisa, but the jewelry made from coins from the French Mint is actually very chic.

The category of goods called accessories is wide, so see also the sections in this chapter on costume jewelry, shoes, and handbags.

CAMILLE LUCIE
232 and 206 rue de Rivol, 1er (Métro: Tuileries).

I hate to start off the chapter with a bargain listing or with big personal confessions, but here we are. I was not looking for this store originally. It is simply next door to the Hôtel Meurice, and it bit me in the behind. When I got addicted, I found another branch up the street and have also seen others popping up all over town. The shops are somewhat TT-looking and may not be your kind of thing. I do understand, but let me confess and then you can decide how you feel.

The store sells copies of the most expensive jewelry; wedding rings are its specialty, although there are also cocktail rings and some other accessories. The prices are two rings for 50€ ($58). Because the rings are not real gold and because I wash my hands frequently and do not remove my rings, I buy two of the same ring. They will last longer if you take better care.

Although I am not married, I sometimes wear a wedding ring in public so outsiders know that I am in a relationship. I buy those rings here and wear "gold" and "diamonds" galore in styles from Europe's most popular names.

For the branch next to the Meurice, call © 01-42-96-41-90, or for the other shop, call 01-42-96-88-26; or log on to www. camille-lucie.com.

FABRICE
33 and 54 rue Bonaparte, 6e (Métro: St-Germain-des-Prés).

Vintage or made with vintage parts, here's jewelry that is ethnic and faux ethnic, chunky and funky, and more, more, more. Fabrice has two stores separated by some other buildings; the prices are pricey, but you get the feeling the stuff is collectible. Every now and then, there's real gold in there with the fun stuff. I was staggered that the object of my obsession was an 18-carat necklace with a price tag of 8,000€ ($9,200). More often, you're looking at items in the 200€ to 400€ ($230–$460) range. © 01-43-26-57-95 or 01-43-26-09-49. www.bijouxfabrice.com.

FRANÇOISE MONTAGUE
231 rue St-Honoré, 1er (Métro: Tuileries).

Located inside a courtyard off the rue St-Honoré, this hidden resource provides retail and wholesale jewelry with a few different looks. Lots of items are made with tons of jewels, including wire collars that you just want to heap around your neck as if you belonged in a Modigliani painting—they're about 109€ ($125) each. There's also resin, mostly fashioned into flower brooches, for about 57€ ($66). Don't miss this one. ℰ 01-42-60-80-16.

OCTOPUSSY
255 rue St-Honoré, 8e (Métro: Concorde).

Very funky handbags and some accessories; a lot of the stock is created with photo-fashion imagery.

PHILIPPE MODEL
33 place du Marché St-Honoré, 1er (Métro: Tuileries).

Although he has just written a book on home style, Philippe Model is most famous as a hat maker. Besides the usual fluff (or unusual fluff, as the case may be) for the racetrack, there's everything from art to wearable.

SHADE
63 rue des Sts-Pères, 6e (Métro: Sèvres-Babylone).

Ali Baba and the young *créateurs* of France have teamed up— Shade has everything from kitsch to fantasia. This store is on a printout given to fashion editors visiting Paris who are looking for the latest. ℰ 01-45-49-30-37.

ACTIVE WEAR

ADIDAS
148 rue de Rivoli, 1er (Métro: Tuileries).

They offer the German brand for shoes and active wear and the Stella McCartney line of gear that is selling out all over the world. ℰ 01-58-62-51-60.

PSG (PARIS SAINT GERMAIN)
27 av. des Champs-Elysées, 8e (Métro: Franklin D. Roosevelt).

This store selling sports souvenirs and activewear represents the local football team Paris Saint Germain (often written PSG), as well as other Europe Cup teams. It's a two-story affair with clothes and accessories, but best of all is the fact that you can buy any shirt and for another 8€ ($9), have your name—or anyone's name—put on the back, while you wait. © 01-56-69-22-22.

RYKIEL KARMA
6 rue de Grenelle, 6e (Métro: Rue du Bac).

As if Nathalie Rykiel's foray into sex toys weren't enough, now she's really aiming for inner peace: she has opened a store that sells workout clothes, especially those for yoga. © 01-49-54-66-21.

AMERICAN DESIGNERS IN PARIS

You can see much American merchandise back home and pay less for it, but in France there's always the chance you'll find your favorite items in shades you can't get in the U.S. Still, I don't suggest you spend too much precious Paris time looking at American-based designers; they're selling status to locals, not merchandise that offers value for money. Yes, in the last 2 years, **Marc Jacobs** has opened his own shop (not just for Louis Vuitton); yes, there's the green label **American Apparel**; and yes, **Nike** is now on the Champs-Elysées. *Eh, oui?*

ART SUPPLIES; ARTS & CRAFTS

The big department stores carry both crafts and art supplies; **BHV** (p. 147) has the best selection. For stores that sell art supplies only, I suggest one legend: Sennelier. The other listings are more arts-and-crafts shops that sell everything. U.S. crafts shops tend to have a larger selection at a better price, but you never know what novelty you'll find.

CREA
55 rue St-Placide, 6e (Métro: St-Placide).

Smack-dab in the middle of 2 blocks of discount stores and just a shout from the department store Bon Marché, this shop is so exciting that my palms itch and my mouth gets dry as I approach. It's got all sorts of supplies and crafts and do-it-yourself notions. The store is part of a chain with branches all over France; the other Paris branches are mostly in residential areas that a tourist is unlikely to visit. They do have classes, demonstrations, and many promotions. Demonstrations are free. They are also in French. ✆ 01-53-63-14-90. www.crea.tm.fr.

LOISIRS & CREATION
Carrousel du Louvre (Métro: Louvre).

This is a major French chain and not the best (I like Crea much better), but this location is easy and if you have kids along, it's going to be a successful visit after the Louvre.

SENNELIER
3 quai Voltaire, 7e (Métro: Assemblée Nationale).

Located right on the Seine (and not too near any Métro stops), this is the most famous atelier of supplies in Paris—and yes, all the big names have shopped here. I find the prices outrageous; most tourists who buy here just want to say they have done so. ✆ 01-42-60-72-15.

CHILDREN'S CLOTHING

If you're the kind of mom—or grandma—who likes to drop a bundle on a single outfit for your little darling, Paris welcomes you and your moolah. You'll have no trouble finding expensive shops where you can swoon from the high fashion and high prices.

Note: French clothes don't fit like U.S. clothes—they're smaller and closer to the body. French kids' clothes are usually marked by the age in years, just like American clothes: 8A means 8 years *(8 ans)*. For an American 8-year-old, buy size 10A. A size chart appears on the inside front cover of this book.

- Don't forget about the **department stores,** which have rather famous children's departments and much more moderate prices. **Galeries Lafayette** has a large array of designer brands for kiddies, even from American designers like DKNY.

- If you're into euro busters, dash immediately to **Monoprix.** Its kids' fashions (boys, girls, and infants) are wonderful and well priced.

- If you like a one-stop kind of destination, hit the rue St-Placide near Bon Marché (Métro: Sèvres-Babylone), which has a branch of just about every kids' clothing brand in France. These are not discounted, but they are all in a 2-block area.

- Some of the trendy boutiques also have kiddie divisions. They include **H&M,** 53 bd Haussmann (Métro: Chaussée-d'Antin or Havre Caumartin). I find the quality is not as good as at Monoprix, but some pieces are just so adorable that you have to snap them up.

- Couture baby wear is the latest thing—not really made to measure, but from the couture houses. **Christian Dior** sells a baby bottle that is adorable—and a great gift.

- If you're looking for children's shoes, you will need a size chart (see inside front cover) and some luck. My favorite source is a cheapie chain called **André,** with branches everywhere—they have copies of all the hot styles that usually cost about 20€ ($23) a pair. Well-made shoes cost an arm and a leg, no matter how small; I call these "fun shoes."

French Chains for Kids

BONPOINT
15 rue Royale, 8e (Métro: Madeleine).
53 rue du Tournon, 6e (Métro: Odéon); and others.

You won't do better than Bonpoint for an expression of style, chic, and quality. This is the leading status symbol for French mothers. While the line held on to classic styles for a very long time, it has since moved into fashion, so that whatever trend Mom is wearing—or the fashion magazines are featuring—can also be found in kids' sizes. Prices are not low.

There are several Bonpoint shops around town. Some specialize in kids' shoes; one has furniture only. A few sell maternity wear. If you're impressed with the clothing, but can't hack the prices, try the outlet store, where last season's collection is sold for a fraction of the uptown price. The outlet is closed on weekends, but is convenient to your Left Bank shopping.

Bonpoint has just opened a new concept store, with museum-like showcases and a children's play area. Don't think play area as you know it; this is a French château from the turn of the 19th century. Honest. Call ✆ 01-47-42-52-63.

DU PAREIL AU MÊME
15 rue Mathurins, 8e (Métro: Madeleine), and others.

I consider Du Pareil au Même (written DPAM sometimes) the best of the mass-market kiddie boutiques, and I curse the fact that my niece has grown up and no longer wears kids' clothes. Most of the line is casual and in strong colors; prices are very affordable. There are stores in every shopping district in Paris. ✆ 01-42-66-93-80. www.dupareilaumeme.fr.

PETIT BATEAU
116 av. des Champs-Elysées, 8e (Métro: George V or Etoile), and about a dozen other addresses.

The famed maker of T-shirts has opened a new flagship. There are now a few U.S. stores, where prices are higher than in Paris.

The line is also available in department stores. © 01-40-74-02-03. www.petit-bateau.com.

TARTINE ET CHOCOLAT
105 rue du Faubourg St-Honoré, 8e (Métro: Concorde).

French-style maternity dresses and layettes, both classic and nouveau. My fave: the big pink hippo in pink-and-white stripes sitting in a playpen, just begging to be taken home to someone's child. Also in the major department stores. © 01-45-62-44-04.

TOUT COMPTE FAIT
101 bis rue d'Alésia, 14e (Métro: Alésia).

After DPAM, this is my favorite of the lot—good colors, good prices, hot styles. There are about 30 branch stores in Paris, and I shop here when I go to La Défense—which may not be for everyone. © 01-45-39-84-85. www.toutcomptefait.com.

Kids' Boutiques & Designer Lines

AGATHA RUIZ DE LA PRADA
9 rue Guénégaud, 6e (Métro: Odéon).

Now don't get carried away; this is no relation to the Italian line Prada. In fact, the Spanish designer was famous before Miuccia Prada became a household name. She is relatively unknown outside of Spain, but has a following in France, where her bright colors are popular in children's wear and accessories. She also does some specialty items for Monoprix. © 01-43-25-86-88.

PETIT FAUNE
33 rue Jacob, 6e (Métro: St-Germain-des-Prés).

Very original baby clothes in the nouveau style. Some have matching shoes and hats. Everything is quite small—to size 2. The clothes are very American, and even the fanciest isn't in the classic style. © 01-42-60-80-72.

CONTINENTAL BIG NAMES

Despite the fact that the French think French fashion is the best in the world, they have graciously allowed other designers to open in Paris. Of course, the Italians have a good number of shops, representing some of the most famous names in fashion; and a handful of the designers are British (John Galliano, Alexander McQueen, Stella McCartney).

Many of the world's biggest names come from other countries yet show their lines in Paris (Valentino, Hanae Mori, Kenzo, Yohji, and so on), so have come to be considered French designers. In most cases, nationality doesn't matter—it's the clothes.

The list below separates the non-French brands by house, not by designer. Note that many of the following names have outlet stores at La Vallée (p. 131), outside of Paris. For French designer brands, see p. 157.

AKRIS
54 rue du Faubourg St-Honoré, 8e (Métro: Concorde).
49 av. Montaigne, 8e (Métro: Alma-Marceau).

ARMANI COLLEZIONI
41 av. George V, 8e (Métro: George V).

BOTTEGA VENETA
14 rue du Faubourg St-Honoré, 8e (Métro: Concorde).
12 av. Montaigne, 8e (Métro: Franklin D. Roosevelt).

BURBERRY
55 rue de Rennes, 6e (Métro: St-Germain-des-Prés).
8 bd Malesherbes, 8e (Métro: Madeleine).

CERRUTI 1881
15 place de la Madeleine, 8e (Métro: Madeleine).

D&G SUPERSTORE (DOLCE & GABBANA)
244 rue de Rivoli, 1er (Métro: Concorde).

DUNHILL
3 and 15 rue de la Paix, 2e (Métro: Opéra).

EMILIO PUCCI
36 av. Montaigne, 8e (Métro: Franklin D. Roosevelt).

EMPORIO ARMANI
25 place Vendôme, 1er (Métro: Tuileries).
149 bd St-Germain, 6e (Métro: St-Germain-des-Prés).

ERMENEGILDO ZEGNA
10 rue de la Paix, 1er (Métro: Opéra).

ESCADA
275 rue St-Honoré, 8e (Métro: Concorde).
53 av. Montaigne, 8e (Métro: Franklin D. Roosevelt).

ETRO
66 rue du Faubourg St-Honoré, 8e (Métro: Concorde).
177 bd St-Germain, 6e (Métro: St-Germain-des-Prés).

FENDI
1 rue François-1er, 8e (Métro: Alma-Marceau).

FERRAGAMO
50 rue du Faubourg St-Honoré, 8e (Métro: Concorde).
68–70 rue des Sts-Pères, 6e (Métro: Sèvres-Babylone).

GIANFRANCO FERRE
38 av. George V, 8e (Métro: George V).

GIORGIO ARMANI (BLACK LABEL)
6 place Vendôme, 1er (Métro: Tuileries).

GUCCI
3 rue du Faubourg St-Honoré, 8e (Métro: Concorde).
23 rue Royale (Métro: Concorde).
350 rue St-Honoré, 1er (Métro: Tuileries).
Rond-Point des Champs-Elysées, 8e (Métro: Franklin D. Roosevelt).

HELMUT LANG
219 rue St-Honoré, 1er (Métro: Tuileries).

JOHN GALLIANO
384 rue St-Honoré, 1er (Métro: Tuileries).

JOSEPH
44 rue Etienne Marcel, 2e (Métro: Etienne Marcel).
14 av. Montaigne, 8e (Métro: Franklin D. Roosevelt).
277 rue St-Honoré, 8e (Métro: Concorde).

KRIZIA
48 av. Montaigne, 8e (Métro: Alma-Marceau).

LAUREL
402 rue St-Honoré, 8e (Métro: Tuileries).
52 rue Bonaparte, 6e (Métro: St-Germain-des-Prés).

MARIELLA BURANI
412 rue St-Honoré, 8e (Métro: Concorde).

MARNI
57 av. Montaigne, 8e (Métro: Alma-Marceau).

MAX MARA
31 av. Montaigne, 8e (Métro: Alma-Marceau).
265 rue St-Honoré, 1er (Métro: Concorde or Tuileries).
100 av. Paul-Doumer, 16e (Métro: La Muette).
37 rue du Four, 6e (Métro: St-Germain-des-Prés).

MISSONI
1 rue du Faubourg St-Honoré, 8e (Métro: Concorde).

MIU MIU
16 rue de Grenelle, 7e (Métro: St-Sulpice).

MOSCHINO
32 rue de Grenelle, 7e (Métro: Solferino).

MULBERRY
45 rue Croix des Petits Champs, 1er (Métro: Palais-Royal).

PRADA
10 av. Montaigne, 8e (Métro: Alma-Marceau).

ROBERTO CAVALLI
*68 rue du Faubourg St-Honoré, 8e (Métro: Concorde);
moving at some future date.*

TOD'S
29 rue du Faubourg St-Honoré, 8e (Métro: Concorde).

TRUSSARDI
8 place Vendôme, 8e (Métro: Tuileries).

VALENTINO
19 av. Montaigne, 8e (Métro: Alma-Marceau).

DEPARTMENT STORES

The biggies offer a lot of bang for your time, but they can get incredibly crowded on Saturdays and in summer. If your time in Paris is limited, go to these stores early and use them to your best advantage: Check out the designer fashions and all the ready-to-wear clothing floors, and you will immediately know what's hot and what's not.

There are common-sense reasons to shop at a department store—aside from the obvious time savings. There are financial benefits, too, if you do all your shopping in one day at one store and earn the required amount for détaxe. *Remember:* Allow at least 15 minutes for the détaxe paperwork, which you must commence in the department store. Expect it to take longer if it's the middle of the tourist season.

Finally, the best news: In the last year or so, the two major department stores have both outdone themselves with eye-popping results. **Lafayette Maison,** just opened in early 2004, is thrilling—even if you're just browsing.

Bazar de l'Hôtel de Ville (BHV)
52–56 rue de Rivoli, 1er (Métro: Hôtel de Ville).

If you think this is a funny name for a store, you can call it BHV (pronounced "beh-ahsh-*veh*"), or remember that the full name of the store tells you just where it is—across from the Hôtel de Ville. The store is famous for its do-it-yourself attitude and housewares. You owe it to yourself to go to the basement (SS) level: If you are at all interested in household gadgets or interior design, you will go nuts.

The upper floors are ordinary enough, and even the basement level can be ordinary (I assure you—I am not sending you to Paris to buy a lawn mower), but there are little nooks and crannies that will delight the most creative shoppers among you. I buy brass lock pieces and string them on necklaces for gifts.

Personally, I think BHV should get rid of fashion entirely and just do home style, but what do I know? You certainly don't come here to buy clothes or accessories, although they are sold. Instead, concentrate on the crafts and art department; excellent office papers, folders, and paper goods; and the adorable Café Brico in the basement.

Open Monday through Saturday from 9:30am to 6:30pm, and until 10pm on Wednesday. Call © 01-42-74-90-00.

FRANCK ET FILS
80 rue de Passy, 16e (Métro: La Muette).

Franck et Fils is a specialty store. It's elegant, easy to shop, uncrowded, and relatively undiscovered by tourists. You can find respectable, classical fashions in an atmosphere geared for madame. You'll feel very French if you browse, although you may get bored if you're expecting something hot or hip. I buy my Chanel-style camellias here: just 10€ ($12) each!

Open Monday through Saturday from 10am to 5:30pm. Call © 01-44-14-38-00.

GALERIES LAFAYETTE
40 bd Haussmann, 9e (Métro: Chaussée-d'Antin).
Centre Commercial Montparnasse, 14e (Métro: Montparnasse/Bienvenüe).

LAFAYETTE MAISON
35 bd Haussmann, 9e (Métro: Chaussée-d'Antin).

LAFAYETTE HOMME
38 bd Haussmann, 9e (Métro: Chaussée-d'Antin).

LAFAYETTE GOURMET
38 bd Haussmann (upstairs), 9e (Métro: Chaussée-d'Antin).

There isn't a more complete department store in France. Come early in the day and take notes, if need be. Before I learned to love the store, I hated it because I got lost and never learned my way around. Don't be intimidated. Trust me, it pays to take some time to familiarize yourself by taking a reconnaissance trip or studying the free store maps available on the ground floor. This is one of the largest stores in the world—it has three buildings.

If you're planning on buying a lot and the thought of all those individual sales slips makes you nuts, you can use a "shopper's card," available at the Welcome Desk.

This is how it works: As you make each purchase, the clerk marks your card with the amount and holds your package at the desk. When you're finished, you pay the grand total. You

don't have to keep opening and closing your wallet and sign-
ing multiple receipts. It's also one of the easiest ways to get
your détaxe, since you pay and claim the credit all at once.

There's only one problem: After you've paid, you must collect all of your packages. It helps if you have marked on the
map where you left them.

Foreign visitors get a flat 10% discount on most purchases
(except food and red-dot items) with a discount card that's available free from the Welcome Desk. (Be sure to present yours
before the sales clerk rings you up.) You can also receive a
coupon for this 10% discount from your U.S. travel agent or
hotel. The export discount is 12% after an expenditure of 175€
($201); do not confuse the flat 10% discount with the 12%
détaxe discount—you're really looking at 10% plus 12%.

When you use the discount card, don't be surprised if you're
sent to a main cash register; there are several on each floor, so
it's no big deal. It's just annoying if you don't know about it.

Galeries Lafayette holds a fashion show on Wednesdays
throughout the year, and on Wednesdays and Fridays from April
to October. It's free, but you need reservations (© 01-48-74-
02-30). The show is in the Salon Opéra. Use the Auber entrance,
then the Mogador escalator, and head to the 7th floor. The fashion show is quite jazzy and good and has no commentary, so
there's no language problem; free refreshments are served. It's
worth doing—it gives you a preview not only of what's available in the store, but also of hot looks and trends.

The store is really a small city spread over three buildings.
There's a post office, a shoe-repair kiosk, a bank (an ATM that
takes U.S. cards is outside on the wall on rue de Chaussée-d'Antin), a penny candy store, souvenir departments, an exposition
space, and a separate museum with real exhibits on culture,
not shopping. The expo space is on the third floor. The store
has been famous for its giant expos for the past century; they
may amuse you. There are salons, there's a spa, there's everything. When I'm asked to categorize this store in terms of an
American point of reference, all I can say is: It's Macy's.

Open Monday through Saturday from 9:30am to 6:45pm, Thursday until 9pm. Also open on the Sundays prior to Christmas and a few other exceptional openings. Closed on French holidays. Call © 01-42-82-30-25 or log on to www. galerieslafayette.com.

Note: The Galeries Lafayette on the Left Bank is a small store catering to locals who work in the area. Its best feature: It opens early in the morning on weekdays. Its second-best feature: It's across the street from **Inno,** my dime-store supermarket. As for the store itself: Yawn.

LE BON MARCHÉ
22 rue de Sèvres, 7e (Métro: Sèvres-Babylone).

Bon Marché is the chicest of the French department stores. It is also divided into separate buildings, like many of the other stores. Building no. 2 is smaller and houses a sensational gourmet grocery store (**La Grande Epicerie**) and more fashion upstairs, as well as the very unique **Delicabar** for lunch or snacks.

Essentially, Bon Marché was re-created in the last decade to represent the needs of the upmarket French woman. This store does not offer a tourist discount card, but will give détaxe, of course. The store reminds me a lot of Barney's New York. Don't miss the basement (SS) level of the main store, which has crafts items, paper goods, children's toys, and books.

Open Monday through Saturday from 9:30am to 6:30pm. Call © 01-44-39-80-00.

AU PRINTEMPS
64 bd Haussmann, 9e (Métro: Havre Caumartin).

PRINTEMPS DE LA MAISON
72 bd Haussmann, 9e (Métro: Havre Caumartin).

BRUMMELL (MEN'S STORE)
Rue Provence and rue Havre Caumartin, behind Printemps de la Maison, 9e (Métro: Havre Caumartin).

PRINTEMPS DESIGN
Pompidou Center museum, 4e (Métro: Rambuteau).

PRINTEMPS NATION
25 cours de Vincennes, 20e (Métro: Porte-de-Vincennes).

PRINTEMPS ITALIE
30 av. d'Italie, 13e (Métro: Italie).

PRINTEMPS RÉPUBLIQUE
10 place de la République, 11e (Métro: République).

Au Printemps is much smaller than Galeries Lafayette, so you really cannot compare the two. The stores think they are competitive; I do not. I'd say Printemps is Saks; Galeries is more Macy's. Keeping with its more upmarket image, the store is always adding on brands and concepts to make you visit—the latest is that superchef Alain Ducasse has taken over the restaurant!

The main store consists of three separate stores: **Brummell**, the men's store, which is behind the main store; the home store, **Printemps de la Maison;** and the fashion store, **Printemps de la Mode.** Brummell has been renovated and is now sensational; there's a great cafe and bar organized by Paul Smith on the top.

The Maison store has more than just housewares—its newly renovated floors of beauty products are just begging you to try them all; there's also a good bookstore and paper shop. The fashion store has floors of luxury brands, as well as space for teens and tweens.

Just like Galeries Lafayette, Printemps has a coupon that entitles foreign visitors to a 10% discount. Ask for yours at the Welcome Desk on the street floor of the main fashion store, and you'll receive something resembling a credit card; you must show your passport. The 10% discount does not apply to food, books, or sale merchandise. This has nothing to do with the détaxe refund; if you qualify for détaxe, you get an additional 12% off.

Printemps hosts a free fashion show on Tuesdays year-round, and on Tuesdays and Fridays from March to October. The show is at 10am on the 7th floor, under the cupola. Commentary is in English and French; the show lasts 45 minutes.

Open Monday through Saturday from 9:35am to 7pm. On Thursdays, the store is open until 10pm! Also open on the Sundays prior to Christmas and some other exceptional openings. Call ✆ **01-42-82-50-00** or log on to www.printemps.fr.

FABRICS, NOTIONS & SUCH

For those who sew, Paris, the home of fancy seams, offers plenty to get creative with. While fabric may not be less expensive than at home, the selection is so incredible that you will be unable to think about price.

If you want a taste of the world of couture or just a silly adventure, you may want to spend a few hours in the **Marché St-Pierre** area in the 18e, a neighborhood that sells fabrics and notions almost exclusively, located on top of the hill on the far side of Montmartre. Couture ends are for sale; shopkeepers are friendly. Some working knowledge of French will be helpful, as well as lots of cash.

The couture fabric resources listed below are famous for their selections (Chanel, YSL, Dior): For starters, there's **Artisanat,** which also sells wool and yarn goods, and then there's **Sevilla,** which can be fabulous if you hit it right. Remember that couture fabrics are not inexpensive—often 100€ ($115) a yard for a silk that may not even be very wide. Prices go up from there.

Bouchara is a more attainable source; they carry the good stuff, but this chain (there's one in every major French city) is more famous for its copycat fabrics at good prices. Should you be somewhat interested in fabric, but not enough to spend much time tracking it down, make Bouchara your first stop. In the basement are some trimmings and possible supplies for your crafts projects. Note that the ground floor is devoted to home style and gives little hint that this is an excellent source for home sewing needs.

If crafts are your thing, don't expect Michael's in France. Hobby stores in the U.S. are more complete and less expensive. On the other hand, **Crea** (p. 139) is fabulous for do-it-yourself supplies for both crafters and artists. You may also have fun at **La Drougerie,** near Forum Les Halles (Métro: Les Halles), for trimmings, beads, and crafts fixings. Expect prices on these supplies to be much higher than in the U.S. Fabrics, however, may be less expensive.

Don't forget the major department stores: BHV has an excellent crafts department, perhaps the best of the French department stores. Bon Marché has a limited crafts department, but I found wonderful beads there and I never saw them anywhere else. You just never know.

ARTISANAT TEXTILE
21 rue des Jeûneurs, 2e (Métro: Sentier).

BOUCHARA
54 bd Haussmann, 9e (Métro: Chaussée-d'Antin).

LA DROUGERIE
9 rue du Jour, 1er (Métro: Les Halles).

MAUPIOU
2 rue de la Paix, 2e (Métro: Opéra).

MOKUBA RIBBON
18 rue Montmartre, 1er (Métro: Etienne Marcel).

RODIN
36 av. des Champs-Elysées, 8e (Métro: Franklin D. Roosevelt).

SEVILLA
38 rue de l'Annonciation, off rue de Passy, 16e (Métro: La Muette).

TISSROY
97 av. Victor Hugo, 16e (Métro: Victor-Hugo).

FOODSTUFFS

If you're looking for an inexpensive gift to bring home, consider taking small but tasty treats or even putting together your own food basket. Foodstuffs are not necessarily easy to pack or lightweight, but they can be rather cheap and look like a lot once you get home and put them in your own basket or wrap them in a clever fashion.

My single best gift in this category is a jar of Maille's Provençale mustard. You can purchase a selection of four Maille's mustards, which makes a great hostess or housewarming gift.

The easiest, and probably the cheapest, place for foodstuff shopping is **Monoprix.** There's a Monoprix on the Champs-Elysées, another behind Printemps on boulevard Haussmann, and yet another at St-Augustin; all locations are central to most hotels on the Right Bank.

If your palate or your pocketbook is advanced, Paris has no shortage of food palaces. As far as I'm concerned, **La Grande Epicerie** (at Le Bon Marché) and **Lafayette Gourmet** (on bd Haussmann) are more reasonably priced than the more famous houses, and more fun to shop. Don't forget the entire rue de Buci, with two grocery stores and many small shops, including a branch of **Oliviers & Co.,** an olive oil specialty shop.

The circle of stores surrounding the place de la Madeleine is almost entirely food specialty shops, including **Maille** and **Maison de la Truffe,** as well as some of the food palaces such as **Fauchon** and **Hédiard.** One block over on rue Vignon is the **Maison de Miel,** the honey shop. You will not starve in Paris, or lack for gifts to bring home.

You cannot bring back any fresh foods; processed hard cheeses are legal, but all others are not. Dried items (such as mushrooms) are legal; fresh fruits and vegetables are not. Foie gras is currently being boycotted as some sort of political payback. Eat yours in France.

For information on stores for wine, see p. 199.

BARTHÉLEMY
51 rue de Grenelle, 7e (Métro: Sèvres-Babylone).

Barthélemy is a shop the size of a large closet, but it smells like cheese heaven and is one of the most famous cheesemongers in France. Everything is fresh and ready to go; if you love cheeses, you will be so happy here that you'll never want to leave.

BOULANGERIE ST-OUEN
111 bd Haussmann, 8e (Métro: Madeleine).

Paris has plenty of good bread shops. So you're wondering what is wrong with me to send you to this slightly out-of-the-way address. Do you trust me? This shop is special because it makes bread in shapes, including the Eiffel Tower! Furthermore, you can get yours with an egg wash, which preserves it (the staff will ask if you want the bread for eating or for display).

The store is about 2 blocks past Madeleine and near the new Monoprix flagship store, so you're going to like it here. It's also near the wine shop Augé (p. 199). *Pronunciation lesson:* If your French isn't that great, you may not know how to say the name. It's just like the flea market in Clignancourt: "sehn-*twehn*." Trust me on this.

FAUCHON
26 place de la Madeleine, 8e (Métro: Madeleine).

Prices are high here, and many items are available elsewhere (have you been to a Monoprix or Inno lately?), but it's a privilege just to stare in the windows. The salespeople are extraordinarily nice. There are three parts to the store: fruits and dry goods; prepared foods next door; and the cafeteria, across the street. Don't forget to check out the tearoom at 30 place de la Madeleine. ✆ 01-70-39-38-00.

FOOD
58 rue Charlot, 3e (Métro: Filles du Calvaire).

As you can guess from the name, this place is about food— but it's mostly a bookstore. It often hosts events with chefs and foodies, and carries some food items. Closed on Monday (and Sun, *bien sûr*); otherwise open from 11am to 1pm and from 2 to 7pm.

HÉDIARD
21 place de la Madeleine, 8e (Métro: Madeleine).

Conveniently located around the bend from Fauchon and Marquise de Sévigné (chocolates), Hédiard competes handily with Paris's other world-class food stores. It's been in the food biz since the mid-1800s, and there is little you cannot buy in this shop. It also delivers, but room service may not be amused. There is another branch (smaller) of Hédiard at the Four Seasons George V. ✆ 01-43-12-88-88.

LENÔTRE
10 av. des Champs-Elysées, 8e (Métro: Clemenceau).
48 av. Victor Hugo, 16e (Métro: Victor-Hugo).
5 rue du Havre, 8e (Métro: Havre Caumartin).
Hôtel Novotel Paris Tour Eiffel, 61 quai de Grenelle, 15e (Métro: Bir Hakeim).

Lenôtre will always mean chocolate and dessert to me, but the store is also a full-fledged deli where you can pick up a picnic. It's open on Sunday (quite unusual) and will gladly guide you through any pig-out. For a price, Lenôtre will even deliver to your hotel. The breakfast special makes it even more fun to be French for a day. As Lenôtre grows, changes, and branches out, it continues to add new concepts, such as cooking lessons, tools, and all sorts of things to try. *Note:* The Champs-Elysées location is not directly on the Champs-Elysées and may be a tad hard to find—it's in what's called the Carré Marigny, across from the American Embassy. © **01-42-65-85-10.**

OLIVIERS & CO.
28 rue de Buci (Métro: St-Germain-des-Prés).
81 rue St-Louis en l'Isle, 4e (Métro: St-Michel, then walk across bridges).
3 rue de Levis (Métro: Villiers); and others.

This chain, begun by the people who created L'Occitane, specializes in olive products—everything from designer tapenade to olive oils from different parts of the Mediterranean. There are French, Spanish, Italian, and even Greek oils, all of which you can taste. A small can of oil costs around 18€ ($21); every now and then, one is on special—there was a big sale on Serbian olive oil last time I was here, no joke. You'll also find soaps, beauty treatments, olive-wood products, and much more—great gift items in all price ranges. O&Co. has some American branches, but prices are much higher in the U.S.

FRENCH DESIGNERS & BIG BRANDS

ANDRÉ COURRÈGES
46 rue du Faubourg St-Honoré, 8e (Métro: Concorde).
40 rue François-1er, 8e (Métro: Franklin D. Roosevelt).
49 rue de Rennes, 6e (Métro: St-Germain-des-Prés).
50 av. Victor Hugo, 16e (Métro: Victor-Hugo).

Courrèges invented the miniskirt and gave us white patent leather boots. Despite his past excesses, he has a very traditional basic line, some dynamite skiwear, and little that is weird or wacky. You can still find some stuff so reminiscent of the 1970s that you don't know if it's new or old merchandise.

AZZEDINE ALAÏA
7 rue de Moussy, 4e (Métro: St-Paul).

Tunisian-born Alaïa shocked Paris fashion with his skin-tight, high-fashion clothes (the Band-Aid dress) and his first boutique in the up-and-coming Marais neighborhood. Now people expect the unusual from him; get a look at the architecture of this place and you'll know he'll never disappoint. The clothes are only for the young and those with figures like movie stars, but the man is on the cutting edge of fashion and retail. Like many shops in the Marais, this one opens at 11am. © 01-42-72-19-19.

BALENCIAGA
10 av. George V, 8e (Métro: George V).

Black dresses are the house specialty, but everything is new and chic and hot, now that Nicolas Ghesquiere has taken over. © 01-47-20-21-11.

BARBARA BUI
50 av. Montaigne, 8e (Métro: Alma-Marceau).
23 rue Etienne Marcel, 2e (Métro: Etienne Marcel).

Barbara Bui is not well known to Americans, but has done so well in Paris that she now has four shops. There are also outposts in New York's SoHo and in Milan. The stores are sparse in their design and chic in their simplicity; there are new boutiques in a row on avenue Etienne Marcel, as well as a cafe (no. 23). If you like Prada, test the waters. © 01-40-26-43-65 or 01-49-23-79-79.

CACHAREL
64 rue Bonaparte, 6e (Métro: St-Sulpice).

Jean Cacharel made his name in America when he introduced charming clothes in precious prints. Thankfully, the line has been re-created and updated by an English design team (Clements & Ribiero) and the results have been spectacular, with an emphasis on color and bold prints. There is also a jazzy bed and bath line now, often found in department stores. © 01-40-46-00-45.

CÉLINE

36 av. Montaigne, 8e (Métro: Franklin D. Roosevelt).
3 av. Victor Hugo, 16e (Métro: Victor-Hugo).

Celine has pretty much lost the horsey motif and the idea of going after Hermès; now it's all sleek, sophisticated, and casual, yet rich, rich, rich. Scarves, bags, and ready-to-wear are the specialties, with an emphasis on creativity in materials, such as string knits. The handbags have been the best bet in recent years. Prices are lower than at Hermès, but they are not modest. © 01-56-89-07-91.

CHANEL

31 rue Cambon, 1er (Métro: Tuileries).
42 av. Montaigne, 8e (Métro: Franklin D. Roosevelt or Alma-Marceau).
21 rue du Faubourg St-Honoré, 8e (Métro: Concorde).

What becomes a legend most? The mother house, as it's known in French, which holds both couture and a boutique at the famed rue Cambon address, tucked behind the Ritz.

There aren't a lot of bargains in this recently renovated store, but serious shoppers will undoubtedly qualify for a détaxe refund. Sale prices in the U.S. may be surprisingly competitive. There's not a total match in terms of selection, so that's the real reason to shop here. Forget savings.

A lot of the accessories—which are the only things that mortals can hope to embrace—are put away in black cases, so you have to ask to be shown the earrings and chains, which is no fun and puts a lot of pressure on you. However, the sales help in this department is usually nice, and the selection is fun. I try to treat myself to a pair of earrings whenever I'm feeling flush; they start at just over 100€ ($115). (There's also a specialty Chanel accessories store at 25 rue Royale; Métro: Madeleine.)

Expect to pay 3,480€ ($4,000) or more for a new suit. If you're game, try a used Chanel suit. A classic is a classic is a classic, no? Check with **Réciproque, Dépôts-vent de Passy,** or **Didier Ludot.** Used suits are not cheap (this is not a new trick): You'll pay around 2,175€ to 2,610€ ($2,500–$3,000). Ludot usually sells the blouse with the suit, but that raises the price of the suit; at Chanel, the blouse is another purchase. *Note:* Used Chanel is less expensive in New York and London.

If by any chance you expect to find faux Chanel in French flea markets, you can forget it. France is very strict about copyright laws; Chanel is even stricter. You want a pair of imitation earrings for 17€ ($20)? You will not find any fakes in France. Call © **08-20-00-20-05** toll-free, or 01-42-86-28-00.

CHARVET
28 place Vendôme, 1er (Métro: Opéra or Tuileries).

Although Charvet sells both men's and women's clothing, it's known as one of the grandest resources for men in continental Europe. Elegant types have been having their shirts tailored here for centuries. You can buy off-the-rack or custom-made. Off-the-rack comes in only one sleeve length, so big American men may need custom-made. The look is Brooks Brothers meets the Continent: traditional yet sophisticated. The shop's mini–department store is filled with *boiserie* (wood paneling) and the look of old money. A men's shirt, like all quality men's shirts these days, costs well over 100€ ($115). © **01-42-60-30-70.**

CHRISTIAN DIOR
30 av. Montaigne, 8e (Métro: Alma-Marceau).
25 rue Royale, 1er (Métro: Madeleine).

What would Monsieur D. (as he was called) say now that Dior is the rage of *teenage girls?* Make room for all Dior has become since its reinvention with John Galliano—and get a load of all the glitz. This large house fills many floors—you can get ready-to-wear, costume jewelry, cosmetics, scarves, menswear, baby items, and wedding gifts, as well as couture. In fact, several little shops cluster around the main "house," and you can wander around, touching everything.

There's a store for fancy jewelry (as in real gemstones) at no. 28, and very small Dior branches at 16 rue de l'Abbaye, 6e (Métro: St-Germain-des-Prés), and 35 rue Royale (Métro: Madeleine). The rue Royale address specializes in shoes and bags. Call © 01-40-73-73-73.

DOROTHÉE BIS
46 rue Etienne Marcel, 2e (Métro: Etienne Marcel).
33 rue de Sèvres, 6e (Métro: Sèvres-Babylone).

The woman responsible for getting this business off the ground was none other than the duchess of Windsor. Sweaters and knits always have been the house specialty at Dorothée Bis. Prices are moderate to those of us used to outrageously high designer tags. There are several retail outlets: for men, women, sportswear, and discount.

EMANUEL UNGARO
2 av. Montaigne, 8e (Métro: Alma-Marceau).
2 rue Gribeauval, 7e (Métro: Rue du Bac).

If you were to translate the colors of the rainbow through the eyes of a resident of Provence, you'd get the palette for which Ungaro is famous. The couture house is a series of three connecting chambers, so you can see many aspects of the line in one large space. Don't be afraid to walk in and take a look. The Ferragamo family now owns Ungaro; their factories in Italy make the shoes. © 01-53-57-00-22.

FAÇONNABLE
9 rue du Faubourg St-Honoré, 8e (Métro: Concorde).

Façonnable has taken over the high street of every French city and moved into vacant space on the Faubourg St-Honoré. Under the auspices of Nordstrom, it has come to the U.S. with a big new store at Rockefeller Center in New York. There are suits, but that's not what one buys here. The best clothes are simply preppy menswear, although there is a lot of room for color in shirts and tops. The basics are basic: navy blazers, khaki trousers, Top-Sider shoes. You get the picture.

GERARD DAREL
22 rue Royale, 8e (Métro: Concorde).

This mid-level designer has numerous free-standing stores and representation in department stores; he also advertises heavily in women's magazines, so you may fall for the ads first. The line is simple and tasteful; the ads are evocative of Jacqueline Kennedy Onassis and actually have more flair than the current collection. Still, the clothes in this bridge line are tailored, excellent for the office, and not outrageously expensive. © 01-45-48-54-80.

GIVENCHY
8 av. George V, 8e (Métro: Alma-Marceau).

Hubert de Givenchy retired, and Julian MacDonald, who has yet to do anything shocking, now designs Givenchy's couture. The couture house is upstairs at 29–31 av. Victor Hugo. The men's store takes up three floors and sells everything. Women's accessories and ready-to-wear are in two separate shops. © 01-44-31-49-91. www.givenchy.fr.

HERMÈS
24 rue du Faubourg St-Honoré, 8e (Métro: Concorde).

Perhaps the best-known French luxury status symbol comes from Hermès. The Hermès scarf is universally known and coveted; the handbags often have waiting lists. I've gone nuts for the enamel bangle bracelets, which are much less expensive in Paris than elsewhere in the world. Since they cost about the same as a scarf, you may want to reprogram your mind for a new collectible. And the tie? It's a power tie with a sense of humor; that's all I can say. The ready-to-wear is now designed by Jean Paul Gaultier.

Remember, in order to get the best price at Hermès, you need to qualify for the détaxe refund. Plan to buy at least two of anything, or four ties (unless you buy a saddle, of course).

If you can't buy anything, but want the thrill of your life, wander the store to educate your eye, then show your copy of this book at the scarf counter, where they'll give you a free, gorgeous booklet called *Comment Nouer Un Carré Hermès* (How to Tie an Hermès Scarf). It's all pictures, so don't worry if you can't read French. They often run out of this booklet, so don't pout (or write me a nasty letter).

Final tips: Don't forget to see if your airline sells Hermès scarves and ties in its on-plane shop; they usually cost slightly less than at Hermès (although the selection is often limited). I recently flew both Air France and Delta, and Hermès was less expensive on Air France than on Delta. If you want used Hermès, see the "Vintage" section on p. 198; **Didier Ludot** is the most famous specialist. Call ✆ **01-40-17-47-17**.

JEAN PAUL GAULTIER
44 av. George V, 8e (Métro: George V).
30 rue Faubourg St-Antoine, 12e (Métro: Bastille).

JUNIOR GAULTIER
7 rue du Jour, 1er (Métro: Les Halles).

This is a mini–department store and tribute to a huge talent. Despite his wackiness, Gaultier is getting a reputation for wearable style. Take in the high-tech shock appeal of Gaultier's unique mix of video tech, fashion, and architecture. The younger line (Junior) is less expensive and not appropriate for anyone over 40. Make that 30. Discount shops on rue St-Placide sometimes sell it. *Also note:* Another Gaultier store is in the Galerie Vivienne, 2e. Call ✆ **01-44-43-00-44** or 01-72-75-83-12.

KENZO

3 place des Victoires, 1er (Métro: Bourse).
16 bd Raspail, 7e (Métro: Rue du Bac).
23 rue de la Madeleine, 8e (Métro: Concorde).
60–62 rue de Rennes, 6e (Métro: St-Germain-des-Prés).
1 rue du Pont Neuf, 1er (Métro: Pont Neuf).

Yes, Kenzo does have a last name: Takada. Yes, Kenzo is Japanese, but he's a French designer. Yes, Kenzo has retired, but the line lives on. The clothes are showcased in big, high-tech stores designed to knock your socks off. The line isn't inexpensive, but there are great sales. ℭ 01-73-04-20-03. www.kenzo.com.

LACOSTE

372 rue St-Honoré, 8e (Métro: Concorde).

Lacoste is often called *le crocodile* in France, which is confusing for those of us who consider it an alligator! This is one of those tricky status symbols that you assume will be cheaper here—after all, it is a French brand—but it isn't. You can pay 74€ ($85) for a short-sleeved shirt in France; this is no bargain. Price the shirts in the U.S. before you buy them in France. ℭ 01-44-82-69-02.

LAGERFELD GALLERY

40 rue de Seine, 6e (Métro: St-Germain-des-Prés).

This is mostly an art gallery, but it also has some clothes and KL-designed accessories. Don't get too excited. ℭ 01-55-42-75-51.

LANVIN

15 rue du Faubourg St-Honoré, 8e (Métro: Concorde).

The House of Lanvin is one of the oldest and best-known French couturiers, due mostly to its successful American advertising campaigns for the fragrances My Sin and Arpège ("promise her anything"). In recent years, the line has been in transition as the house tries to find its place in the modern world. I have no idea how it has stayed in business. ✆ **01-44-71-31-73.**

LEONARD
36 av. Pierre 1er de Serbie, 16e (Métro: Franklin D. Roosevelt).

Léonard is a design house that makes clothes, many from knitted silk—but it's perhaps more famous for the prints on its clothes. These prints are sophisticated, often floral, and incorporated in ties and dresses. A men's tie costs about 80€ ($92), but it makes a subtle statement to those who recognize the print. A discounter named Betty at the place d'Aligre sells Léonard stock.

LOUIS VUITTON
101 av. des Champs-Elysées, 8e (Métro: George V).
6 place St-Germain, 6e (Métro: St-Germain-des-Prés).
57 av. Montaigne, 8e (Métro: Alma-Marceau or Franklin D. Roosevelt).

Louis Vuitton opened his first shop in 1854 and didn't become famous for his initials until 1896, when his son came out with a new line of trunks. Things haven't been the same since.

Nor will you ever be the same after you've seen what's been going on in Paris. Check out the new Champs-Elysées store, built to showcase the ready-to-wear line designed by Marc Jacobs—during construction, the store was dressed as a giant LV handbag. Now the inside of the store looks something like a spaceship and is decorated with vintage trunks and suitcases. There are floors and floors, including a museum. It's truly breathtaking.

On the Left Bank, the front door of the shop is worthy of a half-hour of silent, stunned appreciation. The store is on different levels, and you weave up, down, and around. Toward the front of the store is the house collection of restored but older LV luggage and steamer trunks; these are for sale. You may also bring in your old ones for repair or renovation. Call toll-free ✆ **08-10-81-00-10.**

Loulou de la Falaise

7 rue de Bourgogne, 7e (Métro: Assemblée Nationale).
21 rue Cambon, 1er (Métro: Concorde).

Loulou has been famous for decades as the muse of Yves Saint Laurent. When YSL closed up shop, Loulou opened hers—a small boutique that sells some of her own things (vintage YSL), along with things she finds, likes, and displays. It's mostly accessories, with some clothes; stock varies enormously. Prices are high, but this is the real *ooh-la-la . . .* or *ooh-loulou*. ℂ 01-45-51-42-22 or 01-42-60-02-22. www.loulou-de-la-falaise.com.

Marithe et François Girbaud

38 rue Etienne Marcel, 1er (Métro: Etienne Marcel).

Masters of the unisex look, Marithé and François are still making the only clothes that make sense on either sex with equal style. They have many lines—you may never see everything these designers can do. The main store is a must because of the architecture. **Mouton à Cinq Pattes** sometimes carries discounted jeans.

Nina Ricci

39 av. Montaigne, 8e (Métro: Alma-Marceau).

We can cut to the chase here: Nina Ricci is a couture house that has been trying to remake itself à la Gucci or other, hotter lines. The store has been redone, and sometimes the clothes are streamlined and young. In short, this is not your mother's Nina Ricci. (If you don't need a ball gown, but are looking for a gift for someone you want to impress, consider the gift department, which is small enough to consider with one big glance.) This store is closed Saturday and from 1 to 2pm daily. ℂ 01-40-88-64-51.

SONIA RYKIEL
70 rue du Faubourg St-Honoré, 8e (Métro: Concorde).
175 bd St-Germain, 6e (Métro: St-Germain-des-Prés).

SONIA RYKIEL WOMAN
4 rue de Grenelle, 6e (Métro: Sèvres-Babylone).

Yes, they sell vibrators and sex toys. No, I won't tell you more, except to say this is at the Sonia Woman store.

The main store, for men and women, has the breadth of the SR lines, still famous for knits, but also embellished with leathers, accessories, perfume, and even a 95€ ($109) lariat key chain. Visit the outlet if you're a true fan—you might get lucky. I've been there when it was great and when it was lonely; you simply never know. Sonia's things are unique— they're classics and stay in style forever. The 20- and 30-year-old sweaters have a cult following.

VENTILO
267 rue St-Honoré, 1er (Métro: Concorde).
7 bis rue du Louvre, 2e (Métro: Etienne Marcel).
13–15 bd de la Madeleine, 1er (Métro: Madeleine).

Armand Ventilo is Dries Van Noten for the average woman— a symphony of beads and ethnic chic, with slightly exotic touches that make it fashionable, yet memorable. Paris has a half-dozen Ventilo shops; I've been to most of them, and each one feels different. As a good lesson in the use of space, they reflect the customer's reaction to the clothes. Some of the stores have tearooms; some sell the home line. The Madeleine shop is the new flagship. © 01-44-76-82-95.

YVES SAINT LAURENT
Rive Gauche, 19–21 av. Victor Hugo, 16e (Métro: Victor-Hugo).
38 rue du Faubourg St-Honoré, 8e (Métro: Concorde).

What becomes a legend most? Who knows? Yves is retired, so is Tom Ford. Stay tuned for the new look. Don't forget that

Saint Laurent is also in the perfume and beauty biz—we're talking empire here. The old couture space has been turned into a museum, but the casual line (Rive Gauche) is going strong. ✆ 01-42-65-74-59.

FRENCH MULTIPLES

This section is filled with names and brands you hopefully know little about. From a price standpoint, I've tried to cover from low-end to bridge—everything except big-name designers, which are in the next section of this chapter.

Most of these brands can be found in big department stores, but they also have their own stores with larger selections. In fact, they often have several stores in Paris, so if you find a brand that interests you, ask your concierge if there's a location closer to your hotel than what's listed.

AGNES B.

3 and 6 rue de Jour, 1er (Métro: Etienne Marcel).
6 rue du Vieux-Colombier (Métro: St-Germain-des-Prés).

This international chain of ready-to-wear shops sells casual clothes with enough of a fashion look to make them appropriate for big-city wearing. There are lifestyle stores branching out that feature art galleries, makeup, men's clothing, kiddie clothes, travel gear, and more. ✆ 01-42-33-27-34.

APOSTROPHE

17–19 av. Montaigne, 8e (Métro: Alma-Marceau).

This is a high-fashion line for women with money and style—but more of the former than the latter, plus a need for not too much style, lest they not be taken seriously. It's a big-time career look in France. ✆ 01-56-89-20-80.

COTELAC
19 place du Marché St-Honoré, 1er (Métro: Tuileries).

In my litany of unknown French brands, I translate Cotélac into "yes"—I pop into one whenever I pass by. The store offers young looks with wearable trends and simple chic, which means the clothes are young, but don't look stupid on anyone over 30. It's midrange, price-wise. © 01-42-86-05-31.

CYRILLUS
16 rue de Sèvres, 7e (Métro: Sèvres-Babylone), among many.

This multiple shop offers preppy clothes with a hint of fashion, always in the right colors for the season. It's a French staple for the velvet-headband crowd.

DEVERNOIS
255 rue St-Honoré, 1er (Métro: Concorde).

This is sort of an old-lady brand that offers enough fashion to make it worth looking at. I buy from here because the clothes are comfortable and fit me (I'm large). Each season the selection is different, so it's hard to know if you will love or hate the line. The specialty is knitwear; it's similar to Rodier, but with more colors and prints.

ERIC BOMPARD
46 rue du Bac, 7e (Métro: Rue du Bac).

This brand is known for cashmere in a wide range of colors. No bargains, but colors you won't find in many places.

ETAM
73 rue de Rivoli, 1er (Métro: Pont Neuf).

There's a longer listing for Etam on p. 196, wherein I rant and rave about the flagship store in Paris. Every shopping district in Paris (maybe all of France) has Etam stores—some sell lingerie and others sell fashion, meaning copies of the latest looks at low, low, everyday prices.

GEORGES RECH
54 rue Bonaparte, 6e (Métro: St-Germain-des-Prés).

This is a bridge line that many locals consider designer or big-name. He makes great suits and work clothes for young women who want to look classy, yet stylish. There is a stock shop on rue d'Alésia, 14e (p. 123).

ISABEL MARANT
1 rue Jacob, 6e (Métro: St-Germain-des-Prés).

I have listed the address for the most convenient branch, but if you're into alternative neighborhoods, this designer's shop near the Bastille (16 rue de Charonne; Métro: Bastille) is one of the new storefronts in an up-and-coming area—all in keeping with her image as a hot young thing doing clothes that are a bit daring, but still wearable.

LILITH
5 rue Cambon, 1er (Métro: Concorde).
12 rue du Cherche-Midi, 6e (Métro: Sèvres-Babylone).
outlet shop: 66 rue Parmentier, 10e (Métro: Goncourt).

You must take me with a grain of salt here—I am tall and a tad heavy in the bottom, and I like clothes that are comfortable and can be worn with flats. If you like Eileen Fisher or Armani, a soft color palette, and plenty of layers, you'll go nuts for this inventive designer, who uses myriad fabrics and textures, buttons, pockets, and Euro-Japanese droop to do her own thing. My girlfriend Diane, very short, also wears the brand, so don't shrink from it.

NAFNAF
33 rue Etienne Marcel, 1er (Métro: Etienne Marcel).

Calling all teenage girls.

OXYDE
12 rue de Turbigo, 1er (Métro: Etienne Marcel).

Maybe it's the influence of watching my 20-something kids go shopping, but this casual brand has tons of hippie style that is still metro-chic. Most items cost less than 87€ ($100).

PAUL & JOE
46 rue Etienne Marcel, 2e (Métro: Etienne Marcel).

This is also a designer bridge line and, despite the sound of the name, it's French. Many fashion editors push this brand—it's considered cutting edge with women under 30.

PLEIN SUD
2 av. Montaigne, 8e (Métro: Alma-Marceau).

The designer (Faycal Amor) would like you to think of this as a designer brand; it's hot and colorful, chic and body-conscious, and very rock 'n' roll.

RAYURE
8 rue Francs-Bourgeois, 3e (Métro: St-Paul).

Since no look is more quintessentially French than the white blouse teamed with black skirt (or black trousers), there are several firms that are famous for their tops. Among them is Rayure, which does all-white or all-black tops much like Anne Fontaine, but for less money. Sold in department stores also.

REGINA RUBENS
16 av. Montaigne, 8e (Métro: Alma-Marceau).

I don't have it in me to classify this as a full-fledged designer line, although business must be good enough to have this kind of address. The clothes are for working women who wear suits or classy put-togethers and don't want to look boring, but can't be too over-the-top, either. The store will take special orders if you are hard to fit; there is also a stock shop in the 14e.

RENÉ DERHY

7 rue de Sèvres, 6e (Métro: Sèvres-Babylone).
163 rue de Rennes, 6e (Métro: Rennes).

Bright colors, swirly prints, BoHo ethnic charm with tons of
energy and pizazz. Moderate price range.

STELLA CADENTE

93 quai de Valmy, 10e (Métro: République or Jacques
Bonsergent).

This Stella is not a person named Stella, as in McCartney, but
the Latin word for star—and the shop is one of the stars of
the now-funky/chic Canal St-Martin. The clothes are colorful
and sometimes drapey, often with embroidery, beads, and
feathers.

TARA JARMON

73 av. des Champs-Elysées, 8e (Métro: Franklin D.
Roosevelt).

Gucci copies that are affordable; feminine and sometimes hip
clothes at moderate prices.

ZADIG & VOLTAIRE

1–3 rue du Vieux-Colombier, 6e (Métro: St-Sulpice).

Every time I go into one of these stores, I think it's Zaftig, not
Zadig . . . silly *moi*. This is slim-line fashion for the 20-some-
thing crowd that works and needs clothes that are hot (style-
wise), but not shocking. The stores carry both the house line
and some big-time designer names. There is a spa in the branch
at 18 rue François-1er, 8e (Métro: Franklin D. Roosevelt).

ZAPA

392 rue St-Honoré, 8e (Métro: Concorde).

If you read Russian, or aren't paying attention, you may think
this is Zara, the Spanish retailer. It's not. It's hot and hip, but
still chic and grown-up enough to be frank, yet flirtatious.

Although famous for its dresses, this line does have separates; I bought the best jacket of my life here. Many of the dresses are made with stretchy stuff—good figures required. www.zapa.fr.

HANDBAGS (EVERYDAY)

No one does handbags like the French; *non,* not even the Italians. If you want to splurge on one thing, a handbag is a great notion—especially a brand that isn't well known in the U.S., so you can get a style that few others will have.

Most department stores have enormous handbag departments, usually on the ground floor. It makes more sense to buy a handbag at a department store if you can use the tourist discount card.

If you care about lots of style and a low price, stop by Catherine (see below), which I think has the best cheap—I mean, inexpensive—handbags in the city.

CATHERINE
7 rue Castiglione, 1er (Métro: Tuileries).

These are unbranded handbags, inspired by the world's biggest names—but not exactly fakes, because that would be illegal. They are all made in France and usually cost about 90€ ($104). Obviously, styles and colors change with the season, but if you prefer a 87€ ($100) handbag to a 260€ ($300) one, this should be your first stop. Catherine is a duty-free shop that also sells perfume and makeup (see p. 217 for details). ✆ 01-42-60-48-17.

HERVÉ CHAPELIER
1 bis rue du Vieux-Colombier, 6e (Métro: St-Germain-des-Prés).
390 rue St-Honoré, 8e (Métro: Concorde).

These bags are a cult status symbol and the must-have accessory in Paris, especially in summer as a weekend tote, beach bag, or carry-on. My dog travels in a Sherpa bag, but goes shopping in an Hervé.

Printemps and Galeries Lafayette sell a few bags, but ignore that fact (bad selection) and go only to one of the Hervé stores, where you can see the wide range of yummy colors and combinations. For some reason, there are also cashmere sweaters, but forget them; you came for the bags. Almost all styles cost around 100€ ($115); many are half that price. Call ✆ 01-44-07-06-50.

JUST CAMPAGNE
152 bd St-Germain, 6e (Métro: St-Germain-des-Prés).
342 rue St-Honoré, 1er (Métro: Tuileries).

These casual handbags are especially good for weekend or suburban use; I'm smitten with one that resembles a leather feed bag for a horse and is lined with a nylon pull-string sack inside the feed bag—unusual but fun, and very chic.

LANCEL
8 place de l'Opéra, 9e (Métro: Opéra).
127 av. Champs-Elysées (Métro: Etoile); and other locations.

This is another French brand that many Americans don't know too well, a fact that may change now that the brand has opened a truly huge store on the Champs-Elysées. The handbags are considered a must-have upper-middle-class status symbol in France. They make excellent travel bags—some styles are not real leather, and some models have an outside flap pocket that is perfect for a plane ticket and passport. Lancel has changed a lot recently, so what was once a signature line now seems to compete with Tod's in terms of sleek designs—and, sometimes, prices. There's also luggage, and in the men's space—clothes and accessories and even books, notebooks, and computer gear. ✆ 01-47-42-37-29.

Insider's tip: Buy your handbag at a department store so you can use the discount card.

LOLLIPOPS
40 rue du Dragon, 6e (Métro: St-Germain-des-Prés).

They wholesale and retail, they sell in department stores around the world, and they franchise. They are Lollipops, a line of shoes, small accessories, and bags that are creative and inexpensive, expressive and whimsical, and often great for fashionistas, teens, and tweens. ✆ 01-42-22-09-29. www.lollipops.fr.

LONGCHAMP
404 rue St-Honoré, 1er (Métro: Concorde).

This totally renovated and rejuvenated flagship has teamed with an English designer (shhhh! don't tell the French!), so a classic now has tons of fabulous bags, totes, and luggage. Many leather items are coated to withstand the weather. The logo is a flying greyhound, but the hardware with a piece of bamboo (usually metal, but possibly resin) is more of a status symbol. Although traditionally these bags are in solid colors, some of the new designs are prints or multitones. Available at department stores, too. ✆ 01-43-16-00-16.

RENAUD PELLEGRINO
8 rue de Commaille, 7e (Métro: Assemblée Nationale).

This man is a cult hero who first came to fame when it was revealed he was the genius behind Hermès handbags. He went off on his own over a decade ago, but has moved shop several times. This is the new location. You can't really get going for less than 450€ ($518), but if you want the best in unusual and special, *voilà*. It's all made by hand. There are also shoes. ✆ 01-41-65-35-52.

SEQUOIA
72 bis rue Bonaparte, 6e (Métro: St-Germain-des-Prés).
6 rue Francs-Bourgeois, 3e (Métro: St-Paul).

This brand of handbag considers itself more sophisticated and expensive than a line for teens, but it's still not top-of-the-line French luxe. In the last few years, it has gotten more sophisticated and often been inspired by major looks from the big names. For the set that likes a handbag in the 174€ ($200) range, this bears looking at. Also sold in department stores.

INTERNET CAFES

Note that more and more of Paris is being wired for Wi-Fi, so if your laptop has a wireless card, you don't need an Internet cafe. In fact, I know many a visitor who dresses to the hilt and marches into one of the palace hotels (all wired for Wi-Fi) to enjoy the gilt and do a little e-mail.

If you have no computer with you, you'll do better price-wise by using a cybercafe instead of your hotel's business center. New cafes arrive every week, so ask your hotel concierge for the one closest to you. The ones listed below are the best known, in easy locations for tourists.

EASYEVERYTHING
31 bd Sebastopol, 3e (Métro: Châtelet).
6 rue de la Harpe, 5e (Métro: St-Michel).

Open 24Hsur24, as they say in France, this fabulous resource has cyberstations all over Europe, with more to open in Paris. Clean, neat, bright, easy to use; cafe.

GATE 104
104 bd St-Germain, 6e (Métro: Odéon or St-Michel).

This is the largest Internet cafe in Paris and the newest in terms of equipment, decor, and scene. Hours are Monday through Friday from 8am to 2am, Saturday from 8am to 7am, and Sunday from noon to 2am. The cost is 3€ ($3.45) per hour.

LE WEB BAR
32 rue de Picardie, 3e (Métro: République).

One of the oldest and most established in Paris, with a young crowd and a cafe with DJ.

JEWELRY (COSTUME)

••

The essence of French fashion, aside from couture, is simplicity—consider the basic black skirt and white silk blouse, a staple of every stylish Frenchwoman's wardrobe. Of course, the way to spruce up these basics has always been accessories. Hence the importance of the Hermès silk scarf.

Should you care to go for something glitzier, these sources offer some of Paris's boldest statements. Their specialty is either copies of more serious jewelry or originals that will have value in the marketplace for years to come. The originals reach beyond the basic definition of "costume jewelry." Coco Chanel invented costume jewelry, and designer costume jewelry, whether new or vintage, remains a solid investment—although it can be pricey.

The major designer brands now make their own costume jewelry, so they are not listed below. The sources here give you a range from fabulous fakes to the boldest bangles.

ANEMONE
7 rue de Castiglione, 1er (Métro: Tuileries or Concorde).

Year after year, Anemone is a reliable resource for costume jewelry and earrings. It's across from the Hôtel Meurice and near Catherine. Earrings start around 40€ ($46)—this is Paris, you know. Prices are not give-away, but sometimes you can find good pieces; I bought a YSL gold-tone collar here that I still live in, and it was worth every bit of its 350€ ($403) price tag. It's fun to look in the window even if you don't buy.

BURMA
249 rue St-Honoré, 8e (Métro: Concorde).

If the real thing is beyond you, try Burma. Serious copies, created to fool Mother Nature.

GAS
44 rue Etienne Marcel, 2e (Métro: Etienne Marcel).

This is a small store with very inventive pieces, often made from odds and ends. More fun than couture in terms of a look; possibly a good investment as a collectible. It uses faux gemstones in copper settings; I collect the bees. The earrings don't pinch!

KONPLOTT
57 rue Pierre Charron, 8e (Métro: Franklin D. Roosevelt).

Greek designer, German-owned firm, Parisian kind—costume jewelry begins at 100€ ($115), but many splashier pieces are in the 300€+ ($345+) range. © 01-40-75-02-94.

MICHAELA FREY
9 rue Castiglione, 1er (Métro: Concorde).
167 rue St-Honoré, 1er (Métro: Tuileries).

This Viennese design firm has stores in most European capital cities, but none in the U.S., so you may not know the brand. If you are familiar with the enamel bracelets from Hermès, you are unwittingly familiar with Frey's work. Frey did this enamel work long before Hermès put its distinctive twist on it. Most of the Frey designs are inspired by famous artists or historical finds.

NEREIDES
23 rue du Four, 6e (Métro: St-Germain-des-Prés).

This shop sells a very south-of-France look, casual and resorty, but with bigger pieces than you might wear to work. You'll find various sizes and shapes, a touch of brushed gold, and Etruscan influence.

SWAROVSKI
7 rue Royale, 8e (Métro: Concorde).

Over the years, this crystal maker has provided much of the glitter to Lesage and Chanel. Now, its own brand has an international reputation and a line of jewelry and handbags. Everything is made from top-of-the-line crystals.

JEWELRY (IMPORTANT)

Traditionally, all of the important Parisian jewelers are on the place Vendôme, with a few moving away from the obelisk and stretching toward Opéra.

Two couture houses, both of which made costume jewelry for decades, have launched stores selling the real thing, and I don't mean Coca-Cola. **Chanel** started a few years ago, and **Christian Dior** has come on board. **Cartier** has just opened a large new showroom right on the Champs-Elysées, at no. 154, near the Arc de Triomphe (Métro: Charles de Gaulle–Etoile).

If you want name-brand real jewelry and don't care if it's used, go to the string of specialty boutiques just outside the place Vendôme on the rue St-Honoré. Family heirlooms cram their windows; prices in cash may be juggled slightly.

LINGERIE & BATHING SUITS

Most French specialty stores that sell underwear also sell bathing suits. The department stores have enormous "festivals," selling masses of bathing suits in a designated area (the same space will sell coats in late summer). For the largest selection of bathing suits in Paris, try Galeries Lafayette from May through August. You can even buy some suits a la carte—top and bottom in different sizes, as needed.

There are also a number of multiples (chain stores) that sell underwear and bathing suits (in season). These shops sell either one brand (such as Etam) or many, and aim to serve the mid-market; they are much more expensive than similar stores in the U.S.

Not only was the brassiere invented in Paris, but France has always made the latest in industrial equipment for manufacturing modern underwear. Prices are high, but the technology is unsurpassed. I buy most of my lingerie at **Monoprix**.

ERES
2 rue Tronchet, 8e (Métro: Madeleine).
40 av. Montaigne, 8e (Métro: Franklin D. Roosevelt).

Eres is perhaps the most famous name in bathing suits in France—we're talking high-end, almost couture bathing suits. We're also talking owned by Chanel. As with most bathing-suit lines, Eres also sells lingerie and is responsible for the tulle craze that's still going strong. Some department stores also sell the line; it is extremely chic and expensive, and wonderful. There are boutiques around town, but this is the main shop. It's next door to Fauchon on the place de la Madeleine.

MADE TO MEASURE

ALBANI
3 rue du Duras, 8e (Métro: Champs-Elysées Clemenceau).

One of the few remaining affordable couturiers, M. Albani is an Italian gentleman who works from his atelier right off the rue du Faubourg St-Honoré. You walk into the door, through the courtyard, and spy his door slightly to your right on the far side of the courtyard. M. Albani does not speak English (he's okay in French or Italian), but he has warm eyes, incredible taste, and gifted hands. His cut, especially in suits, has been known throughout the couture world for years.

All clothes made by M. Albani are made to measure, and you can bring a photo, work with him to create a sketch, or look at other things he has made. His specialty is women's suits; bolts and bolts of fabric are leaning against the walls, so you pick the fabric, work out the design, and have your first fitting. You'll need one more fitting later, and he needs a total of 8 working days to make the garment. Make appointments before arrival by phone or fax; no e-mail. This is old-world tailoring, remember? Prices range from 1,500€ to 2,000€ ($1,725–$2,300). The local phone number is ℂ 01-40-07-12-72 (fax 01-40-07-13-63).

MALLS & SHOPPING CENTERS

••

Slowly, Paris has been going mall mad. The shopping center of your teen years does not exist in great abundance in Europe, but Paris is trying out every kind of mall you can imagine. The larger mall structures are often called "commercial centers."

Small malls are springing up in the various train stations, obviously to catch travelers as they move to and fro. Some of the offerings are very enticing—there's a new branch of **Monoprix** in the Gare du Nord and a mall still being built at the **Gare St-Lazare.**

Don't forget that the French had the original versions of the mall, 150 years ago, with their *passages* and *galeries* (see *"Passages,"* below). For outlet malls, see p. 131.

FORUM DES HALLES
11 bis rue de l'Arc-en-Ciel, 1er (Métro: Les Halles or Châtelet).

As we go to press, the contest to redesign this mall has just been opened, so you may need a hard hat by the time you visit. If the mall is open, you might find it pleasant on a rainy day. You'll find it conveniently located directly above a Métro stop, Les Halles, and a stone's throw from the Beaubourg, which you may want to visit.

The Forum des Halles, built to rejuvenate a slum, serves as an exciting monument to youth, style, and shopping. The atmosphere is rather sterile and American—even Tupperware has a store here. The mall is a huge square with a courtyard; it's easy to get lost once inside, though master maps throughout the place will help you find your way. The Forum was built in stages—be sure to see the newest part, which stretches underground. There are fast-food joints in the Métro part of the complex, and real restaurants among the shops in the regular complex.

Although a number of designers and bridge lines have outposts here, the stores are often not as charming as the boutiques on the street can be. If you ran out of here screaming, I wouldn't blame you at all.

Most of the stores open Tuesday through Saturday between 10 and 10:30am and close between 7 and 7:30pm. All stores are closed all day Sunday and until noon Monday.

LE CARROUSEL DU LOUVRE
99 rue de Rivoli, 1er (Métro: Palais-Royal).

This is an American-style shopping mall as well, but it's not too big and it's open on Sundays, so it has many redeeming features. The mall is attached to the Louvre and has many entrances and exits.

For the easiest access, enter from the rue de Rivoli, where a small banner announces the space. This entrance is not particularly prominent, so you may have trouble finding it. The mall is on two subterranean levels; enter and take the escalator down one flight to the food court. Go down another level and you're in a mall like any other in your neighborhood, except this one has **Lalique, Sephora,** and **Virgin Megastore.** There are just over a dozen stores, as well as a branch of the French Government Tourist Office and some excellent museum shops.

PLAZA PASSY
53 rue de Passy, 16e (Métro: La Muette).

It looks like a redone Art Deco–style apartment complex in South Beach, without the blue stucco, but this new mall helps you get a lot done in one neighborhood. It has an upper-class feel to it, especially when you glance around at your fellow shoppers. It's not a big mall or a very special one—it's just that it's easy. Many of the retail tenants are French or American chains, including Gap. I'm not embarrassed to tell you that I think it's super here; it's not terribly French, but it's very much a part of the new French retail scene—global, man, global! I also like the grocery store, **Champion,** on the lower level.

Boutiques are open daily from 10am to 7:30pm; the grocery store is open Monday through Saturday from 8:30am to 8:30pm.

MEN'S SHOPS

Every major shopping area, every major designer, and every department store carries things for men. But when I met a man on an airplane who asked me for a quick and easy list, I scribbled the following names on a napkin for him. I also gave him **Mouton à Cinq Pattes,** a discounter (p. 129).

I warn men to have an honest look in the mirror before they shop in Paris. For the most part, the average American male body is much larger than its French counterpart.

BRUMMEL (PRINTEMPS HOMME)
Rue Provence and rue Havre Caumartin, behind Printemps de la Maison, 9e (Métro: Havre Caumartin).

This is a large, very complete men's department store directly behind Printemps de la Maison. See p. 150.

CHARVET
Place Vendôme, 2e (Métro: Tuileries).

This is not as much a haberdasher as a private club. Every man who is anything in France has his shirts made here. Not to fret, you can also buy off the peg. Amazing assortment of colors and collars. ✆ 01-42-60-30-70.

DUNHILL
15 rue de la Paix, 2e (Métro: Opéra).

HUGO BOSS
115 av. des Champs-Elysées, 8e (Métro: George V).

KITON
29 rue Marbeuf, 8e (Métro: Franklin D. Roosevelt).

LAFAYETTE HOMME
38 bd Haussmann, 9e (Métro: Chaussée-d'Antin).

Ground floor and up are devoted to men's clothing, then a grocery store.

LOFT
12 rue du Faubourg St-Honoré, 8e (Métro: Concorde).

Extremely hip boutique. ✆ 01-42-65-59-65.

MADELOIS
23 bd de la Madeleine, 1er (Métro: Madeleine).

Department store just for men. ✆ 01-53-45-00-28.

NICKEL
48 rue des Francs-Bourgeois, 3e (Métro: Hotel de Ville).

Men's spa; it has its own line of products. ✆ 01-42-77-41-10.

ZEGNA
10 rue de la Paix, 2e (Métro: Opéra).

MUSEUM SHOPS

Almost all Paris museums have gift shops, and there are about 50 museums in Paris. That's a lot of museum gift shops. Some even have their own chains, with branches in various museums. Some just sell slides, prints, and high-minded books or postcards—but several are really with it.

CENTRE GEORGES POMPIDOU
Centre Georges Pompidou, 4e (Métro: Châtelet).

The main gift shop at the entry level is mostly a bookstore, so don't get confused. There are more gifts on the mezzanine, and in sales areas after certain exhibits. The department store Au Printemps runs the shops.

MUSÉE CARNAVALET
29 rue de Sévigné, 3e (Métro: St-Paul).

This museum in the heart of the Marais documents the history of the city of Paris; the gift shop sells reproductions of antique items, many owned by famous people. I have the Georges Sand stemware. Closed Monday.

MUSÉE DES ARTS DÉCORATIFS
107 rue de Rivoli, 1er (Métro: Musée-du-Louvre).

The store sells a mix of books and gift items, all with a wonderful eye toward design. Prices aren't low, but you'll find unique gifts—even a copy of the very first scarf Hermès ever created. There are books on design in several languages. Closed Monday and Tuesday; open Sunday from noon to 5pm.

MUSÉE D'ORSAY
Gare d'Orsay, 7e (Métro: Orsay).

The Musée d'Orsay's gift shop isn't as wonderful as the architecture, but it's damn good; you can buy prints and some reproductions, as well as a scarf or two. Good selection of postcards and gifts (including wonderful art books) for kids.

MUSÉE DU LOUVRE
Palais du Louvre, 1er (Métro: Musée-du-Louvre).

There's a gift shop under that glass pyramid, and it is a beauty, with two levels of shopping space for books, postcards, and repro gifts. *Beaucoup* fun! You do not have to pay admission to the museum to gain entrance. After walking into the pyramid, take the escalator down, and you will be in a lobby reminiscent of a train station. The gift shop is straight ahead.

MUSIC

I've gone nuts for Johnny Hallyday and have bought a number of his tapes and CDs. There are zillions of them (the man's career spans decades), but they can be pricey. In fact, CDs in France are much more expensive than in the U.S., so buy only must-have items you can't get elsewhere. I list some small specialty stores below; the larger electronic palaces like **FNAC** and **Virgin Megastore**—which sell CDs, DVDs, videos, books, tickets, and more—have branches in all major shopping areas.

Jean-Louis Ginibre's Jazz Picks

Paris is my friend Jean-Louis's hometown. He's American now, but he still goes to Paris to buy jazz. His fave, for LPs and secondhand jazz and blues recordings, is **Paris Jazz Corner**. He also suggests that fans check out the stalls at the **Marché Malik** in the flea markets at St-Ouen (p. 261), which are open only Saturday, Sunday, and Monday. Call ahead before visiting these shops to make sure they're open.

CROCODISC
64 rue de la Montagne Ste-Geneviève, 5e (Métro: Luxembourg).

LIBRARIE GILDA
36 rue des Bourdonnais, 1er (Métro: Châtelet).

PARIS JAZZ CORNER
5 rue de Navarre, 5e (Métro: Monge).

PASSAGES

A *passage* (rhymes with massage) is a shopping area, like an arcade in London. Today, passages are the French equivalent of American minimalls; they cut into building lobbies like thruways. In the early 1800s, new buildings were large, often taking up a block. To get from one side of a building to another, pedestrians used a passage. These are inside the building, thus totally covered. Doorways lead through the original structure.

There are passages all over Paris. One of the most famous is the **Galerie Vivienne.** One doorway is on the rue Vivienne, the other on the rue des Petits-Champs. The passage is not surrounded by a greater building, but is directly across from the National Library and near the Palais Royal; it holds a number of cute shops.

Also check out **Cour du Commerce St-Anne,** 59–61 rue St-André-des-Arts, 6e (Métro: St-Germain-des-Prés or Odéon), on the Left Bank. The famous restaurant Le Procope is in this tiny alley. Also here: a tea salon that I suggest for shoppers, **Cour de Rohan,** and a few shops. The shopping isn't so great, but the charm is heart-stopping.

Others to see, if only for the architecture and not the stores: **Galerie Véro-Dodat,** 19 rue Jean-Jacques Rousseau, 1er (Métro: Palais-Royal); **Passage des Panorama,** rue St-Marc, 2e (Métro: Grands Boulevards); and **Passage Verdeau,** 31 bis rue du Faubourg Montmartre, 9e (Métro: Grands Boulevards).

Le Passage du Havre, 109 rue St-Lazare, 8e (Métro: St-Lazare), is a charmless modern *passage,* like an American mall, that has a number of useful shops and a nice, big branch of **FNAC.**

PLUS SIZES

....

Galeries Lafayette has one of the best selections of large sizes in Paris; there are also specialty stores for *les rondes*. Note that H&M has a line called BIB (big is beautiful). I shop at **C&A**, which has inexpensive clothes and tends to go up to size 50, which is a size 20 in the U.S.

CAZAK
4 rue Marignan, 8e (Métro: Franklin D. Roosevelt).

A one-off boutique with mostly fancy clothes and many designer names for work or dress-up. This street is between avenue Montaigne and the Champs-Elysées. © 01-47-20-31-00.

DIFFERENCE
53 rue Ste-Placide, 6e (Métro: Sèvres-Babylone).

The clothes and accessories here are for all sizes—up to 56.

ELENA MIRO
14 av. Victor Hugo, 16e (Métro: Victor-Hugo).
Rue St-Honoré and rue St. Roch, 1er (Métro: Tuileries).

This Italian brand is neither as expensive nor as hip as Marina Rinaldi, but is good for fashion basics, weekend clothes, and some dress-up; from sizes 42 to 56. © **01-45-00-77-62** or 01-42-60-03-90.

MARINA RINALDI
7 av. Victor Hugo, 16e (Métro: Etoile or Victor-Hugo), and many other locations.

The large-size division of the Italian brand Max Mara, this is one of the best made of the plus-size garment brands. Styles tend to be classics, with a selection of dress-up, weekend, and office clothing.

OLIVIER JUNG
*Les Boutiques du Marché St-Germain, 14 rue de Lobineau,
6e (Métro: Mabillon).*

Pronounce the "j" as a "y" and stop by while you're exploring the 6e. The clothes tend to be simple, with clean lines, good
fabrics, and easy-to-wear styles . . . nothing too *trop*. Size range
is from 38 to 56. ℂ 01-46-33-55-30.

FRENCH SHOES (FASHION)

Shoe freaks will find the Little Dragons neighborhood on the
Left Bank (p. 76) a treasure-trove of little stores belonging to
famous designers and hoping-to-be-famous designers. Weave
along these streets and you can't go wrong. Be sure to stop at
the many shops on the rue des Sts-Pères, then make your way
onto rue du Four, with more shops for teens. Don't forget to
shop rue de Grenelle, too.

The department stores all have enormous shoe departments; Au Printemps is trying to make a reputation for its
selection.

CHRISTIAN LOUBOUTIN
19 rue Jean-Jacques Rousseau, 1er (Métro: Les Halles).

How's this for genius: I am watching a late-night chat show
in the glories of my own bedroom when some hot-chickie
starlet, big-maned girly girl comes on the show (I have no idea
who it is), crosses her legs, and lets loose with her chat. I have
no idea what she says or even who the host is. I am lost in the
soles of her shoes, which are bright red, and I know instantly
that she is wearing Christian Louboutin shoes from Paris. Is
there anything more chic? ℂ 01-42-36-05-31.

HAREL
7 rue Tournon, 6e (Métro: Odéon).
8 av. Montaigne, 16e (Métro: Alma-Marceau).
64 rue François-1er, 8e (Métro: Franklin D. Roosevelt).

In style, color, skins, and workmanship, these are among the most exquisite shoes I have ever seen in my life. The prices match. Flats begin around 400€ ($460), while heels are more like 600€ ($690). Still, press your nose to the glass just to understand it all.

PIERRE HARDY
156 galerie de Valois, Palais Royal, 1er (Métro: Palais-Royal).

Small shop; big name. He has created shoes for Hermès, among others, and is beginning international expansion. ✆ 01-42-60-59-75.

RENÉ CAOVILLA
23 rue du Faubourg St-Honoré, 8e (Métro: Concorde).

Italian master of jewel-encrusted shoes, often made in three different heel heights. Shoes start around 435€ ($500) per pair, but *ooh-la-la!* ✆ 01-42-68-19-55. www.caovilla.com.

RODOLPHE MENUDIER
14 rue Castiglione, 1er (Métro: Concorde).

I don't care if you buy here; I don't really even care if you enter. The windows are enough to knock you out. ✆ 01-42-60-86-27.

ROGER VIVIER
29 rue du Faubourg St-Honoré, 8e (Métro: Concorde).

Roger does not design the shoes anymore, but don't let that stop you. Here are three rooms filled with enough high heels to make *Sex and the City* come back on air—in a Paris version. There is a relatively flat, Pilgrim-style shoe that is considered a status item. ✆ 01-53-43-00-00.

SHOES (SENSIBLE)

MEPHISTO
78 rue des Sts-Pères, 6e (Métro: Sèvres-Babylone).

Sensible-shoe folks consider this brand of walking shoe for men and women one of the best in the world. You'll pay about half the U.S. price. They're sold in department stores.

MODA DI ANDREA
79 rue Victoires, 9e (Métro: Chaussée-d'Antin).

This is a discount shoe store selling major brands; there's more about it on p. 128. It sells shoes for men, women, and children—high heels, casual flats, and sensible shoes.

I have bought many versions of chic bowling or running shoes here from major names like Prada, Miu Miu, and Jil Sander at prices about 25% less than regular retail. Shoes are from current seasons.

REPETTO
22 rue de la Paix, 2e (Métro: Opéra).

This is basically a supply house for ballerinas, but it offers much in terms of fashion, including dresses that would be great for black-tie events. This is the firm that introduced *le ballet* into fashion as a shoe, rather than a dance item. ✆ 01-44-71-83-00.

SOUVENIRS

Paris abounds with souvenir shops. I often call them TTs (tourist traps). They cluster around the obvious tourist haunts

(Nôtre-Dame, the Champs-Elysées) and line the rue de Rivoli from the Hôtel Meurice to the front gate of the Louvre.

They all sell more or less the same junk at exactly the same non-negotiable prices. The only way you can get a break is to make a deal on the amount you buy. If you buy a few T-shirts, you may get a discount. The price of T-shirts fluctuates with the dollar: The price varies in euros (note the handwritten signs).

Some of my favorite things to buy at souvenir stands include: a toothbrush with your (or a similar) name in French; a breakfast bowl sponged in blue and white, also with your name in French; boxer shorts with Parisian motifs; T-shirts from French universities; key chains with miniature Eiffel Towers, street signs, Napoleon, and more; and scarves with kitschy tourist-haunt designs that are so bad, they're fabulous.

None of the department-store souvenir departments is very good. Most of the ones on boulevard Haussmann also sell souvenirs from kiosks in front of their stores. Galeries Lafayette has moved its souvenir department several times; right now it's on the ground floor in the far rear, behind the makeup department. It's the best of the department-store souvenir spaces, but lacks the right kind of energy.

AVENUE OF THE STARS
100 rue de Rennes, 6e (Métro: St-Sulpice).

This store sells figurines and gag items, mostly of comic-book characters—but that includes French icons. A reader once asked me where to find Becassine merchandise—*voilà*.

LE THÉ DES ÉCRIVAINS
16 rue des Minimes, 4e (Métro: St-Paul).

This is right near the place des Vosges in the Marais and offers a great gimmick: a selection of teas coordinated to literary talents.

SPECIALTY LOOKS

ANNE FONTAINE
81 rue des Sts-Pères, 6e (Métro: St-Germain-des-Prés), and others.

This is a chain of stores with about a dozen shops in Paris alone—I simply chose the first location on the business card. You can go to www.annefontaine.com for more addresses for this firm, which sells only white and black shirts for women. Most cost about 100€ ($115). (Also see p. 171 for **Rayure,** a copycat brand that costs a little less.) ✆ **01-45-48-89-10.**

A.P.C.
112 rue Vieille du Temple, 3e (Métro: St-Paul).

This store shows off a look—perfect for those who like minimalist chic and Euro-Japanese drape—as well as an area adjacent to the Marais. Prices are more or less reasonable—around 110€ ($127) for just about anything—and you get a lot of bang.

COMPAGNIE FRANÇAISE DE L'ORIENT ET DE LA CHINE
163 & 167 bd St-Germain, 6e (Métro: St-Germain-des-Prés).

This is a chain with stores all over, even in Brussels. Some branches carry the entire line, while some just have clothes or home style. Ignore the boutique in Galeries Lafayette; it doesn't do justice to the line or the look.

As you can guess from the name, the clothes are inspired by the Orient. I have a jacket made of Scottish tweed in a Chinese style—such a brilliant combination of ideas that I wear it all the time. While the clothes are somewhat ethnic, they are not costumey.

ESKANDAR
7 rue Princesse, 6e (Métro: St-Sulpice).

This is my new favorite line, with droopy-drapey Euro-Chinese chic in easy-to-wear clothes created by a Persian designer.

There is also a boutique in London; in the U.S., the clothes are carried at Neiman Marcus. However, this location has gift and tabletop items, as well as the stunning clothes. And did I mention the elastic waists?

FAVOURBROOK
Le Village Royal, 25 rue Royale, 1er (Métro: Madeleine).

This is an English firm that has moved into the French fabric trend and gone wild for Regency. The wares include men's vests, accessories for men and women, and all sorts of sumptuous creations. With a business suit, one of these ties would make a powerful statement.

L'ESCALIER D'ARGENT
42 galerie de Montpensier, Jardin du Palais Royal, 1er (Métro: Palais-Royal).

I found this shop because it's close to the vintage clothing store Didier Ludot. It's also close spiritually—it specializes in 18th-century textiles. It mostly makes ties and vests; ties cost about 60€ ($69). The location only reinforces the magic of the goods; this is Paris at its best.

LITTLE BLACK DRESS
125 galerie de Valois, Jardin du Palais Royal, 1er (Métro: Palais-Royal).

Vintage king Didier Ludot has created a line of new dresses—black only, my dear—inspired by famous vintage choices. Prices average around 200€ ($230).

SHANGHAI TANG
La Maison de la Chine, 76 rue Bonaparte, 6e (Métro: St-Sulpice).

From Hong Kong with love—the Chinese chic created by David Tang has finally come to Paris, where clothing, tabletop, and gift items are sold.

SNEAKERS

··

They're called *les baskets* in French, so forget references to trainers (Brit-speak), sneakers, or running shoes.

CITADIUM
50 rue de Caumartin, 9e (Métro: St-Lazare).

This large store, right behind Printemps and standing over a branch of Monoprix, specializes in all things sport—with a wide range of many brands of sneakers and gear.

LE SHOP
3 rue d'Argout, 2e (Métro: Etienne Marcel).

This store is for young people with a need to grab the latest looks—see the full listing below.

SHINZO
39 rue Etienne Marcel, 1er (Métro: Etienne Marcel).

Located on a street of cutting-edge fashion, this shop specializes in custom-made and collectible *baskets,* but at affordable prices.

TEENS & TWEENS

··

Teens will have no trouble spending their allowances, and all future allowances, in Paris. Many will like the tourist traps along the rue de Rivoli, with sweatshirts and boxer shorts; others will go for the *fripes* and vintage clothing. Any young woman will be mad for **Monoprix,** the big chain of dime stores—all have tons of fashion at pretty fair prices, but they are best for accessories, grooming items, and small items.

Most of the Left Bank is awash with stores that cater to students, some more fashionable than others. American-style clothes are in vogue with the French, so be careful—those Levi's could cost twice what you'd pay at home. For hot, body-revealing looks, check out **Kookaï**, 1 rue St-Denis, 1er (Métro: Châtelet), and 15 rue St-Placide, 7e (Métro: Sèvres-Babylone); and **Morgan,** 165 rue de Rennes, 6e (Métro: St-Sulpice), on the Left Bank, and 81 rue de Passy, 16e (Métro: La Muette), on the Right Bank. **H&M** (p. 8) is my best suggestion—it's one of my favorite stores in the world.

Major global chains that cater to young people, such as the Swedish giant **H&M,** the Spanish firm **Mango,** and the French chain **Pimkie,** have stores all over town. Many mothers prefer to take their teenagers to the major department stores, as the *grands magasins* carry so many different lines in one place.

Au Vrai Chic Parisien
8–10 rue Montmartre, 1er (Métro: Etienne Marcel).
47 rue du Four, 6e (Métro: St-Germain-des-Prés).

The Left Bank shop is tiny, but exactly what you want in a Left Bank store: cozy, with great stuff at moderate prices. When it's on sale, you'll want to buy armloads of these quasi-teen/quasi-adult fashions.

Diesel Concept Store
19 rue Pavée, 4e (Métro: St-Paul).

Although there are Diesel jeans all over town, this is the first Concept Store—deep in the Marais (and open on Sun).

Etam, Cité de la Femme
73 rue de Rivoli, 1er (Métro: Pont Neuf).

Etam is a gigantic chain—do not confuse this flagship store with the zillions of little Etams all over Paris, France, and the rest of the E.U. There is only one City of Women, and this is it.

Etam bought one of the landmark buildings from the late department store Samaritaine and turned it into a five-floor department store with an entire lifestyle worth of design, including a cafe, hair stylist, spa, and beauty department. The

Tammy clothing line was created specifically for hip 9- to 15-year-olds. Prices are low to moderate; high-fashion looks are everywhere.

The cafe is quite good and offers a wonderful view of Paris rooftops, as well as a chance to sip "perfumed" (flavored) iced tea—try rose, the hottest (coolest) taste in town.

KILIWATCH
84 rue Tiquetonne, 2e (Métro: Etienne Marcel or Les Halles).

Near the hottest shops on rue Etienne Marcel and not far from the Forum Les Halles mall, this store is very deep and stocked with an amazing combination of new and vintage clothing. The whole look is pulled together for you under one roof, and you finally understand what being a teen is all about, at least fashion-wise. A marvelous mix that includes jeans, shoes, outerwear—everything you need to be trendy.

LE SHOP
3 rue d'Argout, 2e (Métro: Etienne Marcel).

Don't let the address frighten you—this is easy to find and worth doing, possibly right after you check into your hotel. The store is huge, has loud music blaring at all hours, and hosts quite the teen scene. The clothes are cutting edge; this is where you'll find what's coming up next, as well as the crowd that wears it. Plenty of giveaways for clubs and concerts as well. This is one of the most important stores in French fashion.

MANGO
6 bd des Capucines, 9e (Métro: Madeleine), and many other locations.

Mango has many shops around town; it is a low-cost brand of fashions mostly for teens and young people. Very popular with the French.

Pro Mod
67 rue de Sèvres, 6e (Métro: Sèvres-Babylone), and many other locations.

This French chain is somewhere between Gap and Ann Taylor. It is not that teen-oriented unless your look is BCBG; it's for all female members of the family. In summer, the clothes are perfect for any beach destination. In fall, they're more serious and businesslike, copies of current styles. Everything is priced so you can wear it one season and forget about it the next year.

Zara
2 rue Halevy, 9e (Métro: Opéra).
44 av. des Champs-Elysées, 8e (Métro: Franklin D. Roosevelt); and many other locations.

Zara—a Spanish chain slowly expanding within the U.S.—makes well-priced, chic clothes for work and weekend without being silly and cheap. It copycats the latest jacket shape or skirt silhouette or whatever fashion gimmick is new, so you can look of-the-minute without going broke. There's also a men's line.

VINTAGE
··

Also see "Resale & Vintage" in chapter 6.

Didier Ludot
Jardin du Palais Royal, 1er (Métro: Palais-Royal).
Au Printemps, 9e (Métro: Havre Caumartin).

The most famous name in designer vintage in Paris, with a boutique in the Au Printemps department store and a series of spaces in the Jardin du Palais Royal. The house specialties are Chanel and Hermès; now that YSL has retired, there's a growing cache of the master's work. Also shoes, handbags, scarves, costume jewelry, luggage, and more.

E2
15 rue Martel, 10e (Métro: Gare de l'Est).

This showroom specializes in making new clothes from pieces of vintage works, mixing and matching decades and periods of fashion history. It is made to measure; prices begin around 350€ ($403).

RAG
85 rue St-Martin, 4e (Métro: Hôtel de Ville).

This looks like a head shop, but I've found some great stuff here at good prices. Furthermore, it's in a string of vintage clothing shops, and just a few meters from the Centre Pompidou. I've unearthed everything here, much of it American, but the Hermès scarves for 80€ ($92) are French—and a real find.

YESTERDAY NEVER DIES
53 rue du Four, 6e (Métro: St-Germain des-Prés).

Despite sounding like the name of a James Bond film, this new vintage clothing store sells clothing and accessories, as well as house-made fashions made from vintage clothing. ✆ 01-45-49-14-80.

WINE

AUGÉ
116 bd Haussmann, 8e (Métro: Madeleine).

It's not hard to find a great wine shop in Paris, but this one is special, so try to pop in. This immediate neighborhood has enough of interest to be worth a trip; see **Boulangerie St-Ouen** on p. 155.

AUTOUR DU VIN
1 rue Scribe, 9e (Métro: Opéra).

Conveniently located next to a famous restaurant, this wine shop sells it all, including accessories, and it has tastings. The store is owned by EuroCave, the wine-cooling people.

DERNIER GOUTTE
6 rue de Bourbon le Château, 6e (Métro: St-Germain-des-Prés).

There is only one Juan in Paris, and he is half of the team that owns this small wine shop—an American in Paris by way of Puerto Rico. He is the mentor to just about everyone with good taste on the Left Bank. You can buy by the region, by the price, or by trust.

LAVINA
3–5 bd de la Madeleine, 8e (Métro: Madeleine).

Another of the handful of new wine shops, this one specializes in wines from outside of France. There's also a wine bar inside the store.

LOVIN'
40 rue St-Honoré, 1er (Métro: Pont Neuf).

Read this address carefully and pay attention to the Métro stop—this is not where you think it is, but thankfully is convenient to many places you must visit. The large wine shop has tastings, information services, and a cave that you can use to store your treasures. Monday through Friday, it's open only in afternoons, beginning at 2:30pm; on Saturday, it's open from 10am to 8pm.

TCHIN-TCHIN
9 rue Montorgueil, 1er (Métro: Les Halles).

I've included this special shop because I adore it, but also because I love the entire block, which is in a convenient part of Paris where you will undoubtedly be prowling. This is a wine and champagne shop that specializes in small and unknown labels and specialty champagnes.

Chapter Eight

....

PARIS BEAUTY

Perfume and makeup are still good buys in Paris, often depending on the brand. You also must take into account French style. Don't underestimate the power of novelty, new launches, or experience as a souvenir. You may want to invest in some wild new products that aren't available in the U.S., if only to amuse your friends . . . or you may vote to spend money on spa time, to get a piece of the famed French *bien-être* (well-being).

Because money does matter, remember that you have two big choices for savings—through department stores with their discount schemes or through duty-free shops in town (not at the airport).

Note that the department store **Au Printemps** has redone, expanded, renovated, re-created, and gone nuts with its beauty department—it now takes up three levels of the Printemps Maison store and is the largest beauty hall in the world. In other news, the professional brand **Make Up For Ever** has launched a low-cost line, sold in Monoprix and *hypermarchés*.

Because French stores, like those all over the world, are stuck within the war of the brands, the latest way to bring novelty to French shoppers is to launch American brands. They just keep coming!

VIVE LA DIFFERENCE

••

Makeup in France is different from French makeup in the U.S. This is because makeup (even French brands) sold in the United States must be made according to FDA regulations, regardless of where it's manufactured. When you get to France, the names of your favorite products may be the same or different, and even makeup with the same name may not be identical in shade.

In addition, some products available in France are not sold in the U.S. at all, either because they haven't been launched yet or because the F.D.A. has not approved them.

French perfume is also different in France than in the U.S., mainly because it is made with potato alcohol (yes, you can drink it—just like Scarlett O'Hara), while Anglo-Saxon coun tries use cereal alcohol. Potato alcohol increases the staying power of the fragrance, as well as the actual fragrance—to some small degree. If you've ever shopped for perfume in the Caribbean, you know that certain stores make a big brouhaha over the fact that they import directly from France. Now you know why that's important. The French version is considered the best or most authentic one.

Many American brands that you see in France, such as Estée Lauder and Elizabeth Arden, are made in France (or Europe) for the European market. You may save on these items after the détaxe refund, but generally you do not save on American brands in Europe.

French perfumes are always introduced in France before they come out internationally. This lead time may be as much as a year. If you want to keep up with the newest fragrances, go to your favorite duty-free store and ask specifically for the newest.

If you're stumped for a gift for the person who has everything, consider one of these new fragrances. The biggest spring launch comes in time for Mother's Day in France, which is usually a different day than in the U.S., but always in spring (May or early June).

The converse of this rule also applies. Some older scents are taken off the market in the U.S. and U.K. because sales aren't strong enough. These fragrances are still for sale in France. Just ask anyone looking for Je Reviens.

Some scents never come to the U.S. at all. Guerlain is big on this, as are many other design houses when it comes to their ephemeral scents—the ones that come and go for a season or a promotion. If novelty is your goal, start spritzing.

BEAUTY FOR MEN

I told you to watch out for novelty. But in Paris, makeup and skin care for men are past the novelty stage and even beyond the trendy stage. It's happening, man. There are day spas just for men, treatments at all spas geared specifically toward men (thanks, I needed that), and many, many skin-care products that are packaged for men so they don't think it's sissy stuff.

A study on French spas recently reported that 30% of the clients are men. Firms from Biotherm to Nivea have products just for men.

INSTITUT MARC DELACRE
17 av. George V, 8e (Métro: George V).

Exclusively for guys, and treatments start at 100€ ($115).

NICKEL
48 rue des Francs-Bourgeois, 3e (Métro: Hotel de Ville).

Men's spa, with its own line of products. ✆ 01-42-77-41-10.

ALL BEAUTY, ALL DAY

••

SEPHORA

70 av. des Champs-Elysées, 8e (Métro: Franklin D. Roosevelt).
70 rue de Rivoli, 1er (Métro: Châtelet or Pont Neuf).
Forum des Halles, 11 bis, rue de l'Arc-en-Ciel, 1er (Métro: Châtelet or Les Halles).
50 rue de Passy, 16e (Métro: La Muette).
38 av. du Général LeClerc, 14e (Métro: Alésia).
Carrousel du Louvre, 99 rue de Rivoli, 1er (Métro: Louvre).

This is a large chain of cosmetics and beauty-products shops with stores all over France, in most major European cities, and now in the U.S. as well. The flagship Champs-Elysées store, which is open daily, is the best one to visit. The store in the mall at the Carrousel du Louvre is open Sunday and closed Monday. The hippest store is the one at Pont Neuf in the heart of the rue de Rivoli devoted to the young female shopper—this branch even has spa services and strives to serve the customer more—because the customer tends to be a teen, tween, or 20-something.

Sephora is not a discounter or duty-free, but it offers instant détaxe and a very, very large selection of brands. You may do better price-wise in a department store (with your discount card), but you'll have more fun at a branch of Sephora.

Those are the facts; the emotions are harder to explain. This is simply a shrine to the beauty industry, and a makeup junkie's best fix. The helpful salespeople wear cute uniforms; if you ask for extra samples, you may get them (samples are not automatically given; you must ask); and this is a great source for inexpensive—and inventive—gifts. You can buy prepackaged gift boxes of the house brand or build your own box. The animal-shaped bath gels are great for kids. There is also a small bookshop with books and reference materials related to beauty and fragrance.

Please note the détaxe system here: You will get a refund of slightly over 16%.

BATH & SOAP

··

Since medieval times, the French have been known for their interest in the bathing arts (don't snicker—it's dry cleaning that's expensive in France, not bathwater). It was the French who first learned how to mass-produce soap (in Marseille), and they still make some of the best soap and bath products in the world. An inexpensive gift gimmick is to package together a *gant de toilette,* the French version of a washcloth, with a bar of designer soap or a French soap that has a cute story, like one of the new salad soaps (lettuce and tomato with basil, for instance). The total cost will be about 8.70€ ($10).

Below I have listed some French brands that are known for their bath products and have their own stores; some of them also have U.S. distribution.

DURANCE
224 rue Vignon, 9e (Métro: Madeleine).

A small but luxe soap brand that uses this store to sell not only soap, body and bathing products, but also foodstuffs and Provençale-themed merchandise. ✆ 01-47-42-04-10. www.durance.fr.

LA COMPAGNIE DE PROVENCE
16 rue Vignon, 9e (Métro: Madeleine).

This famous brand from Marseille (sometimes written as LCDP) has finally come to Paris in the form of its own store— the brand has been sold in boutiques and department stores for years. You will recognize the line from its distinctive package, but will also note that it has recently expanded into new scents—I just bought cherry-scented liquid soap. Also note that there are several other soap stores on this street. When I was in the store last, it was mobbed with Japanese tourists who consider this an important status brand to bring home for gifts. I do, too. ✆ 01-42-68-01-60. www.lcdpmarseille.com.

L'OCCITANE
1 rue du 29 Juillet, 1er (Métro: Tuileries).

This is a huge international chain. L'Occitane is a soap manufacturer from Provence and it's not only a line—it's also a mood, a statement, and always a good source for a well-priced gift. There are numerous scented products for men, women, and children, and for body, bath, and home. L'Occitane has also launched color makeup and is beginning a spa business. This branch is close to the Louvre.

INTERNATIONAL BEAUTY BRANDS

ARMANI
Armani stores, including 25 place Vendôme, 1er (Métro: Tuileries), and department stores.

Armani makeup is also available in the U.S.; yes, it's made by L'Oréal, but it's still good stuff.

MENARD
21 rue de la Paix, 2e (Métro: Opéra).

This is a Japanese line and most of the customers are Japanese, but for those who want to know what's new in Paris—*voilà*. There are color cosmetics and skin care; the Embellir Night Cream is said to have benefits from reishi, which helps regenerate new cells. Also sold in department stores and Sephora. ✆ 01-42-65-58-08.

SHISEIDO
3 bd Malesherbes, 8e (Métro: Madeleine).

Don't confuse this listing with the Shiseido-owned perfume shop in the Jardin du Palais Royal. This is a brand-new building in a brand-new location, part of a stretch of new installations that have turned this into one of the city's most interesting retail corners. Shiseido is known for pricey, but well-made beauty treatments and many innovations in beauty and anti-aging products.

SHU UEMURA
176 bd St-Germain, 6e (Métro: St-Germain-des-Prés).

If you consider yourself an aficionado of cosmetics, to be in
Paris and not go here is a sin. Yes, it's even better than Bourjois, more expensive, too. Shu Uemura is one of the most
famous makeup artists in the world and a cult hero in his native
Japan. You can buy his makeup and skin-care products in every
world capital.

Samples, mirrors, and brushes fill this high-tech shop, just
encouraging you to come in and do your face. In makeup, color
is the name of the game here: The hues are spectacular. A single square of color costs about 15€ ($17).

Most department stores also carry the brand; there is a Shu
Uemura Nail Bar in Bon Marché. Le Drugstore, on Champs-
Elysées, also has Shu Uemura makeup.

AMERICAN BEAUTY BRANDS

You'll find American beauty brands in the major department
stores and at Sephora; they are always more expensive in
France than in the U.S. Several international brands are owned
by U.S. holding companies (Lauder owns Darphin, for instance).

A few American firms are opening their own doors here—
one of the latest arrivals is **Fresh,** 5 rue du Cherche-Midi, 6e
(Métro: Sèvres-Babylone).

BRITISH BEAUTY BRANDS

Every now and then, you get a British brand that has turned
French, such as the perfume house **Creed** (p. 213), which
made the switcheroo about 100 years ago.

BODY SHOP
Le Carrousel du Louvre, 99 rue de Rivoli, 1er (Métro: Louvre).

This British icon, despite hard financial times, still has several stores in Paris. Look for them in major trading areas, especially where there are teen and tween fashions.

MARY QUANT
49 rue Bonaparte, 6e (Métro: St-Germain-des-Prés).

The woman who brought us mod back in the 1960s has several new shops in London and free-standing stores in other shopping capitals, such as New York and Paris. Mostly makeup.

FRENCH FACE & BODY

DARPHIN
97 rue du Bac, 7e (Métro: Rue du Bac).

This is a chic, almost secret salon that does facials and treatments (French skin salons never do hair). It sells its own line of natural bath and beauty products, which have made it to America in limited doses—only the rich and with-it know about this line. The salon is big on body shaping and has many hydro-plus (water-added) products to moisturize and balance. Its products are sold in department stores and *parapharmacies* and are known as "the poor man's Sisley." **Note:** Darphin has been purchased by Estée Lauder; I had a note from one reader who says the line is not as good as it used to be, as a result of the takeover.

DECLÉOR
Department stores and parapharmacies.

Decléor is a large line of treatments created around the concept of therapeutic oils, addressing everything from dry skin to aging. I'm not sure if I'm addicted to the benefits or just the scents, but I keep buying. Decléor has teamed with Carita to open its first spa; it's at the Hilton Arc de Triomphe. Non-hotel guests may sign up for treatments.

EXYSTE
26 galerie de Montpensier, Palais Royal, 1er (Métro: Palais-Royal).

This is a small line in a small, new shop in the Palais Royal and is considered a cult brand by Japanese beauty mavens who flock here. The line is made up of natural ingredients, such as wild yams. © **01-42-96-00-18.**

LeClerc
Department stores and parapharmacies.

This brand, known for its makeup for years, has closed its shop and is concentrating on department-store distribution and research and development. The latest launch is a complete line of face and beauty treatments.

PHYTOMER
Parapharmacies.

There is a Phytologie hair treatment center at 33 rue des Arcades, 8e (Métro: St-Augustin or Madeleine), but no free-standing shop. There is also a Phytomer spa in Lafayette Homme, at Galeries Lafayette. *Parapharmacies* carry the firm's beauty products.

SISLEY
Department stores and duty-free shops.

Perhaps the most famous name in French skin care, this line added makeup a few years ago and is a favorite for Americans who adore the fact that the line is about half-price in France. Sisleya, the most famous of Sisley's ritzy wrinkle creams, retails for $300 in the U.S. It's 130€ ($150) in France if you take advantage of all possible deductions. Be sure to buy at a department store with a discount card or at **Catherine** (p. 217).

PARAPHARMACIES

••

These stores specialize in French pharmaceutical brands of makeup and beauty treatments, usually discounted 20%. These are wonderful places to research new products and things you never see in the U.S. All department stores have a *parapharmacie* section, usually adjacent to the makeup department.

EURO SANTÉ BEAUTÉ
37 rue de la Boétie, 8e (Métro: St-Augustin), and other locations.

I love Euro Santé Beauté—I visit one in every French city that has one. More than 200 brands are on sale here, at what I consider one of the better *parapharmacies* in town. Most of the branches are relatively large by French standards. Ask for a price list, which you can pocket and use to comparison shop. This is a large chain; there is also a branch next door to the Hôtel Concorde St-Lazare (Métro: St-Lazare).

FRENCH MAKEUP SECRETS

••

BY TERRY
21 galerie Vérot-Dodat, 1er (Métro: Palais-Royal).
6 rue Jacob, 6e (Métro: St-Germain-des-Prés).
30 rue de la Trémoille, 8e (Métro: Franklin D. Roosevelt).

Makeup addicts, search no more: This is the "in" place to visit and test and swoon over. More and more shops are popping up in Paris, as well as other French cities.

About Bourjois

You've heard of Chanel, sure, but Bourjois? Bourjois is the name of the company that owns the Chanel line of makeup and perfume; it makes a lower-priced line of makeup under the Bourjois name—at the same factories where Chanel is manufactured! This doesn't mean that the lines are identical, but if you can't afford Chanel and want to give this line a whirl, you may be pleased with the investment (about 50% less expensive than Chanel). With the weak dollar, this line is not cheap—it just costs much less than Chanel.

Bourjois is hard to find in the U.S., but it's not hard to find in Paris—if you know where to look. You can buy it at any branch of **Monoprix** or **Sephora**, or at any big French department store. What makes the line so special? For starters: many, many shades of eye shadow sold in big containers, which last forever. The nail polishes and lipsticks are also good.

Terry de Gunzberg gained fame when she created all the colors and makeup for Yves Saint Laurent's beauty line, for which she still consults. After years in the big-time beauty biz, Terry created her own line that is known for the density of the pigment. Because she uses so much pigment, the color is said to last longer than normal makeup.

You can get "made over" in the salon and then pick the choices for your palette (a small plastic container that is fitted to hold assorted color pots). The palette is free if you fill it, but you can also buy a la carte. The shops can create custom colors as well; this is pricey, but makes a status statement.

STEPHANE MARAIS
217 rue St-Honoré, 1er (Métro: Tuileries).

This makeup artist, the latest Shiseido protégé, works with a line of 188 products. He also does fashion shows in Paris, as well as private faces for civilians.

PERFUME & SCENT

ANNICK GOUTAL
14 rue de Castiglione, 1er (Métro: Tuileries or Concorde),
and other shops around town.

The tiny shop on the rue de Castiglione is a Paris landmark, but Annick Goutal has a number of other outlets in Paris and elsewhere in the world. For example, Bergdorf in New York and Harrods in London sell it. Just step into the Belle Epoque–style salon and sniff the house brands, which include perfumes, lotions, and house scents. Be sure to look at the firm's logo, in a mosaic on the sidewalk in front of the store. I'm addicted to the soap called L'Hadrien, the house soap for hotels in the Concorde chain. I like it so much, I've been known to pay cash for it. Despite the fact that Mme Goutal died several years ago, her family carries on the business; new scents are continually launched. The latest is called Songes.

ARTISAN PARFUMEUR
2 rue de l'Amiral de Coligny, 1er (Métro: Louvre-Rivoli).
24 bd Raspail, 7e (Métro: Rue du Bac).
22 rue Vignon, 9e (Métro: Madeleine).

This source makes its name selling hard-to-find brands in Paris, but beware: Many are American or British.

CREED
38 rue Pierre 1er de Serbie, 8e (Métro: Alma-Marceau).

This was a British perfume house when it was founded in 1760; during Victorian times, the firm moved to France. It is now a cult brand that makes scents for royalty and rich people. Prince Rainier asked the house to create a little something for Grace Kelly to wear on their wedding day. Now you, too, can buy it—or any of the other scents worn by celebs, kings, and queens. You can either commission a custom-made scent or choose from the ready-made fragrances.

FREDERIC MALLE
140 av. Victor Hugo, 16e (Métro: Victor-Hugo).

This jewel-box tiny shop sells specialty brews of Malle's own fragrances—there's much emphasis on consultation in choosing the right scent.

GUERLAIN
68 av. des Champs-Elysées, 8e (Métro: Franklin D. Roosevelt).
2 place Vendôme, 1er (Métro: Opéra).
93 rue de Passy, 16e (Métro: La Muette).
29 rue de Sèvres, 6e (Métro: Sèvres-Babylone).
35 rue Tronchet, 8e (Métro: Madeleine).

GUERLAIN INSTITUTS DE BEAUTÉ
68 av. des Champs-Elysées, 8e (Métro: Franklin D. Roosevelt).
29 rue de Sèvres, 6e (Métro: Sèvres-Babylone).
Hôtel de Crillon, 10 place Concorde, 1er (Métro: Concorde).

Perhaps the most famous name in fragrance in France, Guerlain has two types of boutiques in Paris. Some sell products only, while others have salons on the premises. The flagship store on the Champs-Elysées has just been renovated. *Insider's tip:* The *maison* will create your own fragrance for a mere 30,000€ ($34,500).

Perfumes are sold only through Guerlain stores and are not discounted; the brand is rarely found at duty-free stores. If you see it at a duty-free, chances are there is no discount. Some Guerlain fragrances that you'll see in France are not sold in the U.S. There is a brand-new Guerlain spa in the Hôtel de Crillon (p. 61).

JEAN PATOU
5 rue de Castiglione, 1er (Métro: Concorde).

Patou's most famous fragrance is Joy, but the house has numerous scents and now a new-ish store that happens to be a few doors from my favorite duty-free shop for perfume: Catherine. Patou will custom-blend a scent for you. © 01-42-92-07-22.

PATRICIA DE NICOLAI
80 rue de Grenelle, 7e (Métro: Rue du Bac).

A nose is a nose is a nose; this is the granddaughter of the Guerlain family. Fragrance, candles, potpourri, and more. Note the odd hours: It's closed from 2 to 2:30pm daily.

SALON SHISEIDO
142 galerie de Valois, Jardin du Palais Royal, 1er (Métro: Palais-Royal).

If you think this store caters to Japanese tourists, you can forget it right now. This happens to be one of Paris's best-kept secrets, and also one of the must-do addresses that any serious shopper (I mean, sociologist) should seek out, merely from an academic standpoint.

First, a quick history lesson: Shiseido is a Japanese makeup firm. A million years ago, it hired the most famous makeup artist in Paris, Serge Lutens, and let him explore his creativity. This tiny shop, with the most glorious decor in Paris, sells his private inventions and designs. It is best known for his custom-made perfumes. Note that everything is a perfume—there are no derivatives. A bottle of scent costs about 90€ ($104). Beware the stopper; it's not set in too well, so you must pack your fragrance carefully or hand-carry it onto the plane.

To find the shop, walk behind the Comédie-Française (next to the Palais-Royal Métro) into the gardens of the Palais Royal. Go past the creative modern sculptures to the centuries-old gardens. Along each side, you'll see an arcade crammed with shops. The Shiseido salon is in the far arcade across the gardens.

DISCOUNTERS

....

"Discount" is a dirty word in France, and "duty-free" has become confusing. Even a source that discounts, and has done so for years, is suddenly terrified of mix-ups.

Here's the deal: Discount is one thing, détaxe is another, and duty-free is still another.

The big beauty firms do not approve of **discounting,** but they tolerate it up to 15% or 20%. The percentage varies by brand; at an honest store, the staff will explain that the amount of the discount varies.

Détaxe is the tax refund that any non-E.U. passport holder qualifies for after spending 175€ ($201) at any one store in a single day; for a full explanation, see "Détaxe Details" (p. 49).

Duty-free sold at the airport is a flat 13% off—you qualify to buy duty-free only when you are departing the E.U.

A quick overview:

- At Sephora, you get no discount, but you get instant détaxe (if you qualify)—and détaxe is a higher rate than normal.
- At a major specialty *maison,* such as Guerlain, Creed, or Caron, you get no discount, but you do get détaxe (if you qualify).
- At a major department store, you get a 10% discount with the store's tourist discount card (obtain it free at the store's welcome desk); you also get 12% détaxe (if and when you qualify).
- At the airport, you pay exactly 13% less than the department-store full price.
- At the few so-called duty-free shops in central Paris, you get the maximum discount that they allow, which ranges from 15% to 25%, plus the détaxe refund of 13% (if and when you qualify). If you do not spend enough to get the détaxe refund, you get the flat upfront discount—even if you buy only one mascara. The amount of the flat discount varies with the store and the brand.

CATHERINE
7 rue de Castiglione, 1er (Métro: Concorde or Tuileries).

If you've never been to Paris before, listen up. Catherine is my duty-free shop of choice. This is where I do the bulk of my shopping, because of the selection and the way it handles discounting and détaxe.

Catherine is one of the few duty-free shops that not only will give you the discount, but also will advance you the détaxe upfront.

It works this way: Let's say you have spent 175€ ($201).

First you get the 20% or 25% discount on each item bought (Chanel and Dior brands are 20% off, most others are 25%). Once that discount has been deducted, you still have to have a total of 175€ ($201).

If you do, you then qualify for a détaxe discount of an additional 13%.

Call © 01-42-61-02-89. There is no website, so owners suggest that you send a fax to 01-42-61-02-35.

HAIRSTYLISTS

Going to the hairstylist in Paris is fun if you have the time and the patience. While the fanciest salons are expensive, they offer not only a chance to pamper yourself, but also a social history lesson and glimpse at a way of life that you can't be part of, on any level, unless you marry into it. I'd give up a few hours in the Louvre in order to visit Carita.

ALEXANDRE DE PARIS
3 av. Matignon, 8e (Métro: Matignon).
Les Trois Quartiers, place de la Madeleine, 1er (Métro: Madeleine).

Alexandre is legend, perhaps the most famous of the old-school hairdressers. The name is so well known that there's a separate hair-accessories business, with shops all over the world and products sold in major department stores.

For the Avenue Matignon shop, call © 01-43-59-40-09. For the Place de la Madeleine shop, call © 01-49-26-04-59.

CARITA
11 rue du Faubourg St-Honoré, 8e (Métro: Concorde).

Perhaps the most famous name in beauty in all of Paris, Carita offers an entire town house devoted to putting madame's best foot forward. The entrance is on the Faubourg, off the street and set in a little bit.

The great thing about this place, aside from the fact that the reception staff speaks English, is that it's so organized, you can be assured you'll be taken care of. Just walk to the appointment clerk (on street level to your left, once you've parted the waves) and make an appointment. You can also call or fax ahead for an appointment. You can, of course, ask for a particular stylist, but if you don't, not to worry—you'll be in good hands, regardless.

The stylists wear white uniforms; the patrons wear expensive clothes and carry the best handbags in Paris. You receive a paper number when you check your belongings and pick up your smock; don't lose it. This is your client number, which stays with you until you pay the bill.

Note: Patrons do not take off their clothes here; the smock goes over what you are wearing.

The cost of this pampering is the going rate for ultra-fancy in Paris; you can do better price-wise, but never experience-wise. I consider each trip to Carita a souvenir for myself. I come away with a memory and a good hairdo. A shampoo and blow-dry, which includes service (meaning you do not tip), costs about 75€ ($86), or more if you add hair-care products. In France, you pay for each ingredient they put in your hair when they wash it.

Carita added beauty and skin-care products a few years ago and now offers spa services—a natural extension of what it has always done, and done so well. The back desk at street level sells beauty products and accessories.

Carita has branches in various shopping districts of Paris; there is also a Carita spa in the Hilton Arc de Triomphe. Call ✆ **01-44-94-11-00** or send a fax to 01-47-42-94-98.

JEAN-MARC MANIATIS

35 rue de Sèvres, 6e (Métro: Sèvres-Babylone).
18 rue Marbeuf, 8e (Métro: Franklin D. Roosevelt).
Galeries Lafayette, 40 bd Haussmann, 9e (Métro: Chaussée-d'Antin).
Beauty school: Forum des Halles, 2e (Métro: Les Halles).

Still one of the hot shops for models and runway stars, Maniatis has salons in Paris (one is in Galeries Lafayette), as well as a beauty school. The beauty school has a service that offers free haircuts to clients who are willing to let a student practice on them. Men, women, and teens may participate; the stylists make all the choices—you are the guinea pig.

If you want to go for a regular Maniatis session, note that the Right Bank salon is open on Monday; the Left Bank salon is not. You can reach the Rue de Sèvres location at ✆ **01-45-44-16-39,** the Rue Marbeuf location at ✆ 01-47-23-30-14, the Galeries Lafayette location at ✆ 01-42-82-07-09, and the beauty school at ✆ 01-47-20-00-05.

L'ORÉAL CENTRE TECHNIQUE

14 rue Royale, 1er (Métro: Tuileries or Concorde).

Right in the heart of things are L'Oréal's offices and technical center, which is reserved for testing models and VIPs. If you feel like a hair fling, but are watching your budget, you can sometimes volunteer—it costs about 30€ ($35) for color or a cut. The center closes from noon to 2pm, but otherwise you can drop in or phone to ask. The location couldn't be better. ✆ **01-40-20-97-30.**

HAIR SALON CHAINS

....

Jacques Dessange (see below) is a chain of salons with locations all over France. The latest trend is toward less expensive and less formal chains. Many of them do not require appointments, and some have salons in the U.S. Check out **Jean Louis David, Camille Albane**, and **Jean-Claude Biguine**. All three have convenient salons; your hotel concierge will tell you which is nearest. They are all relatively inexpensive (by Paris standards), but do not expect the same quality of work or service that you get at a big-name salon. If you're having a number of services performed and price is an issue, go over a price list with someone who speaks English before you begin. Most Paris salons charge a la carte, which means you can be charged for each shampooing. The price includes service; only regulars top off the bill.

Note: Most of the chains have training sessions at which you can get a free or cheap hairdo. The best of the bunch is **Centre Camille Albane**, 114 rue de la Boétie, 8e (Métro: Franklin D. Roosevelt). For reservations and availability, women ages 20 to 50 can call © **01-43-59-31-32**. Another option is **Jacques Dessange** (© **01-44-70-08-08**), which also does training sessions and imposes similar age restrictions.

CAMILLE ALBANE
17 bis rue de la Boétie, 8e (Métro: Mironmesnil).

This is where I have my hair done now; I use Michaël Galais; his dog's name is Alba; he doesn't speak much English. Closed on Mondays. © **01-42-65-14-85**.

JACQUES DESSANGE
37 av. Franklin D. Roosevelt, 8e (Métro: Franklin D. Roosevelt).

Still famous after all these years, Dessange has a number of shops in Paris and other locations, including the U.S. The clientele is younger and not as fancy as Carita's, but Dessange has a big-time reputation nonetheless. Hollywood's José Eber started here. The beauty and makeup line is available at the salon and at pharmacies. There are hundreds of salons in France; call © 01-43-59-31-31 for the one nearest you.

JEAN LOUIS DAVID
38 av. Wagram, 8e (Métro: Etoile).

This hairstylist revolutionized the business about 30 years ago when he opened no-appointment salons with fixed prices that are fair to low. Jean Louis David has salons in many countries around the world, but the bulk of the business is in France, with a lot of salons in Paris. For the location nearest you, call © 01-58-05-06-03.

LUCIE SAINT-CLAIR
4 av. Pierre 1er de Serbie, 16e (Métro: Alma-Marceau).

This location is the chain's flagship, also called Top International. There's a special that includes a cut, *balayage* (streaks), and blow-dry for about 100€ ($115). The salon offers some spa services. Call © 01-47-20-53-54.

SPA ME

Water, water everywhere and not a drop to drink: Of course not, this is Paris. You drink wine; bathe in water; and celebrate beauty, health, and science in salt water, mud, algae, scented oils, honey, and wine.

Spas have been around France since the Romans marched through, and *maman* trains every French girl to visit the *esthéticienne* (beautician) regularly for *les soins* (the cures). The beauty "cures" are not considered a luxury, but a necessity.

What has changed in France, especially in Paris, is the idea of the day spa—borrowed from New York and translated with French style, as well as French prices. Because *les soins* are part of everyday life in Paris, they are very affordable. Even

Spa Thoughts

Whatever spa you choose, remember some basics:

- In France, body treatments are likely to be done on your naked body. No paper panties.
- Although prices include service, you do tip (give a small token, not a percentage).
- Most spas will try to sell you their products; some will be rather aggressive about it. The products may be less expensive at Monoprix or a *parapharmacie*—and you don't need to buy the products in order to have them respect you in the morning.
- Sometimes a spa will take a walk-in, but it's usually best to book ahead. If you want a jet-lag treatment on arrival, book before you depart for France.
- Smaller spas may not have English-speaking personnel; ask your hotel concierge for help if you do not speak French.

the fanciest spas and salons in Paris are a bargain compared to U.S. prices for the same or similar treatments.

While French families may still sign up for a 1-week cure at famous spas all over the country (mostly in coastal destinations like La Baule, Biarritz, and Monte Carlo), more and more of the working public is taking advantage of the day spa. The customers are almost equally men and women—in France there is nothing sissy about a guy having a spa treatment, especially when he's traveling.

There is a difference between an *Institut de Beauté* and a spa. One is a fancy salon with a few treatments; the other is a full-service place, with many treatments and often a gym. Parisian hotels have the best selection of day spas in Paris; many of them are open to non-guests.

Hotel Spas

Anne Semonin
Hôtel Bristol, 112 rue du Faubourg St-Honoré, 8e (Métro: Champs-Elysées Clemenceau).

This luxury hotel has the best of all worlds: the Anne Semonin spa, next door but in the same building; an Anne Semonin treatment room adjoining the pool and health club; and Anne Semonin products in the guest rooms.

Semonin is an international cult figure; she does not advertise, but is known for her all-natural products and treatments. The best is a jet-lag cure, which consists of a wrap that eliminates toxins. Prices begin at 50€ ($58).

There is a men's spa in Madelois, a men's department store. Barneys and Bergdorf Goodman carry Semonin's products in the U.S. ☎ **01-42-66-63-98.**

Carita Mosaique
Hilton Arc de Triomphe, 51 rue de Courcelles, 8e (Métro: Courcelles).

This is the first full Carita spa in the world—although a test spa exists on a cruise ship, and the real Carita (a hairdresser) is still on the Faubourg St-Honoré, so don't get confused. The spa is named Mosaique in honor of the zillions of glittery tiles inlaid in the enormous spa space with giant treatment rooms and private lockers. Products used are either from the Carita line or by Decléor. You need not be a hotel guest in order to book here. I had a very nice facial (for anti-aging, no less), but the product sales pitch afterward was very aggressive. ☎ **01-58-36-17-17.**

Four Seasons George V
31 av. George V, 8e (Métro: Alma-Marceau or George V).

If you want swanky, nothing in Paris compares to this spa, with its neoclassical decorations and swimming pool. It looks like something out of a decor magazine. Treatments are currently for hotel guests only, but the Four Seasons also offers VIP spa rooms (available by the hour) for small groups, such as a bridal party or family. The hotel also offers a package that includes room, breakfast, and a spa treatment. ✆ 01-49-52-70-00.

GUERLAIN
Hôtel de Crillon, 10 place Concorde, 1er (Métro: Concorde).

Not to be confused with the Guerlain retail spaces all over Paris, this is the last word, a spa unique to this hotel. Non-guests may book the services and even join the gym. ✆ 01-40-07-90-44.

HOTEL MONTALAMBERT
3 rue de Montalambert, 7e (Métro: Rue du Bac).

This hotel's gimmick is a well-being oxygen bar and oxygen drinks. ✆ 01-45-49-68-68.

LES SOURCES DE CAUDALIE
Hôtel Meurice, 228 rue de Rivoli, 1er (Métro: Tuileries or Concorde).

The Hôtel Meurice's Espace Bien-Etre (Space of Well-Being) is a relatively new branch of the Bordeaux wine spa Les Sources de Caudalie. All treatments are made with grape products, proven to have anti-aging effects. You can buy the products at the hotel, any *parapharmacie,* and the nearby Monoprix Opéra.

For your treatment, try a sauvignon wrap, a California grape massage, or a crushed cabernet scrub. Red-wine spa products have relaxing, slimming, or anti-aging properties. There are also facial treatments, as well as special options for jet lag, dry skin, and vitality. I do the 1½-hour facial lifting, since I am at that age. I try to go once a month, and I do use some of the products in between (along with scads of others, as well!).

Prices begin at 50€ ($58), but wraps and massages are mostly about 125€ ($144). Call ✆ 01-44-58-10-77.

TALIKA
Pershing Hall, 49 rue de Charon, 8e (Métro: Franklin D. Roosevelt).

Located right off the Champs-Elysées, the hotel Pershing Hall is so discreet that you might even bypass it. Don't. If you aren't staying there, or dining there, at least check out the latest trend—a specialist spa: eye treatments and rituals, even one that stimulates the growth of your eyelashes. ✆ 01-58-36-58-03.

Day Spas

DANIEL JOUVANCE, ESPACE MER
91 av. des Champs-Elysées, 8e (Métro: Franklin D. Roosevelt or George V).

You don't need to go to a hotel to enjoy a spa day: Daniel Jouvance, who operates a spa in La Baule, the French Atlantic center for *thalassotherapie,* also has Espace Mer, right on the Champs-Elysées. You can test and choose from his wide range of products on the ground level, or go upstairs for traditional Brittany-style treatments, most of which involve the use of water.

The spa offers cures broken down into types (serenity, kinestherapy, skin, and beauty). The 30-minute treatments cost about 30€ ($35), a 70-minute toning treatment costs about 50€ ($58), and half-day combination packages are available. My idea of heaven? Stroll (and shop, of course) the Champs-Elysées, go to the spa for part of the day, then take in a movie. Call ✆ 01-47-23-48-00.

SOTHY'S
128 rue du Faubourg St-Honoré, 8e (Métro: Champs-Elysées Clemenceau).

Not far from the Hôtel Bristol at the far end of this famous street, the tiny Sothy's shop and spa is an insider's delight. Prices for anti-aging treatments begin at 75€ ($86). Although the product line is not well known in the U.S., the full-service spa is perhaps the best destination for a combination of makeup, beauty, and body treatments. ✆ 01-53-93-91-53.

Hairstylists with Spas

JEAN-CLAUDE BIGUINE
10 rue Marbeuf, 8e (Métro: Franklin D. Roosevelt).

The treatment business has become so hot that beauty brands are not the only ones that want a piece of the action. Enter the big-name French hairdressers. Jean-Claude Biguine has expanded his empire from hair to makeup to spas, and offers a full program to rehabilitate you. The daylong package costs 200€ ($230) and includes treatments for body and hair, as well as a manicure, pedicure, waxing, haircut, and blow-dry. ✆ 01-53-67-81-90.

Department Store Spas

The department stores are always at war with one another, seeking out the latest brand names or supporting the classic French lines. Be sure to check for spa news at each store's Welcome Desk.

Galeries Lafayette has the **Phytomer Spa.** Printemps has **Yves Rocher, Nuxe,** and **Shiseido** minispas. La Samaritaine has **Cinq Monde.**

Mass Market Spas

L' OCCITANE
This maker of oils, soaps, makeup, and body products from Provence is slowly adding spa services to some of its spaces around the world, offering pampering and quick-fix solutions in body care. The first one was in London, and now Paris is getting into the rub. Ask at your local boutique for the nearest spa.

Yves Rocher
92 av. des Champs-Elysées, 8e (Métro: Franklin D. Roosevelt).

This makeup, beauty, and hair-care brand has zillions of salons across France. Prices are low; rates for spa services are in keep-ing with the prices of products and are quite fair. This is the line that many teens begin with; as they gain disposable income, they move on to bigger brands. © 01-45-62-78-27.

NAIL BARS

The nail-bar concept is one of the many American retail ideas to take over Paris. It's no longer hard to find a storefront that *posez les ongles* (puts on nails) or claims to do American-style manicures. That doesn't mean you'll get the kind of manicure you are used to—or even a decent manicure.

If you need a quickie repair, most department stores now have their own nail bars, which are often quite glam. **Opi,** the American brand, is considered deluxe in Paris and is featured at several department stores; it has a nail bar at Galeries Lafayette. You can buy supplies to fix your nails at any branch of Monoprix and sometimes in grocery stores.

Chapter Nine

....

MA MAISON

FRENCH STYLE

Over the years, American home design has been tremendously influenced by French style. Guess what? Now Americans are influencing French style. Actually, Americans are influencing French everything, even marketing and store layout.

While country French is now considered classic, my grandmother's idea of decorating had to do with draped silk swags, watered silk, and reproduction Louis. Maybe she knew which Louis it was; surely I did not. Today I live with a jumble of her Louis and my Souleiado mixed with flea-market finds from all over France. I'm not alone.

The young French prefer a more streamlined look; those with money want their lines from, or in the style of, Emile-Jacques Ruhlmann. Minimalism is still working here, partly because of the lack of space in apartments and partly because the arrival of **Armani Casa** has reinforced the Euro-Japanese chic, simple look and made it more French than a look from history or the countryside. In fact, the new food trends often look best served on the popular Zen tableware.

Those going to Paris in search of home furnishings and accessories cannot only choose from among many styles, but also must check out French antiques, brocante, table linens, or merely candles (wait until you see what the French can do with candles). For listings of antiques shops, antiques events, brocante fairs, and flea markets, see chapter 10.

Note: It is against the law to transport paint on an air carrier, so I don't list specialty stores that sell French and English house paints. For everything else, flip this way. You need not do over the house or change your personal style, but please, make room for one lasting souvenir.

SMELLING FRENCH STYLE

French home scents are so affordable and come in so many formats that they make perfect souvenirs. New methods of scent distribution are invented all the time: You'll find everything from perfumed powder for the vacuum cleaner to devices that sweeten the air.

CHRISTIAN TORTU
6 carrefour Odéon, 6e (Métro: Odéon).

Tortu is one of the most famous florists in Paris, sort of the Robert Isabell of the City of Light. He has gone the product route—which makes sense in his line of work—with a wide range of candles and home scents. His brand does not have very good distribution. The shop is in the Left Bank, very close to Souleiado. ✆ 01-43-26-02-56.

DIPTYQUE
34 bd St-Germain, 5e (Métro: Maubert-Mutualité).

If you are not seriously into Diptyque, you can buy the candles at Printemps and save yourself a trip. This tiny store is not in the heart of the Left Bank shopping. In fact, it's sort of in the middle of nowhere, and you must make a special trip. So taxi right here and giggle right back to your hotel with a suitcase filled with gifts and goodies. You'll find candles, soaps, and scents; the candles are a deal at 22€ ($25) each, almost half the U.S. price. Closed Monday.

ESTÉBAN
49 rue de Rennes, 6e (Métro: St-Germain-des-Prés).
20 rue Francs-Bourgeois, 3e (Métro: St-Paul).

One of my favorite scent suppliers is Estéban, which is distributed all over Europe. The store carries diffusers, burners, incense, sprays, scented rocks, and so on. The Marais location is open on Sunday.

LAMPES BERGER
Department stores.

Lampes Berger makes fashionable oil-burning lanterns, not unlike genie lamps. They come in dozens of styles and cost 40€ to 100€ ($46–$115). You buy the scented liquid oil separately for approximately 12€ ($14); there are more than a dozen scents. The process of using this product is more complicated than lighting an aromatherapy candle—but then, this one works.

If you smoke, look into this product immediately—the scent effectively masks the smell of cigarette smoke.

Carrying flammable goods on airplanes is technically illegal (bringing on the lamp itself is not), so you may need to use the toll-free number in the U.S. (provided in the package) to order the liquid.

MARIAGE FRÈRES
30 rue du Bourg-Tibourg, 4e (Métro: St-Paul).
13 rue des Grands-Augustins, 5e (Métro: St-Michel).

Mariage Frères is one of the most sophisticated and expensive teahouses in Paris. It has its own line of tea-scented candles, which are in demand by those willing to spend about 43€ ($50) for a candle. Also sold in department stores. Very chic gift.

SMART SHOPPERS' HOME STYLE

Let's face it, very few people with any smarts at all go to Paris to buy fine antiques. Okay, maybe you're Lord Rothschild and you go to Paris for a few finishing touches for Spencer House. If you're playing in the big leagues, ignore this paragraph. There's no question that Paris has top-of-the-line resources; but the truth is, if you've ever cast a wary eye at the bottom line, you know that Paris has top-of-the-line prices as well. Even Parisians leave town to buy antiques.

People who have price in mind work the wide network of antiques shows, brocante fairs, auctions, flea markets, and weekends in the country, which provide not only wonderful entertainment, but also far better prices than you'll ever find on the Faubourg St-Honoré. Note that there are a number of annual events that charge admission—about 5€ ($5.75), sometimes more.

If you're a serious shopper and plan on some big-time buying, keep the following tips in mind:

- Buy from a dealer with an international reputation.
- Prices are usually quoted in dollars once they top $5,000.
- There is now a value-added tax on some antiques; ask for a détaxe form.
- Make sure you receive the appropriate paperwork so that your purchase can leave the country. The French are not going to let any national treasures slip through their fingers.
- Insure for replacement value, not cost.

LE LOOK

Paris has its share of home-style shops, similar to Pottery Barn, that sell a Euro look at a fair to moderate price. Prices might not be any better than at home (in fact, they could be higher), but you'll find style galore, not to mention items you can't find elsewhere. I am constantly amazed by this look—it was first mastered by the Englishman Sir Terence Conran and owes its success to many American retailing methods.

BOUCHARA
1 rue Lafayette, 9e (Métro: Chaussée-d'Antin).

In terms of home style, this is the low end, but worth visiting if you have a good eye or are in search of fabrics by the meter. Dress fabrics are upstairs; the home style is on the ground floor. It's a good place around Christmastime for ornaments and decorative touches. You can also get pillows in the usual French sizes, which are hard to find in the U.S. This store is next door to Galeries Lafayette's main store.

THE CONRAN SHOP
8 bd Madeleine, 2e (Métro: Madeleine).
117 rue du Bac, 7e (Métro: Sèvres-Babylone).

This is a British shop, but Sir Terence Conran is an expert on French design. The Madeleine store is even more exciting than the Left Bank store; it's newer and has a cafe. Both locations are filled with tons of whimsy and charm. Just browse and breathe the magic: There are books, luggage, foodstuffs, gifts, home style, housewares, pens, paper goods, and more.

FLAMANT
8 place de Furstenberg, 6e (Métro: St-Germain-des-Prés).
279 rue St. Honoré, 8é (Métro: Concorde).

Long a brand name in French home style, Flamant recently opened stores in all of the major French cities. It makes its own furniture, but also has gift and tabletop items. There's a touch of the English in the look, but it is a dream style for many French families. A new branch will be opening on rue St Honoré, 8e. © 01-55-04-88-44. www.flamant.fr.

- ### GENEVIÈVE LETHU
  95 rue de Rennes, 6e (Métro: St-Germain-des-Prés).
  12 rue de Passy, 16e (Métro: La Muette); and others.

Lethu designs some of the most refreshing (and affordable) table-top items in Paris: Her use of color is bold and extravagant, and her prints are exotic without being beyond the pale. She mixes contemporary tabletop and country looks so elegantly that even a formal setting will work. The tablecloths are my favorite, but there's much more from which to choose.

HABITAT
8 rue du Pont Neuf, 1er (Métro: Pont Neuf).
45 rue de Rennes, 6e (Métro: St-Germain-des-Prés).
12 bd de la Madeleine, 9e (Métro: Madeleine).
Centre Commercial Montparnasse, 14e (Métro:
Montparnasse).
35 av. Wagram, 17e (Métro: Ternes or Etoile).

Although Sir Terence Conran developed both, Conran and Habitat are not the same store. In fact, nowadays they're not even similar. Habitat sells lower-end goods and is not my idea of something to plan your trip to Paris around.

LAFAYETTE MAISON
35 bd Haussmann, 9e (Métro: Opéra or Havre Caumartin).

See p. 148 for a full listing on this brand-new department store of home style.

LE CEDRE ROUGE
5 rue de Médicis, 6e (Métro: Odéon).
25 rue Duphot, 8e (Métro: Madeleine).

A chain with shops outside Paris, Le Cèdre Rouge tends to focus on a country-garden look. Affordable style for the masses, but quite classy. Everything is beautifully displayed. This is not just for those who are looking to stock the house; the tote bags and other small items also make good gifts.

MAISONS DU MONDE
Centre Commercial Les Halles, 1er (Métro: Les Halles).
Centre Commercial Quatre Temps (Métro: Grande Arche de la Défense).

This mass merchant may not interest you—the look isn't that different from Pier 1, and you can do well with this sort of thing (Indian and Asian imports) in the U.S. Living in Paris, however, I have found this chain a godsend for getting funky looks and high style at a moderate price. I have bought candles, picture frames, cutlery, and many table accessories here.

MIS EN DEMEURE
27 rue du Cherche-Midi, 6e (Métro: Sèvres-Babylone).
66 av. Victor Hugo, 16e (Métro: Victor-Hugo).

Sort of a hipper, more French Conran's. On my last visit, there were lots of country tabletop looks (items made with twigs) and papier-mâché Christmas ornaments. Some items border on the fabulous; others are ordinary. But when you first step inside and see all the glassware, linens, furniture, and lamps displayed together, you will think it's quite *extraordinaire*.

SPECIALTY LOOKS

A number of chic-er-than-thou shops are so fabulously French that you have to visit them, if only to browse.

ARMANI CASA
195 bd St-Germain, 6e (Métro: Rue du Bac).

Beyond the superstore in Milan, Armani now has a handful of home-furnishings stores in world capitals. The Paris store is especially well positioned near other designer showrooms, many of them Italian, and not far from the designer shops clustered around St-Germain-des-Prés. It sells tabletop and gift items, as well as furniture. There are no bargains here, but at least it doesn't look like expensive Conran (as it does in Milan).

ASTIER DE VILLETTE
173 rue St-Honoré, 1er (Métro: Palais-Royal).
23 rue du Bac, 7e (Métro: Rue du Bac).

Blink and you'll miss this small shop. It is deep, but from the front you could pass it and not know that it's one of the most special spaces in France. It sells a look and a way of being and a mishmash of objects displayed to thrill your heart. The business revolves around hand-thrown whiteware (dishes), but there are also sweaters, gloves, socks, gifts, and objets d'art. The dishes are not inexpensive—a large piece can easily cost 120€ ($138)—but this is the chic look of the moment.

CATHERINE MEMMI
32 rue St-Sulpice, 6e (Métro: Odéon).
11 rue St-Sulpice, 6e (Métro: Odéon).

The look is minimalist, which isn't my thing, but the influence is from Kyoto and the designer's motto is "humble but beautiful." There are clean lines, luxury fabrics, and neutral tones galore; even Galeries Lafayette has a Memmi space. The shop at no. 11 sells more of what Memmi calls *les Basiques*.

GRANGE
5 place St-Augustin, 8e (Métro: St-Augustin).

Grange has been a famous name in French design and home style for over 100 years; its first free-standing boutique is filled with two levels of room sets, furniture, and tabletop accessories. They're mostly large items that won't fit in your luggage, but you might get inspired. There is a Monoprix across the street.

LA TUILE LOUP
35 rue Daubenton, 5e (Métro: Monge).

Just trust me on this one. This shop brims with country French charm. It has a slightly out-of-the-way location, but you can easily wander into the 6e from here. If it's a market day—Wednesday or Friday—stop by place Monge, too.

LE PRINCE JARDINIER
117–121 Arcade Vallois, 37 rue de Valois, Jardin du Palais Royal, 1er (Métro: Palais-Royal).
46 rue du Bac, 7e (Métro: Rue du Bac).

In the far corner of the arcade of shops in the Palais Royal, this store specializes in gardening and country looks. A prince owns it, hence the name. The gardening bags have become the weekend tote of the BCBG chic.

MAISON DE FAMILLE
29 rue St-Sulpice, 6e (Métro: St-Sulpice or Mabillon).
Place Madeleine, 8e (Métro: Madeleine).

This is almost a multiple, since there are now a few in Paris and several in the provinces. And why not? It's a terrific store with a wonderful look. The soothing blend of English, Euro, and chinoiserie will seduce you.

Note: I love the look and feel here, but a shopper might end up paying high prices for British, American, or other imported goods. I can easily find similar things in the U.S. for less—yet when it's all put together, you have a serious browse along with some drooling.

ROSEMARIE SCHULZ
30 rue Boissy d'Anglas, 8e (Métro: Madeleine).

If you check out only one new address this trip, this should be it. It's near Territoire, inside the Galeries de la Madeleine. Be sure to see them both. Emotionally, the two shops are worlds apart. Schultz is a German designer and possibly a florist— her shop sells fabrics, pillows, sachets, and flowers. This is one of the most imaginative stores I've ever been in.

SIA
5 bd Malesherbes, 1er (Métro: Madeleine).

Sia is a mass merchant of style and class; this is its first shop, across from the Madeleine. It is known for fake flowers, and sells all sorts of tabletop items and home style (in department stores, too) at very good prices. I like the plastic container filled with silk rose petals, which you can throw at a bride or scatter on your dinner table.

Simrane
23 and 25 rue Bonaparte, 6e (Métro: St-Germain-des-Prés).

Block prints from India are made into mostly home style, although the smaller boutique of the two stores sells some clothing items. The boutis (bed quilts) are to die for, but then, so are the prices. Because the French Provençale fabrics (called *tissus indiennes*) derived from these prints, the look works very well with all things French. ✆ 01-43-54-90-73.

FABRIC SHOWROOMS

If you are a member of the trade or simply want inspiration, you're welcome to browse in decorator showrooms. Don't be surprised if many of the home-furnishings fabric suppliers want nothing to do with you unless you quickly brandish a business card that proves you are a designer. Most showrooms have U.S. representatives or distributors, and they do not want to undercut their own agents.

This leads to an even more important point: You may find that these same items are the same price (or even less) in the U.S. If you are a member of the trade and present a business card, you can ask for a 10% trade discount.

You may also want to negotiate for the détaxe refund, for which you must qualify when you arrange to ship outside the country. Many firms will not ship to the U.S. at the risk of offending their American agents.

Finally, remember that a huge amount of "French style" is actually British. Some of the best fabric showrooms in Paris showcase British goods! If you discover that your favorite item is British, save money and buy it in the U.K.

If you're just looking, check out the fabric showrooms tucked behind the place des Victoires, not far from the Palais Royal. Walk along the rue du Mail to the place des Victoires. This area borders the Sentier, or garment district (Métro: Sentier or Bourse). **Brunswig & Fils,** 8 rue du Mail, originally a French firm, is now owned by an American family, so it's hard to know where to buy and when you will save.

PASSEMENTERIE & RIBBON

I buy bits of *passementerie*—fringe and braid—at the flea markets, but if you're decorating your home and willing to splurge on the best, Paris has several serious sources.

Au Bon Gout
1 rue Guisarde, 16e (Métro: La Muette).

This store's name means "With Good Taste"—and it's not kidding. It sells braids, buttons, and all the things I love. It's at the low end of the Passy district, so combine a visit here with a trip to the neighborhood. It sells couture buttons, but no CC buttons.

Claude Declerq
15 rue Etienne Marcel, 2e (Métro: Etienne Marcel).

This designer makes new *passementerie* following old color schemes and methods; he will do custom work to match.

Marie-Pierre Boïtard
8 place du Palais-Bourbon, 7e (Métro: Invalides).

A good resource for simple *passementerie* in a chic, totally Parisian environment.

PASSEMENTERIE DE L'ILE DE FRANCE
11 rue Trousseau, 4e (Métro: Ledru Rollin).

This is just past Bastille, but right on Napoleon in terms of style. It opens at 9am; closed Saturday and Sunday.

TABLETOP & GIFTS

Everywhere you look in Paris, there's another adorable shop selling gifts or tabletop items. No one sets a table like the French. The department stores often have exhibits or even classes in table arts; you can take notes—or pictures.

DINERS EN VILLE
27 rue de Varenne, 7e (Métro: Rue du Bac).

If you take my advice and stroll the rue du Bac, you'll find this store on your own and congratulate yourself for being such a clever bunny. This small, cramped two-room store is filled with the kind of French tabletop merchandise you and I adore. There's nothing in this store I wouldn't buy.

EN ATTENDANT LES BARBARES
50 rue Etienne Marcel (at Victoires), 2e (Métro: Etienne Marcel or Palais-Royal).

Great shop for chic, cutting-edge gifts. I'm most impressed with the items (especially candlesticks) made from resin. Stop by, if only to gawk.

LA DAME BLANCHE
186 rue de Rivoli, 1er (Métro: Tuileries).

Nestled between the tourist traps on the rue de Rivoli is this tiny shop selling reproduction faience, Limoges boxes, and Louis-style porcelain.

MURIEL GRATEAU
Galerie de Valois, Jardin du Palais Royal, 1er (Métro: Palais-Royal).

Muriel once designed ready-to-wear for Charles Jourdan; now she has her own place. There are linens in more colors than the rainbow, plus beautiful textiles. Her linen napkins come in 36 colors.

RESONANCES
3 bd Malesherbes, 1er (Métro: Madeleine).

I find this store very American (part of the New Paris), but because it's easy enough to get to and next door to the Sia store, you may want to pop in. Résonances sells gifts, tabletop design, office design, cards, and novelties. This store has branches in every major French city and another Paris store in the Carrousel du Louvre.

SABRE
13 rue du Marché Saint-Honoré, 1er (Métro: Tuileries).
4 rue des Quatre Vents, 5e (Métro: Odéon).

Although this resource sells dishes and other tabletop items, it is most famous for cutlery. Some pieces boast ceramic handles and come in gingham squares or prints, but the best by far are the marbleized resin bistro sets, made in fashion colors that are so chic, you'll lose your mind. I have a set in orange and red shades; I have a friend who did place settings with a rainbow of differing shades. Carried in department stores or in either of its two new Paris boutiques ✆ 01-42-97-56-88 or 01-44-07-37-64. www.sabre.fr.

KITCHEN STYLE

Paris is rightfully renowned for its table arts; luckily for tourists, there are a number of kitchen-supply houses within a block or two of one another, so you can see a lot without going out of your way. Price is not the object here; selection is everything. Note that most of the kitchen shops open at 9am (sometimes earlier), so you can extend your shopping day by beginning with these resources. The "kitchen neighborhood" is a block and a cross street; you can easily start at one and walk to the others. Remember, rue Montmartre is not in Montmartre; it is near Forum des Halles. And Etienne Marcel is a great shopping street.

A. SIMON

48 rue Montmartre, 2e (Métro: Etienne Marcel or Les Halles).

Note to regulars: A. Simon has moved. There's a blue-jeans store in the old space, across the street. A major supplier of kitchen and cooking supplies for over 100 years, this store is conveniently located down the street from the Forum des Halles mall. You can buy everything from dishes to menus here; I buy white paper doilies by the gross—many sizes and shapes not available in the U.S.—at fair prices. Touch everything in this wonderland of gadgets and goodies. © **01-42-33-71-65.** www.simon-a.com.

DEHILLERIN

18–20 rue Coquillière, 1er (Métro: Musée-du-Louvre or Les Halles).

Perhaps the most famous cookware shop in Paris, Dehillerin has been selling cookware for over 150 years. It deals mostly with the trade, but you can poke around and touch the copper, cast iron, tools, gadgets, and more. Or someone may even help you. Try out your French—it goes a long way here. The store opens at 8am and closes for lunch. © **01-42-36-53-13.** www.dehillerin.com.

DUTHILLEUL & MINART

14 rue de Turbigo, 1er (Métro: Etienne Marcel).

This shop sells professional clothing for chefs, kitchen staff, waiters, and so forth. It's a great resource for creative fashion freaks or teens. You can buy anything from kitchen clogs to aprons; a *toque* (cap) costs around 10€ ($12), while the *veste chef* (chef's jacket) is around 26€ ($30). There are various styles of aprons (which make good gifts) and many wine-related items. You'll find it around the corner from the other kitchen shops, right at the Métro stop.

LA CORPO
19 rue Montmartre, 1er (Métro: Etienne Marcel or Les Halles).

This one isn't my favorite, but it, too, has a vast selection of kitchenware, including much equipment. While you may be tempted, remember that electric gadgets are a no-no. Still, there are lots of enticing pots, pans, and supplies.

MORA
13 rue Montmartre, 1er (Métro: Etienne Marcel or Les Halles).

Similar to A. Simon, but with more utensils (more than 5,000 in stock), Mora has a salon for bakery goods, which sells *fèves* (charms that go into the *gâteau de roi*, or king's cake, for Epiphany) in small and large packages. It has a huge paper-goods section as well.

CANDLES

One of the first stores in Paris that bowled me over with just how clever the French can be was a candle shop, **Point à la Ligne.** Now that line is available at any French department store and in the U.S. Still, when you wander Paris, you will find extravagance and wit, often at an affordable price, at shops selling candles.

I now travel with my own candles, which I light in the bathroom while I soak in the tub or place by my bedside while I read. (Do remember to snuff out the candle before you go to sleep!) I used to buy **Rigaud** candles at my favorite duty-free shop, Catherine, but I now use other brands—I am always testing what's new.

Rigaud was the leading brand of scented candles when no one else was into them, and it is still at the top of the market in terms of status and quality. Most of the big fragrance houses (**Guerlain, Manuel Canovas, L'Occitane, Roger & Gallet**) sell scented candles in addition to perfume or soaps. For more home-scent resources, see "Smelling French Style," on p. 229.

POINT À LA LIGNE
67 av. Victor Hugo, 16e (Métro: Victor-Hugo).
25 rue de Varenne, 7e (Métro: Rue du Bac).

Probably the most famous of the contemporary candle makers in Paris, Point à la Ligne has candle sculptures, as well as ultra-skinny, enormously chic, long tapers that make sensational birthday or celebration candles on a cake. In sum, all sorts of fabulous things. The products are available in all French department stores. *Note:* Point à la Ligne specializes in novelty candles, not scented candles.

DELUXE LOGO STYLE

Want a chic souvenir? Purchase something from a famous French address. Several shops, cafes, and even tourist attractions sell attractive logo merchandise.

BOUTIQUE CRILLON
Hôtel de Crillon, 10 place de la Concorde, 8e (Métro: Concorde).

The Crillon is one of the most famous hotels in Paris. Even if you aren't staying here, you may want to visit to have tea or to shop. Because the hotel is part of the Concorde chain, which is owned by a famous French family (ever heard of the name Taittinger?), the gift shop sells products made by other companies in which the Taittinger family has an interest. Accordingly, you'll find an amazing array of French luxury goods—Annick Goutal and Baccarat, to name just a couple. Also here are Crillon logo goods that you wouldn't dare steal from your room—robes, slippers, note cards, and such.

Even without its association with the Hôtel de Crillon, this would be a good group of shops. Better yet, the hotel gift shop is open Sunday and is open late during the week.

BOUTIQUE DU CAFÉ DE FLORE
26 rue St-Benoît, 6e (Métro: St-Germain-des-Prés).

The Café de Flore is one of the three famous Paris bistros on the Left Bank (the other two are Les Deux Magots and Brasserie Lipp), and so far it's the only one that has opened its own gift shop. The tiny store, around the corner from the cafe, is just adorable. You get a free chocolate when you wander in (you can buy a box), and you can browse among dishes, serving pieces, paper goods, and all sorts of gift items. Rumor has it that this store may close because of the value of the real estate, but since you'll be in the neighborhood anyway, have a look.

COMPTOIR DE LA TOUR D'ARGENT
2 rue du Cardinal Lemoine, 5e (Métro: Maubert-Mutualité).

La Tour d'Argent, one of the most famous restaurants in Paris, has withstood the comings and goings of new rivals. Whether you eat here or not, you may want to shop next door, where you can get a picnic-to-go or a gift basket to take home. It also has ashtrays, crystal, china, and more.

LE MEURICE
228 rue de Rivoli, 1er (Métro: Tuileries).

It's the dishes and ashtrays that make me swoon at the Meurice. Since no one smokes anymore, the ashtrays are good butter dishes. While the hotel sells many items through its new logo boutique, I prefer the small tabletop items. ℰ 01-44-58-10-10. www.lemeurice.com.

SALON DU THÉ BERNARDAUD
11 rue Royale, 8e (Métro: Concorde).

This is tricky, because an entire Bernardaud china shop is at this address. What I'm recommending are the porcelain logo souvenirs sold at the front counter of the tea shop.

CHINA, CRYSTAL & SILVER
••

French crystal and porcelain have been the backbone of French luxe for centuries. Prices can be fair in France, but the shipping will kill you. Come with a price list from home—a sale in the U.S. may wipe out any French savings.

BACCARAT
11 place des Etats Unis, 16e (Métro: Iena).
11 place de la Madeleine, 8e (Métro: Concorde).
10 rue de la Paix, 2e (Métro: Opéra).

Baccarat's headquarters moved into a palace and began a chain of new store openings that has turned Paris upside down. This place is not only swank, but also has a Philippe Starck restaurant. The location is a bit off the tourist track, but it's worth seeing if you don't mind being out in public with your mouth open.

BERNARDAUD
11 rue Royale, 8e (Métro: Concorde).

If you're making the rounds of the hoity-toity tabletop houses, don't miss Bernardaud, which means Limoges china. Especially impressive are the newer contemporary designs with Art Deco roots. If you don't have to ship, you can save over New York prices. The tea shop is farther back in the *passage.*

CRISTAL LALIQUE
11 rue Royale, 8e (Métro: Concorde).

One glance at Lalique's crystal door and there's no doubt that you've entered one of the wonders of the world. Get a look at the Lalique-designed Olympic medals created for the 1992 Winter Games. The headquarters is sort of like a museum: People come to stare more than to shop. The prices are the same as at factory sources on the rue de Paradis, by the way, so don't think you can beat the tags here. Besides, you get to apply for détaxe, everyone is friendly and speaks English, and they ship to the U.S. This is an excellent case of a brand name that has expanded like mad—there's everything from jewelry to handbags to belts to perfumes.

CRISTAL VENDÔME
1 rue de Castiglione, 1er (Métro: Concorde).

Right underneath the Inter-Continental is a factory-direct store that will ship to the U.S. (You can phone in an order once you have bought in person, a service the factory does not offer.) It sells various lines (Baccarat, Lalique, Daum, and more), which makes shopping easy. The store offers tax-free prices, the same as at the airport. I priced a Lalique necklace and found it to be almost half the U.S. price.

DAUM
4 rue de la Paix, 2e (Métro: Opéra).

There's a lot more to Daum than large, lead-crystal cars, and this two-level shop is a great place to discover just how much more. The extra space allows the display of inventive glass art and colored-glass pieces that will surely become collectors' items one day.

ROBERT HAVILAND ET C. PARLON CRISTALLERIES ROYALES DE CHAMPAGNE
Village Royal, 25 rue Royale, 8e (Métro: Madeleine).

This shop is a little bit hidden and very, very fancy. It's best not to bring the kids. Check out the way in which the printed patterns are mixed and matched—it's the essence of French chic.

ORIENTAL INSPIRATIONS

Paris went Zen in its craze for Japanese-inspired tabletop items and dishes about 3 years ago. Giorgio Armani's new home-style shop, **Armani Casa** (p. 234), has reinforced that look. If you don't want to pay 43€ ($49) for a salad plate, try the resources below.

COMPAGNIE FRANCAISE DE L'ORIENT DE LA CHINE
167 bd St-Germain-des-Prés, 6e (Métro: Rue du Bac).
260 bd St-Germain-des-Prés, 7e (Métro: Rue du Bac).
170 bd Haussmann, 8e (Métro: Ternes).

This store has a few locations in Paris and some in other cities (such as Brussels); it sells clothes and tabletop accessories, sometimes in the same store, or in separate stores. On the Left Bank, the stores are separate. The goods are mostly Chinese, as the name suggests, and very chic.

MUJI
99 rue de Rivoli, 1er (Métro: Louvre), and other locations.

This Japanese firm hit it big in London before coming to Paris, where its many shops sell a department store's worth of merchandise. It has storage units, paper goods, gifts, and tabletop items. There are Muji stores in every major shopping district in Paris; some are better than others.

PROVENÇAL FABRICS

If you aren't headed for Provence, Paris has a selection of traditional country French prints. Most street markets sell less expensive wares.

BLANC D'IVOIRE
50 rue du Bac, 7e (Métro: Rue du Bac).

As the name might suggest, pale is the rule in this shop of reproduction French *boutis* (quilts) and classic antique linens from Provence. There are a few bright pieces, but no hot primary colors. The machine-washable quilts cost a few hundred euros/dollars and have a wonderful old-fashioned feel. This line is also sold in department stores.

LES OLIVADES
95 rue de Seine, 6e (Métro: St-Sulpice or Odéon).

I have been told that Les Olivades was started in the mid-1970s when someone in the Souleiado hierarchy departed and began a new firm. Indeed, Les Olivades reminds me of the Pierre Deux/Souleiado look, although the colors (pastels and the like) are more muted. Les Olivades sells much the same merchandise—fabric by the yard, place mats, tablecloths, napkins, umbrellas, travel bags, and so forth. While the goods are not cheap, they are about 30% less expensive than at Souleiado in France.

SOULEIADO
78 rue de Seine, 6e (Métro: Mabillon)
Forum des Halles, 1er (Métro: Châtelet)
85 av. Paul-Doumer, 16e (Métro: La Muette).

You have to be a real Pierre Deux freak to know that Pierre Deux is the name of the American franchise for these prints, but is not the name of the company in Europe. So remember the name Souleiado, which will get you happily through France.

The flagship rue de Seine shop is everything it should be. You will be in country French heaven. Be sure to see all parts of the shop (there are two rooms); the main shop winds around another showroom in the far back, where more fabrics are sold by the meter. There is a showroom for the trade next door. The Passy shop on avenue Paul-Doumer is almost as good, but not quite as quaint. Nonetheless, it is chockablock with the look we love—plenty of fabrics, plus clothing and all the tabletop accessories in the world.

TABLE LINENS

JEAN VIER
66 rue de Vaugirard, 6e (Métro: St-Sulpice).

Specializing in Basque country linens, Jean Vier features natural and bleached linen run through with a colored stripe, or several. There's also towels, bath supplies, candles, and more. ✆ 01-45-44-26-74.

LE JACQUARD FRANÇAIS
12 rue Richepance, 1er (Métro: Madeleine).

Be still, my heart; this is flutter time if you love table style and fabrics and color as much as I do. The brand is well known (it's available at department stores, where you can use your tourist discount card), but this is the first free-standing store. It carries the entire line. There are hanging samples to touch and three video screens to watch. The patterns are all made with a jacquard loom (as you can guess from the name); they are incredibly sophisticated, very French, and fabulous for gifts.

BED LINENS

••

Continental bed sizes are metric, but why should that stop you?
Just bring your tape measure. Or, if price is truly no object,
have Porthault custom-make your sheets.

Descamps
44 rue du Passy, 16e (Métro: La Muette).

Descamps no longer has stores in the U.S., but higher-end
American department stores sell its products. You may not find
prices much better in Paris. Still, every time I visit Paris, I buy
a few items (such as oblong terrycloth bath mittens) that aren't
available back home. I also buy Primrose Bordier (that's the
designer's name) home scent here. There's one in every trading area in Paris. The outlet shops are named Texaffaires;
there's one on rue du Temple across the street from BHV
(Métro: Hôtel de Ville).

D. Porthault
18 av. Montaigne, 8e (Métro: Alma- Marceau).
370 rue du Faubourg St-Honoré, 8e (Métro: Concorde).
163 bd St-Germain-des-Prés (Métro: Rue du Bac).

Porthault was making fancy bed linens long before the real world
was ready for patterned sheets—or the notion that a person
could spend 870€ ($1,000) on bedclothes and still be able to
sleep at night.

　　Porthault sells two lines in America: One is identical to what
you can buy in France (but costs more in the U.S.); the other
is contracted by the Porthault family and is available only in
the U.S. The French laminated products are not sold in the U.S.;
the American wallpaper is not sold in France. The Montaigne
shop has a whopper of a sale in January, when it unloads everything at half the retail price, or less.

　　The shop on the Faubourg St-Honoré is tiny and doesn't
have the selection or the feel of the mother store or the factory shop. If you're headed for Lille, note that discontinued

prints cost a fraction of their regular price at the factory outside Lille. If you're a fan, this is a trip you will never forget. I'm still drooling; thankfully, I bought a lot of bibs.

FRETTE HOME COUTURE
49 rue du Faubourg St-Honoré, 8e (Métro: Concorde).

Very fancy new showroom for the Frette linens and home line. It stocks pajamas, robes, and all your nesting needs.

OLIVIER DESFORGES
26 bd Raspail, 7e (Métro: Sèvres-Babylone), and others.

This is Descamps's main competitor, with fewer stores in France and none (to my knowledge) in the U.S. Sometimes the line has a country look to it. Don't miss this one if you adore sophisticated bed linen. There are several Paris shops.

YVES DELORME
Le Louvre des Antiquaires, 2 place du Palais-Royal, 1er (Métro: Palais-Royal).

Yves Delorme makes linen sold under the Palais-Royal label in the U.S.; he has a boutique on the street level of the Louvre des Antiquaires, as well as in Monaco and Lyons. This is luxury linen that isn't as wildly priced as other premium French lines (such as Porthault and Descamps), but is still chic. Bed-linen freaks won't care about the prices; the total look has a certain French charm that makes it a must-have.

DEPARTMENT OF HOME STYLE

Naturally, the Parisian department stores carry many of the brands listed in this chapter. Furthermore, Au Printemps has a store, **Printemps Maison,** with many floors devoted to home wares. Galeries Lafayette has launched its home-style store, **Lafayette Maison,** which has been mentioned in just about every chapter of this book.

BHV has the largest selection of items for home decorating, from the basement (SS) hardware level to many floors of home and decor goods. It also has departments for storage style, furniture refinishing, and more.

Le Bon Marché is the most chic of the department stores and has many lines the others do not carry, including Alain Ducasse kitchenware. It even has different patterns of mass-market merchandise—there's a Geneviève Lethu pattern that only this store keeps in stock.

La Samaritaine is in the middle of a makeover, so who knows what the future will bring? But it currently has the best selection of bed linens of all the Parisian department stores.

For more information on the department stores, see p. 146.

Chapter Ten

....

ANTIQUES & FLEA MARKETS

ANTIQUES & BROCANTE

Paris is one of the world's capitals for antiques. One of the pleasures of shopping here is browsing the wide variety of antiques shops. Whether you're buying real antiques or just some "old stuff," remember that U.S. Customs defines an antique as something that is at least 100 years old. If a piece does not come with provenance papers, you must have a receipt or a bill of lading from the dealer that says what the piece is, its origin, and its age. The French government is rather stringent about what can be taken out of France; it even tries to keep some designer *fripes* (used clothes) in the country.

Expensive museum-quality antiques are generally sold in the tony shops along the rue du Faubourg St-Honoré and in the 16e, although there are plenty of high-end dealers on the Left Bank. Mid-priced antiques are predominantly found in antiques shops on the Left Bank, in the antiques *villages,* and at the markets of St-Ouen. Brocante (junk) is mostly sold at street markets, fairs, and flea markets (see p. 259 for a list of fairs and flea markets).

If you just want to browse and get the feel of the serious antiques scene, get over to the Left Bank. A grouping of very important dealers sits between the river and the boulevard St-Germain. They may be a tad more expensive than others in

Worth a Trip

Besides specialty events, there are a few other kinds of antiques events that I recommend, if you have the strength. They are slightly out of town or on the fringes.

- **Chatou** is a fair in the town of Chatou held twice a year—March and September—on dates announced in the antiques magazines. Take the RER A1 train (direction St-Germain-en-Laye) there and walk from the station (it's well marked). The trick, of course, is to be able to carry your purchases back on the train with you—or to move to Paris and have them delivered. There is a shipping office. For event dates, call © 01-47-70-88-78.

- **Versailles** is known for the palace of the Sun King and even for its hotel, spa, and restaurant, but few people ever talk about the antiques *village* right in the heart of town.

- **Stadium shows** are similar to the Rose Bowl Swap Meet in Pasadena. They take place at stadiums in the outskirts of Paris and are fabulous for their low prices and huge selections. Few are served by public transportation—I hire a car and driver. The shows usually have shipping offices.

town, but these are the real guys with the real reputations who don't even look up from their newspapers when you walk in. They can tell from your questions just how serious you are, what you know, and, often, whom you know.

If you want to familiarize yourself with the notions and motions of French-style antiques shopping, get to a large news agent and look at the half-dozen magazines devoted to antiques and brocante. The most popular is *Aladdin,* but all give the schedules of big shows, fairs, specialty antiques events, and such. You can also check the Friday edition of any of the Paris newspapers for the brocante schedule.

Antiques *Villages*

A *village* in Paris is not a subdivision of an arrondissement, but a place for good antiques. *Villages* are buildings that house many antiques dealers under one roof. If you need a rainy-day occupation, a trip to any *village* probably will do it; some are even open Sunday.

LE LOUVRE DES ANTIQUAIRES
2 place du Palais-Royal, 1er (Métro: Palais-Royal).

At this virtual antiques department store of some 250 dealers, you may have more fun than at the museum! At least you can shop here. Many mavens claim this is the single best one-stop source in Paris—quality is high and dealers have reputations to protect. You can even bargain a little. There are enough affordable small pieces that you're bound to find something you like without having to pound the pavement. A restaurant and a shipping agent are indoors. Sophisticated, civilized, nothing junky at all. Closed Sundays in August; otherwise, the Sunday scene is from a movie—the other shoppers alone make it worth a visit. Clean bathrooms, too.

LE VILLAGE SUISSE
54 av. de la Motte-Picquet, 15e (Métro: Motte-Piquet).

You won't find any gnomes making watches here, or handing out chocolate bars, just a lot of dealers in the mid- to high-price range, with some very respectable offerings. Le Village Suisse is near the Hilton, the Eiffel Tower, the foodie street rue Cler, and l'Ecole Militaire, so don't be baffled by the address. There are 150 shops in an area 1 block long and 2 blocks wide—it's sort of like a mall that rambles from building to building. Prices are not outrageous, but they aren't low, either; most stores offer shipping. There are no cute or funky shops here, but several are theme-oriented, selling nautical items or antique jewelry, for instance. Sunday is a big day here.

VILLAGE ST-PAUL
Rue St-Paul, 4e (Métro: St-Paul).

This *village,* near a block or more of street stalls selling antiques, can be a little hard to find. It's hidden in a medieval warren of streets between the Seine and the church of St-Paul, close to Marais and Bastille. The *village* is between the rues St-Paul, Charles V, des Jardins St-Paul, and Ave-Maria.

Get off the Métro at St-Paul and walk toward the river. Or walk along the quai going toward the Bastille and take a left when you spy the first antiques shop on the corner of the rue St-Paul. If you're coming from the river, you have the advantage of being able to see the VILLAGE ST-PAUL sign that spans the street across the rooftops.

Hours are generally Thursday through Monday from 11am to 7pm. Prices can be steep, but the variety of the merchandise, combined with the charm of the neighborhood, makes this a delightful way to pass the time. It makes a good stop to piggyback with your visit to the Marais. Yes, there's life on Sunday afternoons.

Auction Houses

For years, the big name in Paris's auction world was the **Hôtel Drouot.** But ever since Sotheby's gave up its Monaco offices and moved to Paris, and the government allowed others to play in the big leagues, the scene has become much more competitive. **Christie's** and **Sotheby's** are now fairly substantial players; **Tajan** isn't quite as big a name, but has some popular auctions (I went to its Barbie auction; what a scene!).

When an entire estate is being auctioned—usually due to death or bankruptcy—and there is usually nothing "important" (as the dealers tend to say) for sale, you can find bargains. This tip will be most useful for those trying to furnish a home here in France, not for those shopping for shipping.

HÔTEL DROUOT
9 rue Drouot, 9e (Métro: Le Peletier).
15 av. Montaigne, 8e (Métro: Alma-Marceau).

Drouot is a weird and fascinating place. At the entrance, an information counter has catalogs and notices of future sales; three TVs on the ground floor show different parts of the building. There is an appraiser who will tell you, free of charge, if an item you bring in is worthy of auction; he will appraise it for you on the spot in a small private room. If you agree with the estimate, you can set a date for your auction. The seller pays an 8% to 10% commission to the house.

Auctions take place on weekdays in summer and daily the rest of the year. They always begin at 2pm and usually end around 6:30pm. Previews are held on Wednesday until 11am. When you read auction catalogs in Paris, note that Hôtel Drouot listings with an R after them (for Richelieu) refer to the old location; an M refers to the avenue Montaigne location. You can buy Drouot's magazine at newsstands and get an instant look at the auction of the month.

The auction rooms are various sizes; all are carpeted and have art, tapestries, or both hanging on the walls. The clients sit on chairs to watch the bidding. Most of the clients are dealers; I've never noticed a very jazzy crowd here, even at a Goya auction. All business is in French. If you are not fluent, bring your own translator or expert, or book a translator (✆ 01-42-46-17-11) ahead of time.

You needn't register to bid; anyone can walk in, sit down, and bid. Paddles are not used. Some dealers occasionally use shills to drive up the price. The auctioneers are familiar with all of the dealers and could possibly choose to throw a piece their way; dealers may even pool in on items. All auctions have catalogs, in which the lots are numbered and defined. You do not need a catalog to enter a preview or an auction, as you do in New York. The conditions of the sale are plainly printed (in French) inside the first page of the catalog. You can pay in cash up to 1,500€ ($1,725). French people may write local checks; Americans cannot write checks on U.S. banks. If you have only American dollars on hand, there's an exchange bureau in the house. If you pay cash, you can leave with your item.

Brocante Shows

Brocante is the French word for junk; it does not include antiques. Those who sell brocante are not antiques dealers—this is very strict in the French sense of things. An American might not notice the difference.

Brocante is sold wherever you go in France, from local markets to fancy shoe stores. **Sadema,** 86 rue de Lille, 7e (© 01-40-62-95-95; fax 01-40-62-95-96; Métro: Solferino), is an organization that hosts brocante shows. These shows are annual or semiannual, most frequently held at the same time (more or less) and place each year. They are announced in the papers (check *Figaroscope*) and in weekly guides such as *Pariscope*. You can call, write, or fax for the schedule. Some shows are weekend events; others last up to 2 weeks.

Sadema is not the only game in town; other organizations also sponsor shows. One such agency is Joel Garcia (© 01-56-53-93-93). Some are fancier and charge more. In fact, the cost of admission mirrors how tony the dealers are: The higher the fee, the more expensive the dealers and their wares. Annual shows include:

- **Ferraille de Paris:** Held in the Parc Floral de Paris (Bois de Vincennes), this good-size indoor fair takes place toward the end of February. It includes a lot of affordable merchandise and approachable merchants. There's everything from empty perfume bottles to the kitchen sink—the French country kitchen sink. Métro: Porte Dorée.
- **Brocante de Printemps:** This March event usually lasts 10 days; it heralds the coming of spring, of course. Métro: Edgar Quinet.

- **Brocante à la Bastille:** This event does not take itself or its merchants too seriously. This fair is usually held on both sides of the canal. Pay near the place de la Bastille; there are bridges to the other side. Usually held for 10 days in April or May, and particularly fabulous in fine weather. I'd fly in just for this one. Métro: Bastille.
- **Brocante de Paris:** This huge event is the talk of the town for those who hope to get a designer bargain. It runs for 10 days in May. Métro: Brochant.

FLEA MARKETS

Paris is famous for its flea markets, although I think only two of them are worth getting hot and bothered over. Many people think of the markets in St-Ouen as the only game in town; I think Vanves is better. I give you the information about Montreuil in order to be complete—I don't suggest it.

PUCES DE MONTREUIL
Av. André Lemierre and av. Gallieni, 20e (Métro: Porte de Montreuil).

I have included this market because I want you to know that I know it exists and that I've been there. But it's really only for die-hard flea-market shoppers. It's a junk fair of sorts, so there are very few diamonds here—and those are artfully hidden. You could hunt for hours before throwing up your hands in disgust, having found nothing.

This immense market absorbed three other nearby markets with a huge path of illegal vendors that stretched from the nearest Métro station all the way across a bridge to the beginning of the market proper. There's a good selection of *fripes*, Victorian bed linens, old hats, new perfumes (look, Mom, who needs détaxe?), work clothes, cheap clothes, records, dishes, junk, junk, and more junk. Did I mention there is a lot of junk? This is a really low-end market without any charm whatsoever. Dealers work this one very thoroughly—it runs a good

10% to 20% cheaper than St-Ouen, but it's 50% harder to find anything. This is for those with a strong heart and a good eye; princesses and blue bloods need not apply. Open Saturday and Sunday morning through evening.

PUCES DE VANVES

Av. George Lafenestre, av. Marc Sangnier and av. Maurice d'Ocagne, 14e (Métro: Porte de Vanves).

When people tell me they are headed to the flea market in Paris, I always ask, "Which one?" They look at me like I'm an idiot, then stammer and finally say it's "the big one" or "the famous one." That means they are headed to St-Ouen, which is a lot of fun.

However, I think the number-one flea market in Paris is Puces des Vanves. This market is not like any other; it's more like a bunch of neighbors who've gone in together on a multifamily garage sale stretching for a mile or so. The market is L-shaped: On the main part of the street are the licensed vendors who pay taxes to the city; on the branch part are the illegal tag-sale vendors, who are, of course, the most fun.

The tag-sale goods are of lesser quality, but together with the licensed vendors, they make for wonderful strolling and browsing. If you don't have much time or can't stand the strain of St-Ouen, try this neighborhood affair that's perfect for a weekend. Saturday is the best day to shop Vanves. Early birds get the worms, of course; I'm here at 9:30am.

The main part of the market is on the avenue Georges Lafenestre. With the legal and the illegal guys, there are almost 200 vendors here. A crepe stand is at the bend in the road; the Sunday food market on avenue Marc Sangnier enhances the experience. *Note:* The basic part of the market closes at noon, but some dealers stay on. In the afternoon, around 1 or 2pm, a new bunch of dealers moves in to sell new (cheap) ready-to-wear, shoes, socks, towels, and so on. Open Saturday and Sunday from 9am to 1pm.

THE MARKETS OF ST-OUEN
St-Ouen (Métro: Porte de Clignancourt; Bus: PC1).

Also known as the Marché aux Puces or "the famous flea market," St-Ouen comprises several markets, each with its own dealers and each with its own special feel.

The St-Ouen markets grew from a series of little streets and alleys. Today, more than 30 hectares (75 acres) of flea market sprawl through this suburb. Each market most frequently bears the name of the street on which it rests, even though you may be hard-pressed to find the original street sign. The markets themselves are usually well marked; they often have doors on two different streets.

These are not garage sale–style street vendors: Usually the stalls open onto the street or a walkway, but have some covered parts; even the informal markets are sheltered. You will see limited street action and selling off makeshift tables. However, as you walk from the Métro to the flea market, you will see candy stands and blue-jeans dealers. The first market you see is not the flea market you're looking for; ignore these dealers.

Places to eat are numerous, bathrooms are not, and more pickpockets or rowdy boys abound than the French government would like to admit. I was once terrorized with lighted cigarettes and burning matches held by teenage boys who wanted to chase me. While they burned holes in my clothes, I refused to run or surrender my packages. I mention it because it happened to me, so it could happen to you.

If you feel you need a system for working this vast space, try mine: Start with the big guns (Biron, Cambo) and the markets in that area, then walk back so that Malik is one of your last stops. In fact, if you like the Marché Malik as little as I do, you'll be happy to run from there and call it a day.

To do it my way, turn into the market streets on the rue des Rosiers (with your back to the Métro station you came from, turn left). Work this street until the good stuff peters out; then cut to the left by way of the Marché Paul Bert. Then go right on the rue Vallès. At that point, retrace your steps by cutting through Malassis. Note that there are free-standing antiques stores, as well as big (and small) markets. Open Saturday through Monday from 8:30am to 7pm.

Note: Business has been bad with fewer American visitors at St-Ouen, so various promotional deals and events are popping up. The **Mondial de l'Antiquité** lasts for a few days in October, including one day when people sell from trucks—it's wild and well priced. To promote business with Americans, often the markets offer parity days, when the U.S. dollar is at parity with the euro in figuring prices.

MARCHE ANTICA (99 rue des Rosiers)   Just a little bitty building refinished in the Memphis Milano teal-blue-and-cream look. This market abounds with cute shops selling small collectibles of good quality at pretty good prices. It's on a corner of the Marché Vernaison, at rue des Rosiers and rue Voltaire.

MARCHE BIRON (85 rue des Rosiers)   The fanciest market in the place is one of the first markets on rue des Rosiers. Biron should be the first stop for dealers who are looking for serious stuff. If you come here and are looking for fleas, you may be turned off—it's quite hoity-toity.

MARCHE CAMBO (75 rue des Rosiers)   Another serious market, but a little less refined—the dealers are usually busy hobnobbing with one another and may ignore you. You'll see furnishings in various states of refinishing and find dealers in various states of mind—some know what they have and are hard-nosed about it; others want to move the merchandise and will deal with you. They are particularly responsive to genuine dealers who know their stuff and speak some French. The selection is less formal and more eclectic than at Biron (next door); there are rows of stalls along lanes or aisles.

MARCHE DAUPHINE (140 rue des Rosiers)   A newer *village* of some 300 shops opposite the Marché Vernaison, this

St-Ouen Markets

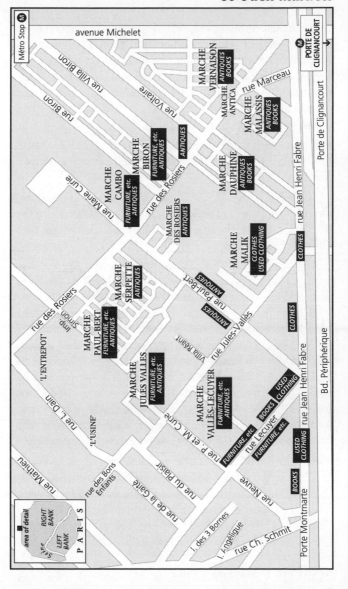

Métro Stop Ⓜ

avenue Michelet

Ⓜ **PORTE DE CLIGNANCOURT** →

rue Villa Biron

rue Biron

rue Voltaire

rue Marie Curie

MARCHE VERNAISON ANTIQUES BOOKS

MARCHE ANTICA

MARCHE MALASSIS ANTIQUES BOOKS

rue Marceau

MARCHE CAMBO FURNITURE, etc. ANTIQUES

MARCHE BIRON, etc. FURNITURE, etc. ANTIQUES

ANTIQUES

rue des Rosiers

MARCHE DAUPHINE ANTIQUES BOOKS

Porte de Clignancourt

rue Jean Henri Fabre

MARCHE DES ROSIERS ANTIQUES

MARCHE MALIK CLOTHES USED CLOTHING

CLOTHES

MARCHE SERPETTE ANTIQUES

rue Paul-Bert

ANTIQUES

rue des Rosiers

Imp. Simon

MARCHE PAUL-BERT FURNITURE, etc. ANTIQUES

Villa Réard

ANTIQUES

CLOTHES

rue Jules-Valles

'L'ENTREPOT'

MARCHE JULES VALLES FURNITURE, etc. ANTIQUES

Bd. Périphérique

rue L. Dain

'L'USINE'

MARCHE VALLES-LECUYER FURNITURE, etc. ANTIQUES

rue P. et M. Curie

FURNITURE, etc.

BOOKS

USED CLOTHING

rue Mathieu

rue du Plaisir

rue des Bons Enfants

rue de la Gaité

rue Lecuyer

FURNITURE, etc.

USED CLOTHING

rue Neuve

rue Jean Henri Fabre

BOOKS

Porte Montmartre

Porte Montmartre

f. des 3 Bornes

f. Angélique

rue Ch. Schmit

PARIS
RIGHT BANK
LEFT BANK
area of detail
Seine

is one of the first places to hit when you get to the market area. It's enclosed, with a balcony, industrial lighting, and a factory-like, high-tech atmosphere under a glass rooftop. A shipping agency is on hand. Some dealers are affordable; I found a button dealer and a specialist in vintage designer clothing that flipped me out for *fripes*.

MARCHE DES ROSIERS (3 rue Paul Bert)   A very small market specializing in the period between 1900 and 1930. There are about 13 small stalls in an enclosed horseshoe-shaped building.

MARCHE JULES-VALLES (7 rue Jules Vallès)   I like this one, although it's small and junky; reproduction brass items for the home mix with real antiques and real repro everything else. Cheap, cheap, cheap.

MARCHE PAUL-BERT (96 rue des Rosiers)   Are we having fun yet? If not, send the husband and the kids for pizza and go for it on your own—this is too good to not enjoy. Marché Paul-Bert is more outdoorsy than the rest; it surrounds the Marché Serpette in three alleys forming a U. This market is both outside and inside, with lower-end merchandise, including Art Deco, *moderne,* and country furniture. Most of the items here have not been repaired or refinished. There could be some great buys, but you need to have a good eye and know your stuff. Piles of suitcases, carts, dolls, and buttons in bins. Yummy. If you visit only one market, want to start with the very best, or think the weather may turn on you, start here.

MARCHE SERPETTE (110 rue des Rosiers)   This market is in a real building, not a Quonset hut. There is carpeting on the floor, and each vendor has a stall number and a metal door. There are also nice, clean bathrooms on the second floor. Serpette is on the edge of the Marché Paul-Bert, but you can tell the difference because this one is totally indoors and is dark and fancy.

MARCHE VERNAISON (99 rue des Rosiers)   I like this market a lot, although the new building puts me off a bit. There isn't that much I want to buy; I just like to prowl the various teeny showrooms. There are a few fabric, textile, trim, and needlework mavens who always have things I covet. You may not realize at first that this sprawling market alone constitutes a *village*, with its own streets and byways. A good first stop, it has a lot of natural charm and many affordable places; it's also first if you follow my walking path.

HELPFUL HANDS

If you're interested in these market sources—and ones that might only be open to the trade, you might want to call a local expert who arranges everything and even does the bargaining for you. My friend **Carole Carlino** has been taking dealers around Paris and the provinces for almost 20 years. Her home phone number is © **01-30-73-06-85**; her cellphone is 06-80-63-71-74.

You can latch onto a shopping tour that will take you to the flea markets; these are usually general tours that aren't too expensive and provide someone who may speak French better than you do. You can go to www.chicshopping.com for some ideas as to what tours are offered.

Need a shipper for items of furniture, not household goods? Try **Alain Franklin** (© **01-40-11-50-11**).

These sources speak English, some are even American, have been in business for decades, work with the trade, and will teach you shipping tricks, how to use a coupon booklet, and everything else you need to save a bundle while you send over a haul.

INDEX

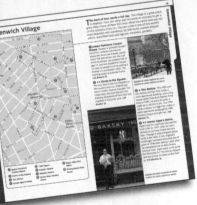

FROMMER'S® CRUISE GUIDES

Alaska Cruises & Ports of Call

Cruises & Ports of Call

European Cruises & Ports of Call

FROMMER'S® NATIONAL PARK GUIDES

Algonquin Provincial Park
Banff & Jasper
Grand Canyon

National Parks of the American West
Rocky Mountain
Yellowstone & Grand Teton

Yosemite and Sequoia & Kings
 Canyon
Zion & Bryce Canyon

FROMMER'S® MEMORABLE WALKS

London
New York

Paris
Rome

San Francisco

FROMMER'S® WITH KIDS GUIDES

Chicago
Hawaii
Las Vegas
London

National Parks
New York City
San Francisco

Toronto
Walt Disney World® & Orlando
Washington, D.C.

SUZY GERSHMAN'S BORN TO SHOP GUIDES

France
Hong Kong, Shanghai & Beijing
Italy

London
New York

Paris
San Francisco

FROMMER'S® IRREVERENT GUIDES

Amsterdam
Boston
Chicago
Las Vegas

London
Los Angeles
Manhattan
Paris

Rome
San Francisco
Walt Disney World®
Washington, D.C.

FROMMER'S® BEST-LOVED DRIVING TOURS

Austria
Britain
California
France

Germany
Ireland
Italy
New England

Northern Italy
Scotland
Spain
Tuscany & Umbria

THE UNOFFICIAL GUIDES®

Adventure Travel in Alaska
Beyond Disney
California with Kids
Central Italy
Chicago
Cruises
Disneyland®
England
Florida
Florida with Kids

Hawaii
Ireland
Las Vegas
London
Maui
Mexico's Best Beach Resorts
Mini Mickey
New Orleans
New York City

Paris
San Francisco
South Florida including Miami &
 the Keys
Walt Disney World®
Walt Disney World® for
 Grown-ups
Walt Disney World® with Kids
Washington, D.C.

SPECIAL-INTEREST TITLES

Athens Past & Present
Best Places to Raise Your Family
Cities Ranked & Rated
500 Places to Take Your Kids Before They Grow Up
Frommer's Best Day Trips from London
Frommer's Best RV & Tent Campgrounds
 in the U.S.A.

Frommer's Exploring America by RV
Frommer's NYC Free & Dirt Cheap
Frommer's Road Atlas Europe
Frommer's Road Atlas Ireland
Great Escapes From NYC Without Wheels
Retirement Places Rated

FROMMER'S® PHRASEFINDER DICTIONARY GUIDES

French

Italian

Spanish